PRAISE FOR *WHAT WE STAND TO LOSE*

"In privatizing New Orleans' public schools, education officials and charter school advocates labeled them completely dysfunctional, saying they failed generations of children. Buras disproves this baseless claim and the accusation that Black teachers were the prime reason for the system's failure. Dispelling such allegations, she documents the illustrious history of a Black high school, revealing its notable achievements. *What We Stand to Lose* is a must-read and a disturbing example of the marginalization of Black people and their institutions that has plagued America for centuries."

—RAYNARD SANDERS, coauthor of *Twenty-First-Century Jim Crow Schools: The Impact of Charters on Public Education* and executive director of the Claiborne Avenue History Project

"In the pages of this book, Kristen Buras bears witness to the vibrancy of a community school in Black New Orleans. Written with humility as well as brute honesty, she reveals the state-sanctioned death of an institution that affirmed life for young people and their families. It is a story that must be told and can never be forgotten."

—DAVE STOVALL, author of *Born Out of Struggle: Critical Race Theory, School Creation, and the Politics of Interruption*

"Education is a political battleground where schools are treated as capital assets and teachers as low skill operatives who 'deliver' prepackaged curricula. Buras's powerful and moving book explodes these shameful lies and reminds us of the rich and irreplaceable work of Black teachers who care, who are there for children, who EDUCATE in the best sense of that word."

—DAVID GILLBORN, author of *White Lies: Racism, Education and Critical Race Theory* and editor of the journal *Race Ethnicity and Education*

"In *What We Stand to Lose*, Kristen Buras brilliantly weaves the story of urban public education in New Orleans through the lens of George Washington Carver Senior High School. This book stands as a powerful generational study of a school and its community, offering critical insights into the politics of public education—past, present, and future. Masterful!"

—DERRICK ALRIDGE, coeditor of *Schooling the Movement: The Activism of Southern Black Educators from Reconstruction through the Civil Rights Era* and associate editor of the *Journal of African American History*

"Against racist, pathologizing narratives that justify closing schools in Black communities, Kristen Buras offers a powerful counter-narrative of New Orleans' Black educators' commitment to community building and self-determination. Through the story of one school, Buras compels us to see what is under attack and what we must collectively fight for: Black public education integral to the Black freedom struggle."

—PAULINE LIPMAN, author of *The New Political Economy of Urban Education: Neoliberalism, Race, and the Right to the City*

"*What We Stand to Lose* is a timely, compelling book on the history and impact of Black public schools and what is sacrificed when they are closed. Kristen Buras masterfully narrates a story of the power of teaching and community, despite the sociopolitical challenges that have undermined and continue to threaten the equitable pursuit of Black education. Given the current attacks on public schools nationwide and the enduring costs incurred by communities and neighborhoods, this must-read book is a clarion call to recognize the value of Black teachers and schools."

—KEFFRELYN BROWN, author of *After the "At-Risk" Label: Reorienting Educational Policy and Practice* and cofounder of the Center for Innovation in Race, Teaching, and Curriculum, University of Texas-Austin

WHAT
WE
STAND TO
LOSE

WHAT WE STAND TO LOSE

BLACK TEACHERS,
THE CULTURE THEY CREATED,
AND THE CLOSURE OF
A NEW ORLEANS HIGH SCHOOL

KRISTEN L. BURAS

BEACON PRESS, BOSTON

BEACON PRESS
Boston, Massachusetts
www.beacon.org

Beacon Press books
are published under the auspices of
the Unitarian Universalist Association of Congregations.

28 27 26 25   8 7 6 5 4 3 2 1

This book is printed on acid-free paper that meets the uncoated paper
ANSI/NISO specifications for permanence as revised in 1992.

Text design and composition by Kim Arney

Library of Congress Cataloging-in-Publication Data
Names: Buras, Kristen L., author.
Title: What we stand to lose : Black teachers, the culture they created,
and the closure of a New Orleans high school / Kristen L. Buras.
Description: Boston : Beacon Press, [2025] | Includes bibliographical
|references and index. |
Identifiers: LCCN 2025007313 (print) | LCCN 2025007314 (ebook) |
ISBN 9780807019498 (trade paperback) | ISBN 9780807019511 (ebook)
Subjects: LCSH: Carver Senior High School (New Orleans, La.) | African
American schools—Louisiana—New Orleans. | School failure—Louisiana—New
Orleans. | African American teachers—Louisiana—New Orleans. | African American
students—Louisiana—New Orleans. | African Americans—Education—Louisiana—
New Orleans. | African Americans—Social networks—Louisiana—New Orleans. |
African Americans—Civil rights—Louisiana—New Orleans. | Racism in education—
Louisiana—New Orleans. | New Orleans (La.)—Race relations.
Classification: LCC LC2803.N4 B8 2025 (print) | LCC LC2803.N4 (ebook) |
DDC 371.82996073—dc23/eng/20250221
LC record available at https://lccn.loc.gov/2025007313
LC ebook record available at https://lccn.loc.gov/2025007314

The authorized representative in the EU for product safety and compliance
is Easy Access System Europe 16879218, Mustamäe tee 50,
10621 Tallinn, Estonia: http://beacon.org/eu-contact

For Reverend Willie Calhoun, a 1968 graduate of G. W. Carver Senior High School, in honor of all you have done to rebuild post-Katrina schools and communities in New Orleans, and with gratitude for what you have taught me throughout this struggle together

School is composed of many individuals who lend their services for the success . . . of the institution. The yearbook is dedicated to those staff who have given their services in the school since its inception. We salute these individuals, for without their support, Carver would have been forgotten in the annals of history.

—Dedication in the 1978
G. W. Carver Senior High School yearbook
(Personal Collection of Avis and Vermon James)

POEM

PRINCIPAL MOORE
LOWER 9TH WARD, NEW ORLEANS

EXCERPT

In the Library at the School

> *A young woman flaunts herself*
> *Across the book shelved floor.*

Doctor Moore comes upon her.
> *Her with her attitude.*

He invites her to leave.
He places his hand on her shoulder.

"Don't touch me!" she snarls.
> *Shrugging him off.*

"I am Clergy!" He said holding firmly.
"I can touch you! I can Bless you!"
"I know your Mama, too!"

Discipline in New Orleans.

I can touch you. I can Bless you. I know your Mama, too.

Amelie Prescott (1942–2023), a veteran teacher and founder of Mos Chukma Arts-as-Healing Institute in New Orleans, wrote this poem after witnessing Dr. Lindsey Moore, principal of Martin Luther King High School and former principal (and 1965 graduate) of the historic Carver Senior High School, discipline a student in 2017.

CONTENTS

CHAPTER 1

"THEY DON'T KNOW THE HISTORY"

Why Re-membering Carver Senior High School Matters

One could reasonably conclude that, prior to [Hurricane Katrina in] 2005, public education in New Orleans had no history—at least in the minds of post-Katrina reformers. . . . The reformers do not mention the names of those [teachers and students] who came before, nor do they mention past accomplishments. They don't know the history. . . . [This] helps to block from memory the efforts of determined individuals who spent their underpaid educational careers working against incredible odds to educate all children.

—AL KENNEDY, "The History of Public Education in New Orleans Still Matters"[1]

Those [Carver] teachers, they saw in you what you didn't see in yourself. They applauded that, and they always told you to think outside the box, that you can do this, you're better than this. The world was yours if you listened to those teachers.

—TRENESSE MOSLEY,
a 1981 graduate of Carver Senior High School[2]

If traditional teachers and principals in a school can rally themselves and admit that *they failed* . . . they can be a part of the [post-Katrina] turnaround. If not, [they] can leave.

—MARY LANDRIEU, US senator of Louisiana (italics added)[3]

The teachers—a majority of them black—were terminated. All of them. In November 2005, about three months after Hurricane Katrina struck New Orleans, officials announced that 7,500 public school teachers and employees would lose their jobs in early 2006.[4] It was an astounding move for a city that needed to rebuild its public school system. At least 80 percent of Orleans Parish public schools had been either damaged or destroyed during the storm.[5] Most of the students were black.

Officials never asked students, parents, teachers, or others in the most deeply affected communities—where homes and neighborhoods were wiped out—what they thought should happen amid such destruction. Just the opposite: plans for rebuilding began in elite white policymaking and business circles before displaced black communities could return to New Orleans or take part in the dialogue about what would happen to their schools.[6]

The reason became clear soon enough. City residents were informed that, for too long, New Orleans public schools had been in shambles. Something had to be done for the good of the children. As it turned out, black teachers were being blamed for the struggles of previous decades. *They* had failed the students. If only they had been caring and competent enough, all would have been well. Louisiana senator Mary Landrieu told the Center for American Progress in 2011 that New Orleans' teachers and principals should either "admit" culpability or "leave."[7] Of course, those in power terminated the city's teachers before they could meaningfully respond to such finger-pointing.[8] Low standardized test scores and high dropout rates were pinned on the teachers quicker than lightning.[9]

While there was sufficient evidence that the city's public schools were falling short by traditional measures, no evidence linked those problems to the shortcomings of any teachers. The entire history of racism in New Orleans, including first denying enslaved blacks the right to an education and then strategically neglecting black public schools after their establishment, was never mentioned by officials.[10] Neither were teachers and students asked how they viewed their schools, how they defined success and failure, and what was needed to eliminate existing challenges.[11]

Rather than providing evidence of alleged faults, officials fired teachers en masse without due process.[12] A very simple equation was offered that defined the problem with the city's public schools and envisaged the solution:

Past = Traditional Teachers and Public Schools = Bad
Reform = New Teachers and Charter Schools = Good

To be clear, "new teachers" and "charter schools" meant terminating veteran teachers and closing the public schools where they taught. Accepting this definition of the problem—and the solution—was problematic on many levels. Those in power were offering a version of the past devoid of history. It seemed important to determine if the dominant narrative met the historical litmus test. What did students experience in these "failing" schools? What kinds of teachers worked in the classrooms of New Orleans? What did they do—or fail to do? And what exactly was the historical context in which the city's schools were situated?

In the opening quote, historian Al Kennedy suggests that past accomplishments in New Orleans public schools have been ignored.[13] This is not a minor point. Rather, it implies the narrative of failure rests not on historical evidence but a series of decontextualized assertions about public schools. I set out to test such assertions, with data, by investigating the history of George Washington Carver Senior High School, including its post-Katrina closure due to alleged failure and charter school expansion. I collected archival documents and conducted oral history interviews with students and teachers covering the school's fifty-year history, from 1958 to 2005, when Katrina struck; methods are detailed at the end of the chapter. I also documented the process of Carver's closure, which unfolded from 2005 to 2014.

This history is important because the firing of veteran teachers and closing of public schools based on unsubstantiated allegations of failure are pressing concerns in New Orleans and many other cities. In communities of color across the nation, urban neighborhoods have been under assault by policymakers and privatizers seeking to replace experienced, unionized teachers and close public schools by chartering privately managed ones and hiring inexperienced recruits to teach.[14] Specifically, charter schools are public schools operated under charter, or contract, by private entities, often for profit, with limited state oversight.

Carver as a long-standing black educational institution—deemed a failure, closed, and replaced by charter schools—represents thousands of school communities nationally that have experienced closure or reconstitution as charter schools. Indeed, this destructive experience has occurred in Chicago, Detroit, Philadelphia, New York City, Camden, Newark, Milwaukee, Indianapolis, Cleveland, Boston, and Washington, DC; it has occurred in Memphis, Nashville, Little Rock, St. Louis, Atlanta, and Houston; Phoenix, Oakland, and Los Angeles, among others, have not been spared either.[15] This book lays bare what is at stake and fundamentally challenges the notion of failure at the heart of current urban school reforms.

In fact, despite the broad assault on culture and civil rights represented by racially targeted school closures, the literature is relatively small.[16] In a review of research on school closures, published from 2000 to 2019, scholars Eve Ewing and Terrance Green note that studies have documented how closures map onto race and class disparities, reflect racialized policies of privatization, and negatively affect communities of color. Other studies have documented community responses to closure. However, they find that research on the responses of "the people most proximal to [the] immediate effects" of closure, such as students, teachers, and school leaders, is largely absent.[17] Further, it is evident that existing literature focuses on the process of school closure and its aftermath, without in-depth histories of schools closed since the early 2000s. This book highlights the missing voices of students and teachers and offers a robust account of school life long before the doors were forced shut. As an institutional history, *What We Stand to Lose* demonstrates the cultural value of school communities over time, including the ways they have navigated and excelled despite racism and state neglect. This is, then, partly a history of the role of black teachers in the freedom struggle and the ways in which current reforms, and the people who support them, strategically undermine that struggle.[18]

In this chapter, I describe the post-Katrina takeover of New Orleans public schools by Louisiana's state-run Recovery School District and affiliated entrepreneurs in the charter school sector. As I detail, in just a decade, New Orleans was transformed into the nation's first all-charter school district and a national "model" for teacher termination, school closures, and charter school expansion. I underscore that New Orleans' takeover—and the story of Carver—signal a racially targeted assault on historic public schools and teachers affecting black and brown urban neighborhoods nationwide. The book's epilogue provides a stark picture of school closings and takeovers in cities beyond New Orleans.

Finally, after detailing the takeover of the "failing" New Orleans public schools and offering some introductory words on Carver, I turn to a brief history of black public schools in the Jim Crow South and New Orleans to set the stage for my historically grounded investigation of Carver. This is key because the robust culture created by black teachers at Carver over the course of five decades is part of a much longer legacy of institution building by African American teachers and communities. Ultimately, I argue that allegations of failure made by outsiders do not correspond with the valuations of experienced insiders who underscore Carver's successful history despite endemic racism in New Orleans. I conclude this chapter with an overview of Carver's school culture and the critical aspects examined in subsequent chapters.

I consider this book to be a strategic intervention in the ongoing debate over teacher termination and school closings, which have reached epidemic levels.[19] It is essential to weigh officials' negative valuations against historical evidence and the experiential knowledge of those who built or were familiar with these institutions.[20] This book powerfully illuminates the competing definitions of success and failure at play, definitions that Ewing rightly argues are racialized and, therefore, problematic in the context of top-down school reform that ignores community perspective and experience.[21] Top-down reform without community input is precisely what happened in New Orleans.

TAKEOVER OF NEW ORLEANS PUBLIC SCHOOLS

On September 12, 2005, only about two weeks after Hurricane Katrina struck the Gulf Coast, the conservative Heritage Foundation released a report on "principled solutions for rebuilding lives and communities" there. It offered the following guidelines for restructuring education:

> New approaches . . . such as enhanced choice in public education should be the norm. The critical need now is to encourage investors and entrepreneurs to seek new opportunities within these [hurricane-affected] cities. The key is to encourage private-sector creativity—for example, by declaring New Orleans and other severely damaged areas "Opportunity Zones."[22]

Immediately following the release of this report, President George W. Bush delivered a national address from New Orleans urging Congress to create a Gulf Opportunity Zone in Louisiana, Mississippi, and Alabama, where the government "will take the side of entrepreneurs as they lead the [region's] economic revival."[23] The next day, the Heritage Foundation weighed in on "how to turn the president's Gulf Coast pledge into reality" and called for Congress to "use existing federal charter school funding to encourage the development of charter schools."[24] Following calls for charter school expansion in affected areas, the US Department of Education offered rebuilding monies, but only for charter schools, not traditional public schools.[25]

Countless reports followed the Heritage report, calling for the expansion of charter schools in New Orleans.[26] If the federal government planned to "take the side of entrepreneurs," who would take the side of the displaced New Orleans communities, teachers, and students, and embrace their vision for building a new-and-improved educational future? It would not be Louisiana's state leaders.

State leaders in Louisiana had their own vision of how to reconstruct New Orleans public schools. In November 2005, Governor Kathleen Blanco called a special legislative session in Baton Rouge. It was the occasion for passing Act 35, which redefined what constituted a failing school so that most New Orleans schools could be deemed failing and placed in the state-run Recovery School District (RSD). Act 35 allowed 107 of 128 of the city's public schools to be folded into the RSD, though only 13 schools were considered "failing" before the legislation was passed. This was accomplished by shifting upward the state's cut point for school failure, from a school performance score of 60 to 87.4, just below the state average.[27]

It is important to note that the RSD, created in 2003 (two years before the storm), had not assumed control of schools in Orleans Parish. For legislators, post-Katrina New Orleans presented the ideal time to not only take over schools but redefine failure in a way that maximized their power over the greatest number of schools in the city.[28] Significantly, the state had never previously demonstrated an interest in using its power to adequately resource or equalize black public schools in Orleans Parish.

Around this same period in 2005, Blanco signed Executive Orders 58 and 79, suspending certain provisions of charter school law, such as the need to consult and obtain the votes of affected faculty, staff, and parents before converting an existing public school into a charter school.[29] This would further marginalize the voices of teachers and students, disenfranchising affected communities with precision and speed.

Next came the efforts of local power brokers, who aspired to "reform" the public schools of New Orleans. Mayor Ray Nagin, a black official backed by the city's white business leaders, established the Bring New Orleans Back (BNOB) Commission. The education subcommittee, consisting of local real estate moguls, architects, charter school advocates, and Teach For

America representatives, was tasked with developing a plan for the schools. Teach For America (TFA) is an edu-business that staffs high-needs urban schools with uncertified teachers who work under two- to three-year contracts.[30] The BNOB Commission's education subcommittee issued its plan in January 2006, advocating a "world-class public education" in the form of an all-charter school district.[31]

Turning New Orleans into an all-charter school district would require coordination on the ground. Enter New Schools for New Orleans (NSNO), an entrepreneurial venture and charter school incubator founded in early 2006. NSNO sought founders to *start* charter schools, principals to *lead* charter schools, teachers to *teach* in charter schools, members to *serve* on charter school boards, and philanthropists to *contribute* to these efforts.[32] Needless to say, the teachers that NSNO sought were not the traditional teachers allegedly responsible for the "failure" of pre-Katrina public schools. In fact, NSNO founder, Sarah Usdin, had earlier taught as a TFA teacher, worked as TFA's executive director in Louisiana, and acted as a founding partner for The New Teacher Project, another venture to supply temporary recruits to teach in urban classrooms.[33] In short order, the Eli and Edythe Broad, Bill and Melinda Gates, and Doris and Donald Fisher Foundations awarded $17.5 million jointly to NSNO, TFA, and another NSNO affiliate called New Leaders for New Schools to recruit new teachers and principals and open new charter schools in New Orleans.[34] Everything was to be new-new-new. The "old" was cast as uniformly bad, without any consideration for black teachers' efforts or racism and its effects on black schools and communities.

Local, state, and federal officials, in coalition with national foundations financed by wealthy white philanthropists, clearly saw New Orleans as an opportune place to implement entrepreneurial reforms that would transform the public schools into a marketplace of "school choice." Black communities, however, would have little say or choice in the matter. How would this takeover and transformation be legitimated? And how would the slate be cleared to enable such reform to proceed?

BLAMING AND TERMINATING BLACK TEACHERS

If the public schools in New Orleans were failing, then someone had to be responsible. State officials and education entrepreneurs blamed black veteran teachers. Official proclamations did not focus on white policymakers' historic neglect of black education as an explanation for challenges in the city's public schools. Instead, this history was ignored while veteran black teachers were blamed for every conceivable problem. Regarding criticisms of the RSD and the expanding charter school sector in New Orleans, Usdin proclaimed, "There seems to be incredible amnesia in this community about what we had before."[35] Usdin was not speaking of the separate and unequal schools that predated Katrina by at least a century but rather of the alleged failings of the teachers and principals "we had before." Her own amnesia regarding perpetual state neglect of black education was glaring. Equally concerning was the vacuous proposition that black teachers brought nothing of value to the city's public schools.

Linda Johnson, president of the Louisiana Board of Elementary and Secondary Education (BESE), indicated that the state takeover was "the only way to terminate . . . central office employees, eliminate the collective bargaining agreement and leverage the opportunity to start anew."[36] Likewise, RSD superintendent Paul Vallas praised the temporary recruits provided by TFA as well as nonunionized charter schools, making clear: "I don't want the majority of my teaching staff to work more than ten years. The cost of sustaining those individuals becomes so enormous."[37] The mass termination of teachers was viewed as a cost-saving mechanism to decrease expenses related to laddered pay, benefits, and pensions, which new transient teachers would not expect and experienced black teachers, according to Johnson and Vallas, did not deserve.

The move to hire new teachers—most of them white and from outside the community—was not motivated by economics alone. It was clearly connected to a low cultural valuation of black veteran educators. BESE member Chas Roemer professed, "Charter schools are now a threat to a jobs program called public education."[38] His reference aligned with wider characterizations of African Americans as shiftless and dependent on state welfare, and implied that lazy and incompetent veteran teachers, who once relied on public schools for employment, could no longer count on collecting a salary in exchange for an alleged failure to perform. Such comments made clear that veteran educators and the teacher union were viewed as the primary cause of the challenges faced by New Orleans public schools before 2005.[39]

In November 2005, the Orleans Parish School Board (OPSB), pressured by the state, announced that the district's teachers would be terminated in March 2006. This action involved 7,500 veteran educators and support staff—a large portion unionized through United Teachers of New Orleans (a local affiliate of the American Federation of Teachers)—and dissolved the collective bargaining agreement with OPSB. Veteran teachers rehired in the RSD, including charter schools, would be treated as first-year employees with respect to pension in the state teacher retirement system.[40]

In 2005, black veteran teachers constituted approximately 75 percent of New Orleans public school teachers. By 2008–09, veteran teachers in the RSD plummeted to 46 percent.[41] In his study on teacher quality in New Orleans, Howard Nelson reported, "Both the RSD and many charters decided to hire new teachers enrolled in alternative certification [programs] and some teachers with no certification at all."[42] In 2010–11, five years after Katrina, nearly 40 percent of the city's teachers had been teaching for three years or less. The percentage of white teachers had nearly doubled, from 24 to 46 percent.[43]

Racism was a central dynamic in teachers' mass termination and the takeover of New Orleans public schools. The findings in *Oliver v. Orleans Parish School Board*, a class action lawsuit initiated in New Orleans' Civil District Court on behalf of terminated teachers, were telling.[44] To repeat, state officials had faulted veteran teachers for public school problems. The district court, however, affirmed that fired teachers had no record or notice of unsatisfactory performance prior to state takeover; all were in "good standing" and "met or exceeded all state requirements."[45] Additionally, although thousands of veteran educators were available to teach post-Katrina, the Recovery School District (RSD) asserted there was a teacher shortage and BESE approved a TFA contract nearly simultaneously with teachers' termination.[46] Meanwhile, state superintendent Cecil Picard told federal authorities that monies would be used to pay the salaries and benefits of out-of-work teachers. Nonetheless, "the State diverted [over $500 million] to the RSD" and offered signing bonuses and housing allowances to out-of-state recruits, some as high as $17,500.[47] In sum, black teachers who had served the schools for decades and lost their homes in Katrina were terminated, while recruits lacking community roots and teaching experience were hired in their stead—and paid generously to relocate.

The state's treatment of teachers and public schools in majority-black Orleans Parish was unique when compared to similarly affected white districts.[48] The nearby, largely white St. Tammany Parish had 5,600 public school employees and schools comparably damaged by the storm. Gayle Sloan, that district's superintendent, described state education officials as "very supportive." All of St. Tammany's public schools had reopened by October 2005, even if it meant finding alternative locations due to storm damage. Not a single employee was terminated, and all were paid while schools remained closed. By contrast, when the superintendent of New Orleans proposed to reopen schools, the request was rebuffed by Picard, and teachers were put on leave without pay, then terminated.[49]

After the teachers were removed, it followed that the "failing" schools should be either closed or reconstituted as charter schools. By 2014, the so-called reformers had reached their goal: RSD-New Orleans became the nation's first all-charter school district. Not a single neighborhood public school remained open in the district.[50]

The historic all-black Carver Senior High School was one of many public schools closed in New Orleans. I now briefly introduce Carver and turn to a history of black educational institutions that predated it, enabling us to see Carver as part of a longer legacy of institution building by black teachers. Pushing back against characterizations of "failure" requires an intimate portrait of what came before.

CARVER SENIOR HIGH SCHOOL: FAILURE OR BURIED TREASURE?

By official accounts, Carver epitomized the "failure" that presumably explained the mass termination of teachers and the closing and chartering of public schools. From the outside, Carver could hardly be considered a model high school, surrounded by train tracks and located near the Desire public housing development, one of the largest and ostensibly most dangerous of its kind in the nation. Consider a 1980 depiction of the Desire community in the city's major newspaper, the *Times-Picayune*:

A baby screams in the night. A rat has bitten him while he sleeps in a Desire Housing Project apartment. . . . [Drug] addicts and pushers loiter daily on the corner. . . . Sometimes it is impossible to reach a nearby grocery store without being offered several kinds of dope. . . . The social and economic ills that plague these residents every day—most of them children and teen-agers—are like an urban cancer. . . . Most families earn less than $4,000 a year. . . . They don't know what a neighborhood is, or what success means.[51]

The children, teenagers, and families in Desire were part of the Carver school community, which suffered stigma as a project school with a host of educational problems.[52] In 1981, New Orleans public schools superintendent Robert Arends reported that many students lied about their addresses to facilitate attendance at other schools, with "the implication being that they don't want to go to Carver."[53]

As 1986 Carver graduate Kelly O'Guinn explained to me, "The area around Carver gets classified as kind of a rough neighborhood."[54] Yet, from the inside—meaning the perspectives and lived experiences of Carver stu-dents—a more complex narrative existed. O'Guinn continued, "The teachers, I felt like they always cared about you. They cared about your well-being."[55] "Carver wasn't the bad school that most people thought it was," said Dwan Julien, a 1991 graduate. "The impression that people have of the school is not really what it was."[56] Hasan Sparks, a Carver senior in 1993, said Carver "deserved better recognition" and called it a "buried treasure."[57]

A nuanced perspective was provided by Lolis Eric Elie, a black New Orleans–born journalist whose father was a highly regarded civil rights attorney in the city. In 2002, Elie wrote about a visit to the Carver campus, where he discovered no operative fire alarm system, an intercom system that only worked in parts of the school, a gym without air-conditioning or heat, an auditorium that was shut down in the mid-1990s after flood-related damage and never repaired by the cash-strapped district, and a rusty tin roof covering an outside walkway that threatened to collapse on students.[58] Despite such neglect, he described the mood of the school as "warm and inviting," and commended Theodore Jackson, principal of Carver Se-nior High School, for his "firm and caring" tone with students. Despite the accumulative effects of disinvestment, Elie noted, "The grounds are well-manicured, thanks in part to the horticulture class in which students learn to take care of trees."[59]

These competing narratives—those from the inside and those from the outside—made Carver an ideal focus for study. There is something else that led me to study Carver. I am the cofounder and director of the New Orleans–based Urban South Grassroots Research Collective (USGRC), a research alliance with long-standing African American cultural and educational groups committed to equity.[60] Through USGRC, I heard stories from Carver graduates about their school pride, teacher care, student success, and lifelong camaraderie. The school's mascot was the Carver RAM, standing for righteousness, achievement, and mastery (Figure 1.1). It was clear that being a Carver RAM meant having a deep sense of belonging and accomplishment; Carver was a place that mattered. It was difficult to reconcile these stories with the mainstream narrative of failure circulated by policymakers, pundits, and charter school proponents. I wanted to dig deeper.

In *What We Stand to Lose*, I highlight the testimony of Carver students and teachers over the school's fifty-year history. In doing so, I document an intergenerational culture that nurtured self-determination and an abiding sense of community in the face of endemic racism. Alumni report that teachers exemplified a dual commitment to the mastery of academic content as well as the development of civic character in the context of life circumstances as African Americans, including the need to confront white racism and systemic racial barriers. The archival record substantiates student-teacher testimony.

In the following chapters, I document the robust culture of the historic Carver school and illuminate the wider context of racial inequity in which it operated. To be clear, Carver's history is important in its own right. However, I also believe this history speaks to present debates on school reform in New Orleans and cities across the nation. Veteran teacher termination in urban school districts is rampant, as is the closure of traditional public schools in black and

FIGURE 1.1 Emblem of the school mascot, the RAM, in the 1962 Carver yearbook[61]

brown neighborhoods.[62] The story of Carver from the inside should compel each of us to question narratives circulated from the outside. Kennedy suggests that those firing the teachers and closing the schools do not know the history.[63] Or perhaps they consciously ignored it.

Joyce King, Ellen Swartz, and colleagues discuss the significance of what King calls *heritage knowledge*.[64] Heritage knowledge or group memory "is the repository of knowledge, traditions, experiences, and cultural retentions of people of African ancestry and other liminal groups—long ignored and devalued as a strategy of oppression."[65] They go on to emphasize:

> At the center of [our work must be] the concept of "re-membering"—a process for recovering history by putting back together the multiple and shared knowledge bases and experiences that shaped the past. . . . The absence of Indigenous voice and accurate scholarship in school knowledge continues to position African people on the Continent and in the Diaspora . . . as people without a history—as if thousands of years of African cultural production did not [exist].[66]

Re-membering Carver means centering heritage knowledge over and above the white majoritarian narratives that circulate so widely.

I next offer a glimpse into knowledge on black education during the Jim Crow era of legalized racial segregation. Carver's history, after all, is part of a much bigger story of the struggle to build and sustain black schools in the context of white supremacy. This brief history is a first act of re-membering. The rest of the book, focused on Carver's history, is a second act. I conclude this chapter with a short description of my research methods and provide an overview of the rest of the book.

RE-MEMBERING BLACK SCHOOLS IN THE JIM CROW SOUTH

Black education in the US South is the product of dreamers and revolutionaries. Enslaved by whites, African Americans sought literacy, education, and freedom, even when it threatened to cost them their lives. It was unlawful to teach an enslaved person to read or write; anyone engaged in such a practice would be penalized severely. This did not stop people of African descent from forming secret schools throughout the South. Nor did an oppressive racial order stop free people of color in the Deep South from establishing their own educational institutions and pathways.[67]

After emancipation, the struggle for black education continued. Most Southern whites, however, were determined to subvert and undermine any attempt at black self-determination. Jim Crow or racial segregation by law was institutionalized by the US Supreme Court in the 1896 *Plessy v. Ferguson* decision. The New Orleans–based Citizens Committee, along with shoemaker and education activist Homer Plessy, set in motion the case that challenged segregation on Louisiana's railcars.[68] The Supreme Court ruled that "separate but equal" should prevail, although "equal" was nowhere to be found. A segregated school system took root.[69]

The classic rendering of a black school in the racially segregated South is Vanessa Siddle Walker's history of the Caswell County Training School in North Carolina. In *Their Highest Potential*, she details the school's origins, history, and closure.[70] Her account presents the "emic perspective," providing "the community's evaluation of its former school" as opposed to "using some externally imposed variable to define the school as 'good.'"[71] This resonates with what I earlier noted were students' experiences of Carver Senior High School from the "inside" as opposed to negative depictions from the "outside."

First known as the Yanceyville Colored School, the Caswell County Training School was chartered by law in 1897 as an elementary institution. It resided in a two-story house purchased for $400 by several prominent black community members.[72] By 1919, the school became so overcrowded that children sat on boxes due to inadequate seating and space.[73] A larger school was desperately needed, and two teachers—Elsie Green Palmer and Novella Evans—contributed the first funds to build it. Additionally, a high school was needed for students to advance beyond the elementary grades. Requests made to the white school board for a high school were repeatedly ignored and ultimately met with the offer that the board would contribute some amount if the community contributed.[74]

N. L. Dillard, who became Yanceyville's principal in 1930, would play a critical role in establishing the high school.[75] He began by leading Yanceyville—then a school of eighty children in grades one through seven—with three female teachers. Principal Dillard immediately engaged the community in the life of the school, inviting them to activities, holding PTA (Parent-Teacher Association) meetings, and publicly recognizing students' accomplishments.[76] He took it upon himself to add high school grades to the existing elementary school; meanwhile, a group committed to establishing a high school approached the North Carolina Department of Education.[77]

In 1934–35, the school was renamed the Caswell County Training School (CCTS) and recognized as a state-accredited high school.[78] The struggle was far from over, however. Rising enrollment—driven by the desire of black youth for education—created new challenges. At the existing school, teachers had to share rooms. There was no school gym and no shower. There were no lockers, and no lunchroom until 1946–47. There was little storage for books and academic supplies. Evon Reid, a music teacher there in 1950, had to float from space to space and carry music materials with him throughout the day.[79] In fact, there were 400 high school students and 125 elementary students in a meager ten classrooms.[80]

It took more than a decade of struggle with the school board to build a high school. For example, the students in the CCTS agriculture department once cut down trees donated by black farmers to help build the school. According to teacher R. A. Benjamin, the board used the lumber to rebuild a white school that had recently burned down.[81] In 1951—fourteen years after the campaign began for a new high school facility—school construction was finally completed.[82]

Throughout the school's history, black teachers worked tirelessly to educate their students. To facilitate student development, the principal and teachers focused not singularly on the classic curriculum but also on an array of opportunities. When the school first opened with only four teachers, it offered boys and girls glee clubs, a literary society, a drama club, and a Hi-Y club. Baseball and basketball teams also existed, along with a school newspaper.[83] The debating team was tasked with doing comprehensive research on the debate question. Then, according to Alean Allen Rush, a former debate team member, "Mr. Dillard and Mrs. Taylor too would come in and really interrogate you."[84] As one competition approached, in preparation, students not only debated at school but met where Mrs. Taylor lived. Walker writes, "There the teacher fixed dinner for them, and from 4 to 6 p.m. they would go through mock debates."[85] The local paper reported that CCTS won the competition.[86] Over the school's history, there were at least fifty-three clubs, all run by teachers.[87]

There was also the whole-school chapel or assembly. Students were given the chance to exhibit talents among other students and taught life lessons as well. Teacher Lucille Richmond remembers Dillard lecturing students:

> In this world today, the world you are going out in, you are going to have to be good, and extra good. You're going to have to be better. I don't care how many degrees you can go out and get, you are going to have to be better than the white man.[88]

Students remembered teachers for their genuine care. Teacher Reverend Wiley recalled that students "felt free to come to you. They would talk about more than just class. They would talk about personal problems."[89] The teachers were there to listen and lend guidance. Teachers also contributed financially to meet the needs of students. One such teacher reported buying clothing when students in her class needed it. Band director Leonard Tillman sometimes paid other band directors to work with students, who he felt would benefit from exposure to various conductors.[90] None of this negated a rigorous academic learning process in which students consistently described their teachers as "hard on them."[91] Meanwhile, Principal Dillard knew all his students' names. Former student and later school secretary Novella Graves recalled Dillard out by the buses, in the hallways, just about "everywhere."[92] He counseled students and supported them in attaining their aspirations, often accompanying them and their parents on visits to college campuses.[93]

In 1969, CCTS was closed. As a result of court-issued desegregation orders, the school was slated to become a desegregated junior high school. Four months before the last class graduated, Dillard passed away. Many believed the stress of desegregation, and his concerns about what would happen to black students, contributed to his passing.[94] While the white school board invested little in educating black children, the black principal, teachers, and parents offered everything. What is notable, Walker argues, is what they "were able to create despite the inequalities they faced."[95]

CCTS did not stand alone. A host of segregation-era schools—from Dunbar High School in Washington, DC, to Booker T. Washington High

School in Atlanta to Frederick Douglass High School in Baltimore to Central High School in Louisville—have been documented as providing positive school environments despite limited financial resources and other historic inequities.[96] All were characterized by exemplary teachers with high expectations for student success, a curriculum that included both vocational and classical training for students and a solid extracurricular program, and dedicated, astute leadership by the school principal.[97]

Similar contributions have been documented by Alridge, Hale, Loder-Jackson, and fellow historians in *Schooling the Movement*, which chronicles the work of Southern black educators long before and during the Civil Rights Movement. They show that black teachers "engaged in *intellectual and pedagogical activism* in their classrooms and communities, promulgating ideals of freedom and liberation . . . through teaching, leading, researching, and mentoring."[98] For instance, historian Jarvis Givens documents how black teachers developed pedagogic practices and curricula that challenged the white supremacist ideology embedded in dominant forms of knowledge. He shows how teachers "made efforts to introduce students to important events and figures from the Black past" and address concerns more broadly through "teachers' associations, summer school classes, and groups of educators who organized themselves in their local communities."[99] In 1912, Leila Amos Pendleton, a teacher in the Washington, DC, public schools, published her own textbook entitled *A Narrative of the Negro*. The book "offered students a story of persistent persecution of Black life and, simultaneously, one of Black people's ongoing resistance in their quest for freedom." Pendleton's book was recommended by *The Crisis*, the official magazine of the newly founded National Association for the Advancement of Colored People (NAACP): "The colored American would do well to put this book in the hands of his children, to let them know that they, too, have great men and splendid women. . . . These people are ours."[100]

Education researcher Sonya Douglass Horsford interviewed black school superintendents who attended segregated schools during their youth.[101] All felt grounded and positively influenced—even inspired—by the experience. As highly accomplished education leaders now, they attested to the value of the education they received growing up from knowledgeable, deeply committed black teachers. Dr. Steele recalled having "the best teachers you could find" as they knew "we were going to be somebody."[102] Dr. Clark referred to her teachers as "advocates, motivators, and leaders" who "insisted on excellence."[103] Dr. Baker explained that his teachers took "time with you in and out of school," shared "wisdom," and provided "encouragement." Baker told the story of a ninth-grade semester when he received an A in every class, except for a C in algebra. He lamented his grade with his math teacher, who was sympathetic but did not bend. Baker recalled her response: "[I cannot] give you what you didn't earn, but if you want to learn algebra, I'll teach it to you."[104]

In reflecting on historic, racially segregated, all-black schools, Walker concludes:

> Many of the schools' characteristics appear to have been a direct response to the challenges they faced and intimately connected to the oppressive circumstances in which they operated. In their world, there was a clear "enemy"—racism. . . . All the training and modeling by teachers and principal were aimed at helping themselves and their students overcome that enemy.[105]

Nonetheless, she goes on, "the more traditional and widely accepted portrait" of historic all-black schools is one of "almost complete inferiority."[106] In short, those inside the schools saw things differently than those on the outside, as they experienced black teachers' investments firsthand. Black teachers in Jim Crow New Orleans were no exception when it came to the depth of their commitment.

RE-MEMBERING BLACK SCHOOLS IN JIM CROW NEW ORLEANS

In the *Journal of African American History*, Monica White explored the cultural capital of teachers in New Orleans public schools during the era of segregation.[107] She writes that, during the late 1950s and early 1960s, African American teachers:

> sought to create academic excellence in their teaching of African American children in New Orleans. In a segregated society they engaged in activity fostering social justice and providing important services as did many other African American professionals of that time. . . . These educators and other

professionals made use of the "cultural capital" that was made available to them by parents and community leaders who shared the cultural value that education was the path to freedom.[108]

Four teachers and two students were interviewed for their thick description of the period. Various themes surfaced through White's investigation, including teachers' sense of mission and unity of purpose in fighting racial oppression; standards of professionalism, which made teachers pillars in their community; teaching practices that maintained high standards for all students; and a curriculum responsive to the world facing the students.[109] A student named Yolanda summed it up: "It was the commitment. Teachers then knew that [for] the kids they worked with, education was their ticket out. So they [the teachers] took it personally."[110] Teachers' investments, along with those of parents and community, accounted for the educational success of all-black schools in the immediate post-*Brown* years. Such efforts were critical, as a tumultuous period of white resistance unfolded after the 1954 US Supreme Court ruling in *Brown v. Board of Education* deemed racial segregation unconstitutional.

Kennedy presents the legacy of black educators in New Orleans, including their contributions to the development of young student-musicians and the city's distinct jazz tradition.[111] Born in 1888, Camille Lucie Nickerson was the daughter of William Joseph Nickerson—a music teacher who trained Jelly Roll Morton, headed Southern University's music department, taught orchestra at Straight University, and ultimately, offered lessons after school at Thomy Lafon Elementary School in addition to at his home. Camille Nickerson, a pianist, attended the teacher training program at Southern and taught at the public elementary Marigny School. Kennedy writes that in 1917:

> Nickerson gathered twelve of her advanced "female piano students" in her studio and formed the B-Sharp Music Club. Now in its eighty-fifth year, B-Sharp continues as an organization devoted to music appreciation and performance. Over the years, its membership has included many public school teachers and principals. . . . The B-Sharp membership became an extended cultural, social, and educational network that promoted music in the community and in the schools.[112]

Such efforts were critical because the Orleans Parish School Board supported music programs in black schools only if there were no associated costs.[113]

Part of the lineage of black musician-teachers, Valmore Victor taught at Lafon Elementary and Ricard Elementary from 1928 to 1953. Victor "played everything" and taught piano, saxophone, and trumpet.[114] Among his students was Ellis Marsalis, the late internationally renowned jazz artist. Victor also began what was likely one of the first elementary public school marching brass bands.[115] Then there was Osceola Blanchet, a science teacher for forty-five years at McDonogh No. 35 High School, founded in 1917, New Orleans' first publicly funded black high school. He also offered music lessons during lunch period and after school.[116] Importantly, Kennedy explains:

> It was not just music that Blanchet taught to the students. He was always trying to open up the whole spectrum of the arts to them. Although African American students were seldom invited to the Delgado Art Museum, Blanchet took his students there anyway. He made sure McDonogh 35 students visited the Cabildo and many other places of historical and cultural interest. He introduced them to different philosophies, and he challenged them with discussions about world religions. For years he painstakingly prepared a weekly bulletin that was posted throughout the school. In addition to the regular school announcements . . . [he informed] students about famous paintings, definitions of unfamiliar words, notes about operas, lists of poems, and suggestions of books for the students to read.[117]

Blanchet retired in 1969, but into his elder years, he continued to mentor musicians.

Education historian Raphael Cassimere Jr. attended Joseph Clark Senior High School in New Orleans from 1955 to 1959. Drawing on his own recollections, those of other students and teachers, and select documents, Cassimere provides a description of Clark's early years, from 1949 to 1970.[118] Principal Jesse Richards led the school for eighteen years, serving students from several black public housing developments—Lafitte, St. Bernard, and Desire.[119] Clark faced overcrowding. With one-thousand-plus students, a split schedule was instituted, with multiple shifts and major space constraints: "Physical education classes held dance classes in the basement, which was also used for the occasional 'sock hop.' . . . Locker rooms [were used] for regular classes. . . . The band room also served as a classroom for non-music classes. The library was always crowded with students on study break, and sometimes it was used for classes when regular classrooms were unavailable."[120] Discarded textbooks and school equipment from white schools were often used at Clark.[121]

Despite insufficient material resources at Clark and the inordinate responsibility of schooling so many students, Cassimere underscores the tenacity of the principal and faculty. As for Richards, he "seemed to be everywhere," not only in school hallways but in neighborhoods scouring the streets for absent students.[122] At schoolwide assemblies, Richards's commentary usually ended on a moral or political note. Cassimere recalled his guiding message: "Despite racial slights, we could achieve even amidst adversity. It was incumbent upon us to maintain our dignity and discipline at all times."[123] Students were told that they "had to be twice as good as whites to succeed" and were exposed to ample African American role models through Richards's talks and visitors meant to inspire. The teachers were likewise stellar, with advanced degrees and deep commitment. Herbert McCullum, a Clark teacher, earned his doctorate and later led Carver Senior High School.[124] A notable number of Clark students belonged to civil rights organizations, such as the NAACP Youth Council and the Congress of Racial Equality (CORE), including civil rights activists A. P. Tureaud Jr., Jerome Smith, and Oretha Castle Haley.[125]

As elaborated in the next chapter, white segregationists in the 1950s were under pressure to build more black public schools, hoping to quiet demands for racial integration. This partly explains why Carver Senior High School was built. Almost half of Clark's teachers transferred to Carver when it opened its doors in 1958, including Milton Becnel, who became Carver's first principal. As Cassimere suggests, the Clark spirit likely contributed to Carver during its first few years.[126] Both schools ultimately created cultures aimed at maximizing student potential despite the discriminatory conditions that shaped their campuses and the lives of their students in New Orleans.

Kennedy notes in his essay "The History of Public Education in New Orleans Still Matters": "The history of New Orleans Public Schools shows that when times were at their toughest, teachers stepped up to guide children, comfort them, deal with their personal and family issues, provide desperately needed nutrition during school hours, and offer alternatives to suspension and failure."[127] He offers as one example Fannie C. Williams, who led Valena C. Jones Elementary School from 1921 to 1954. Under Principal Williams, the school provided a nutritional program and medical care to students, offered access to library books via a bookmobile, and took students on cultural outings. She even brought Eleanor Roosevelt and Mary McLeod Bethune to meet the children at her school.[128] In addition to acknowledging Williams, Kennedy provides a long list of respected black educational figures in New Orleans—George Longe, Minnie Finley, Charles Kilbert, Maude Dedeaux Crocker, Yvonne Busch, Lawrence Crocker, Joseph Davis, Duncan Waters, Vorice Waters, Charles J. Hatfield, Felix James, Anna B. Henry, and Myrtle Banks—a list he says "barely scratches the surface" of the city's notable teachers. He concludes: "The sheer magnitude of the historical obstacles caused by the racial climate of New Orleans, and the tales of teachers, community members, students, and school administrators who worked long and hard to combat racism, should not be lost."[129] In King and Swartz's words, they must be "re-membered."[130] What were the historical obstacles confronted by teachers and students at Carver Senior High School in New Orleans? Is there something worth re-membering at Carver or was it the "failure" that officials and charter school advocates suggested?

WRITING A HISTORY OF CARVER: MY METHODS

I was born and raised in New Orleans. For twenty years, I have worked with USGRC in post-Katrina New Orleans to document the effects of mass charter school expansion, teacher termination, and public school closures on black communities—and to push back.[131]

Through USGRC, I have been privy to many conversations about what things were like in the city's all-black schools prior to Katrina. Veteran teachers, with unshakable commitment and community knowledge, prevailed over the difficult circumstances resulting from endemic racism. I heard stories from Carver alumni, who were deeply troubled by the school's closure and the proliferation of charter schools, not to mention the mass firing of the city's black teachers post-Katrina and their replacement by young, inexperienced white recruits from beyond the city.[132]

These stories prompted my historical research on Carver. Through oral history interviewing and archival research, I sought to answer the following questions:

- What was it like to be a student or teacher at Carver, including experiences inside and outside the classroom?
- What was the culture of Carver and how did specific traditions contribute to it?
- According to students and teachers, did Carver successfully educate students?

Over a two-year period, from 2017 to 2018, I conducted oral history interviews with nineteen Carver alumni spanning the school's long history (Figure 1.2). Additionally, I conducted oral history interviews involving twelve Carver teachers, most with thirty-plus years of teaching experience spanning the full range of subject areas (Figure 1.3). For deceased teachers, I sought interviews with children, former students, and colleagues and relied on archival and secondary materials. Methodologically, oral history interviews were gathered as counterstories in the critical race tradition, either as first-person or third-person accounts that center the experiential knowledge of people of color who daily confront racism.[133] Oral history accounts were contextualized with primary and secondary sources.[134]

Specifically, I conducted research, with a focus on Carver, in the Orleans Parish School Board archive at the University of New Orleans' Louisiana and Special Collections. I also reviewed materials on teacher Charles Hatfield at Tulane University's Amistad Research Center. Further, I gathered materials from alumni and teachers that I interviewed. I obtained secondary sources, when available, on Carver, Carver's teachers, and the surrounding neighborhood, including articles from the New Orleans *Times-Picayune* newspaper archive from 1958 to 2005.

Interviews were audio-recorded, transcribed, and analyzed using an ad hoc method of different approaches and techniques for meaning categorization and generation.[135] Documents were likewise read and analyzed as material evidence, generally for (in)consistency with participant testimony and other relevant details.[136] The elements of Carver's culture were surfaced through this analysis (Figure 1.4).

DECADE	STUDENTS	YEARS TO GRADUATION[137]	RACE/ GENDER	INTERVIEWS PER DECADE
1958–59	Merricks, Althea	1958–1959	BF	
	Lewis, Theron	1959–1962	BM	(2)
1960s	Joseph, Rhea	1960–1963	BF	
	Charles, Ernest	1962–1965	BM	
	Blackburn, Irvin	1965–1968	BM	
	Polk, Mary	1965–1968	BF	
	Calhoun, Willie	1965–1968	BM	(5)
1970s	Smith, Leonard	1969–1973	BM	
	Shaw, Ella	1971–1974	BF	
	Riley, Herlin	1971–1974	BM	(3)
1980s	Royal, Kenneth	1976–1980	BM	
	Mosley, Trenesse	1977–1981	BF	
	O'Guinn, Kelly	1982–1986	BF	(3)
1990s	O'Guinn, Denise	1986–1990	BF	
	Julien, Dwan	1987–1991	BF	
	Sparks, Hasan	1989–1993	BM	(3)
2000s	Gladney, Adrienne	2002–2004	BF	
	White, Catherine	2001–2005	BF	
	Lynch, Martaz	2003–2006	BM	(3)
			10 BF, 9 BM	**T=19**

FIGURE 1.2 Carver Student Interviews

TEACHERS	SUBJECT TAUGHT	EXTRA-CURRICULAR	ADDITIONAL ROLES	TOTAL YEARS TAUGHT	YEARS AT CARVER	DEGREE	RACE/GENDER
Enos Hicks	Physical Education	Lead Coach		37	1958–1976	MA	BM
Charles Hatfield	Language	Yearbook	Union Leader	27	1958–1979	PhD	BM
Yvonne Busch	Music	Band Director		32	1958–1983	MA	BF
Lamar Smith	Science		Community School Principal, Union Organizer	34	1958–1986	MA	BM
Lenora Condoll Gray	Social Studies	Close Up		38	1958–1996	BA	BF
Vermon James	Math	Student Council		27	1961–1988	MA	BM
Marilyn Pierre Degrasse	Business Education	Future Business Leaders of America	Cooperative Office Education Coordinator	8+	1962–1970	BS	BF
Danielle Foley	Health	Lead Coach	Athletic Director	37	1971–2005	MA	BF
Clarence Righteous	Horticulture	Horticulture Club		33	1972–2005	MA +45	BM
Avis James	Accounting	Dillard Talent Search	Counseling	32	1973–2005	MA	WF
Carol Righteous	English	Drama		26	1974–2000	MA	BF
Lindsey Moore	Principal (1965 Grad)		Health Clinic, Childcare Center	55	1985–1997	PhD	BM
TOTAL							12

FIGURE 1.3 Carver Teacher Interviews

SCHOOL CULTURE AT G. W. CARVER SENIOR HIGH SCHOOL, 1958–2005

OWNERSHIP OF PLACE

- Navigating and embracing a given space (school, neighborhood, or geographic locale) based on personal experience and historical knowledge
- Situating place, consciously and proactively, within a broader political context

INTERGENERATIONAL NETWORK

- Developing and sustaining meaningful relationships across time
- Appreciating connections between past, present, and future generations

ETHIC OF SELF-DETERMINATION AND ACHIEVEMENT

- Fostering a sense of inner authority, intrinsic capacity, and self-determination
- Embracing high expectations and supporting achievement

DUAL COMMITMENT TO ACADEMIC CONTENT AND CIVIC CHARACTER/CONTEXT

- Valuing traditional measures of education (content mastery), while also demonstrating concern for development of the whole person (civic character and consciousness)
- Accounting for students' life circumstances (race, income, social context) as part of the pedagogic process

COMMUNITY-BUILDING TRADITIONS

- Planning and participating in long-standing practices and programs that facilitate mutual association and shared mission
- Partaking in events that are culturally rooted

POSITIVE FEELING AND AFFILIATION

- Possessing positive emotions and feelings of well-being in relation to a community
- Defining self through a collective identity, tied to an enduring sense of belonging, affiliation, and commitment

FIGURE 1.4 School Culture

OVERVIEW OF THE BOOK

The remainder of this book chronicles the robust culture of Carver Senior High School over a half century. This culture was characterized by an ownership of place; an intergenerational network; ethic of self-determination and achievement; a dual commitment to academic content and civic character in the context of racial inequities; community-building traditions; and positive feeling and affiliation. In sum, I reveal an intergenerational culture that nurtured self-determination and community against all odds. Rather than centering a decontextualized narrative of failure, I turn to the testimony of those who experienced a historic school firsthand—and had the most to lose. In the tradition of oral history and critical race theory, experiential knowledge matters. As opposed to assuming a scorched earth approach, like that of charter school proponents, the value of historical memory is foregrounded. In doing so, it is possible to reveal an education model indigenous to the community.[138]

In chapter 2, I take a moment to situate black public schools in New Orleans within a history of white supremacy, then follow with background on Carver's founding in 1958, including the racially motivated decision of education authorities to locate the school complex "back in a corner someplace" near the Desire housing development. With this context in mind, I explore the first aspect of Carver's robust culture—ownership of place—and reveal how students and teachers consciously embraced the school and surrounding neighborhood despite its location on the city's geographic margins.

In chapter 3, I profile five teachers at Carver from its very beginning in 1958. In doing so, I reveal how additional aspects of Carver's school culture—an intergenerational network, ethic of self-determination and achievement, and a dual commitment to academic content and civic character in the context of racism—were fostered by veteran educators at Carver. These short biographies also reveal how the work of Carver teachers grew out of their life histories as black people in New Orleans.

In chapter 4, I explore in greater depth how an intergenerational network shaped school life at Carver. Here, I draw on the testimony of students and explore the experiences of a broader group of teachers, including those who joined Carver's faculty in later decades and taught a range of subjects, as well as a Carver student-turned-Carver principal. In this and subsequent chapters,

I present student and teacher testimony chronologically, highlighting the continuity of Carver's school culture over time.

In chapter 5, I chronicle Carver's ethic of self-determination and achievement, again including the voices of students and teachers. Here it becomes clear how deeply committed teachers were to the educational success of students—and the many things they did to support student achievement. Importantly, I briefly touch upon Carver's lack of material resources, as teachers sought ways to mediate the deficiencies that resulted from a lack of state investment in black public schools. (The lack of material resources is taken up more thoroughly in chapter 9.)

Chapter 6 provides an in-depth view of the school's dual commitment to academic content and the development of civic character. I show how teachers accounted for the complex life circumstances of the black students in their care. The pedagogic process involved more than subject matter; consciousness and the capacity to navigate and even challenge racism mattered too. In short, teachers attended to a range of student needs, whether personal, developmental, familial, racial, or socioeconomic.

In chapter 7, the school's community-building traditions are described and charted. By students' and teachers' accounts, Carver engaged in long-standing practices and programs that facilitated mutual association and shared mission among those in the school. Partaking in such activities and events, some of them culturally rooted in New Orleans, helped turn a school building into a cohesive community.

Chapter 8 illuminates how, taken together, these aspects of Carver's culture fed into one culminating reality: a community of positive feeling and affiliation. It is evident that students and teachers possessed heartfelt and affectionate feelings for Carver, which signaled the overall sense of well-being they experienced at school. Rather than a group of isolated individuals, they shared a collective identity as Carver RAMs, a deep sense of belonging, and an abiding commitment to the school community. To be sure, their connection to Carver and one another is an enduring one.

In chapter 9, I explore the context of systemic resource deprivation that defined life at Carver, and its relationship to traditional measures, such as test scores and dropout rates. Considering the history of racism and strategic disinvestment in Carver (and other black public schools in New Orleans), I argue that the robust culture at Carver evolved against incredible odds and that problems at the school were attributable to the challenges generated by meager financial resources for black schools, poor conditions in public housing, and related issues, rather than the failure of teachers. In this regard, I lean on the testimony of students and teachers, who underscored deteriorating conditions at the school and the effects of systemic neglect. This evidence, ignored by officials in the post-Katrina context, casts doubt on the claim that it was the teachers who failed rather than the policymakers who perpetually and systematically underfunded Carver and other black public schools in New Orleans.

In chapter 10, I highlight the post-Katrina experience of veteran teacher termination, school closure, and the fate of Carver. This includes an account of Carver's reopening under Louisiana's Recovery School District, its subsequent phaseout and closure, and the takeover of Carver's namesake and campus by a charter school network with novice teachers and a harsh disciplinary culture with a "No Excuses" approach. The visionary effort by the historic Carver community to rebuild the school and advance its legacy—and resistance to its closure—feature centrally. Additionally, the perspectives of Carver teachers and students on the post-Katrina moment are incorporated to illustrate the human toll of the disrespect and disenfranchisement they faced. Returning to King's notion of heritage knowledge, I conclude that re-membering Carver's legacy is critical.[139] This history challenges charter advocates' decontextualized narrative that public schools like Carver were "failing" and highlights the long-standing existence and value of black educational traditions—and the teachers who created and sustained them.

Finally, in the book's epilogue, I briefly chart the scope of school closings in urban communities of color across the nation. I share details on the destructive effects of school closings in various cities. In this way, the experiences of the Carver school community in New Orleans are linked to those of communities struggling to defend neighborhood public schools in other places. The pushback of various communities is explored. Ultimately, it is evident that what we stand to lose are the cultures, legacies, and institutions at the heart of the struggle for self-determination and equity by racially oppressed communities.

Carver was a place born out of this struggle, as I show in the next chapter.

CHAPTER 2

"BACK IN A CORNER SOMEPLACE"

Placemaking in the Carver School Community

> One of the things you may notice is the location of all the black
> schools. . . . Do you see any schools on a main thoroughfare?
> They're all stuck back in a corner someplace where nobody
> could actually see them or know where they are. . . .
> In spite of that, so many of our kids succeeded.
>
> —LENORA CONDOLL GRAY,
> Carver Senior High School social studies teacher[1]

To understand the culture that Carver teachers created and sustained with students, it is critical to map the place where school life unfolded. Carver was founded amid the struggle to end Jim Crow. The racial caste system of New Orleans pervaded every aspect of life—where African Americans lived, went to school, were employed, and more. Just a century before Carver's founding, Louisiana's public education system was established for white students only. Reconstruction-era schools, which opened formal education to blacks, were derided and often destroyed by white supremacists in the years that followed. *Plessy* cemented a racially segregated and unequal public education system in New Orleans, shaping classrooms for decades to come.[2] This is part of the history of Carver, built by a white school board intent on preserving a segregated school system by "equalizing" facilities for black students and teachers in the years preceding *Brown*. The Desire housing development, adjacent to the Carver complex, was planned by New Orleans' white housing authorities on the city's outskirts.[3]

Carver's teachers knew this history well. They, their parents, and their grandparents had lived it. When Carver opened, in fact, a cohort of teachers transferred there from the overcrowded Joseph Clark Senior High School. Carver, located in a part of the Upper Ninth Ward that initially lacked paved streets or electricity, was indeed back in a corner—just as Condoll described. Yet teachers and students found ways to make Carver their own; it was their corner of the world, and from there, they would build on the expansive dreams of those who came before. The echoes of ancestors who once occupied a Maroon colony in the same vicinity, linking formerly enslaved peoples with free people of color in New Orleans, were part of this place-making history.[4] The punctuated voices of the Black Panthers, who made Desire their home base in the struggle for self-determination, likewise echoed on these grounds.[5] Carver may have been built by a racist school board, but it was *made* by the people who called it home.

This placemaking process was a foundational aspect of Carver's culture. To appreciate what this meant, it is helpful to first situate Carver in the context of Jim Crow New Orleans. Following this, the story of Carver's founding and early years, and the sense of place-based ownership that teachers and students fostered, are explored.

CARVER IN THE CONTEXT OF JIM CROW NEW ORLEANS

For most of their history, public schools in New Orleans were not intended for black children or their teachers; they were considered the property of Southern whites. The history of slavery, legalized segregation, resistance to desegregation, white flight from the city, and ongoing racism translated into perpetual state neglect of African American education. This neglect, however, did not go unchallenged, as African Americans created educational spaces of their own and fought for support of black public schools.[6]

In the mid-1840s, a state constitutional convention called for the free public education of white children in Louisiana. Before the Civil War, white policymakers in New Orleans did not invest in black schools. The education of enslaved blacks was prohibited by state policy and free blacks had to organize their own schools. During Reconstruction, blacks fought for the integration of public schools, only to meet white resistance.[7] In late 1874, the New Orleans chapter of the White League encouraged white students "to boycott schools to which blacks had been admitted and to remove them forcibly from their classrooms."[8]

With weakening federal commitment to Reconstruction, the Ku Klux Klan's terrorism advanced with attacks on the recently acknowledged rights of

African Americans. Newly freed blacks were subjected to white violence that destroyed churches and schools, the infrastructure of the black community. In 1896, the Supreme Court's decision in *Plessy v. Ferguson* solidified the legal apparatus of segregation.[9] Despite historic mobilizations for educational equity by African Americans, a segregated and unequal system of public education took root.

In 1900, the New Orleans school board decided to limit public education for blacks to the first five grades.[10] Beginning in 1916, Louisiana decided to supervise public education for blacks through the newly established Division of Negro Education (DNE). The DNE's mission was shaped in large part by John Rockefeller's General Education Board, a group of Northern white philanthropists who advocated for elementary, agricultural, and industrial education for Southern blacks.[11] Outside of rural Louisiana in New Orleans, where urban blacks often learned skilled trades, industrial education was useless.[12] Louisiana's DNE was not abolished until 1963, but evidence exists that many black vocational teachers redefined the curriculum and taught "reading, 'riting, and reckoning" when beyond state supervision.[13]

The city's first black public high school, McDonogh No. 35, which did not open until 1917, was largely the result of African American demands. Booker T. Washington, the city's second black public high school, did not open until 1942; it followed on the heels of the Grace Report.[14] Headed by Alonzo Grace, the Citizens' Planning Committee completed a comprehensive study of New Orleans public schools during 1938–39. Paid for by the Orleans Parish School Board and local citizens, this report of findings was issued in 1940.[15]

Regarding black elementary school buildings—twenty-three out of twenty-five were visited—the Grace Report concluded that most required complete replacement. It also noted the schools were provided with only "a minimum supply of educational materials and books" by the state.[16] Only four schools had a separate room for a library, and six reported no library books at all. Only eight had an auditorium, none had a gymnasium, and the majority had very small playgrounds. Only seven had facilities to serve hot lunches.[17] In terms of black public secondary schools, McDonogh No. 35 was the city's only senior high school, with two junior high schools. At McDonogh No. 35, "practically every pupil studies two years of English, history, mathematics, science, music, art, and physical education," a program "founded on the belief that all pupils are preparing for college."[18] Only one-fourth of the school's graduates, however, were able to continue on.

For black teacher training, the Grace Report specified (in one illustration) that Valena C. Jones Normal School had seventy-three black student teachers enrolled in 1938, with the faculty experience ranging from fifteen to thirty years. There was a two-year curriculum with thirty-five course offerings, but the campus lacked "a library, laboratories, recreation rooms, gymnasium, auditorium, and other essential facilities for the adequate preparation of teachers."[19] Of forty-two graduates in 1936–37, only thirteen had found teaching positions by 1938. The report concluded many would have found positions "if class sizes in the elementary school were reduced."[20] For those who taught in black high schools, the median length of classroom experience was twelve years, with female high school teachers at seventeen years and female elementary principals at twenty-two years, revealing the central role of veteran teachers in sustaining black public schools in New Orleans.[21]

With *Brown v. Board of Education* in 1954, the Supreme Court overturned *Plessy* and deemed "separate but equal" unconstitutional in public education. As before, this led to massive resistance by local and state authorities as well as white citizens. By May 1960, federal judge Skelly Wright had yet to receive desegregation plans from the Orleans Parish School Board. Louisiana's governor and legislature passed a host of laws against desegregation, including a bill that authorized closing all the state's public schools to avoid desegregation and another prohibiting the provision of state funds to desegregated schools.[22]

Thus, Judge Wright issued a desegregation proposal of his own. In November 1960, two all-white schools were set to be desegregated in New Orleans—William Frantz Elementary and McDonogh No. 19. White parents quickly withdrew their children and harassed African American children on the front lines of the desegregation struggle, including Ruby Bridges at Frantz and Leona Tate, Gail Etienne, and Tessie Prevost at McDonogh No. 19.[23]

THE FOUNDING OF CARVER SENIOR HIGH SCHOOL

Designated a "Negro school" by local authorities, Carver Senior High School opened in 1958 in the wake of *Brown*, racially targeted state neglect, and white resistance to desegregation. This same year, seven new schools for black students opened, including the Carver complex.[24] There was a pressing need for access to both housing and schooling in the black community of New Orleans. Central City had become a densely populated, all-black tract, with scant land for additional housing, inadequate school capacity, and woefully dilapidated school buildings. The little land that remained was expensive, and white neighborhoods were off-limits.[25]

In the early 1950s, white school and housing officials planned a housing project and school village "in a swampy section of the Ninth Ward that was cut off from the rest of New Orleans."[26] While housing officials and white residents sought black containment in certain areas, school officials aimed to build and "equalize" schools to ease demands for desegregation.[27] Charles Colbert, architect and head of the school district's planning division, was intent on reducing land costs. His proposal suggested a "school village" on "an isolated ninety-acre tract in the city's Ninth Ward, roughly six miles from Central City."[28] The tract was bought for $300,000 in 1952, almost $6 million to $8 million less than the same amount of land in Central City. However, the area was surrounded on four sides by railroad tracks in addition to nearby drainage canals. Colbert's plan was presented in 1952 before *Brown* was decided by the Supreme Court.[29]

This same year, the Housing Authority of New Orleans learned it would receive $24 million under the 1949 federal Housing Act to build an 1,860-unit black housing development near the area proposed for the school village.[30] In short, the Desire Housing Project and Carver school complex would be built as part of a coordinated scheme. Colbert emphasized that "the price of real estate in this outlying section . . . would enable the Board to give the Negroes a school with facilities such as they had never had before—a football field, gymnasium, track space, etc."[31] He emphasized as well that the board "would be able to assist in city planning by helping to direct populations," a clear statement on preserving racial and geographic segregation.[32] Notably, Carver's building contract was approved one month after the *Brown* decision.[33]

The proposed sites for the Carver complex and Desire had problems that extended beyond geographic isolation. Historian Walter Stern writes that the area "was hardly suitable for large-scale human habitation" as it was partly a public dump and the rest swamp land.[34] There were no streets, except Louisa-Piety on the south end of what would become Carver, and train tracks bordered the area. The building contract went to Curtis and

Davis Architects and Engineers. Before Carver's opening in 1958, the board also contracted with Curtis and Davis to build Helen Sylvania Edwards Elementary School on the same site to serve kindergarten through grade six. As a swamp, land conditions were so poor for building that seventy-foot pilings had to be drilled into the ground for the foundation.[35]

Desire faced structural challenges as well, mostly due to poor construction. Opening in 1956—two years before the Carver complex did—the faux brick on Desire's 262 buildings covered only wood and plaster, which gave way to termites and decay. Floors were not reinforced with concrete, thus sinking began before families even moved in. By 1957, all units were nonetheless occupied.[36] More than ten thousand of Desire's fourteen thousand residents were children; school overcrowding thus resulted in a system of part-time attendance.[37]

Nathaniel Curtis and Arthur Davis, native New Orleanians and Tulane School of Architecture graduates, designed the Carver school complex. Their plan book for Carver Junior-Senior High School contains a sketch of buildings, along with ground-level details.[38] They explained, "Although the major street plan for the city predicts that the [school] site will be bounded on all sides by thoroughfares," access was limited, with the "L&N Railroad . . . form[ing] a barrier to the north." Utilities, including "gas, water, electricity, drainage, and sewerage" were "expected to be brought."[39]

At the outset, Carver Senior would accommodate grades ten through twelve, while grade nine and middle school grades resided at Carver Junior. Carver Senior encompassed 122,000 square feet, with fifty-four classrooms designated for different areas of study. The curriculum reflected in the architects' planning book included English, foreign language, speech, journalism and business English, social studies, math, business education (shorthand, typing, bookkeeping), science (biology, physics, chemistry), home economics, industrial arts (electrical shop, woodworking, masonry, mechanical drawing, blueprinting, automotive shop, welding), music, art, and physical education (with a gym to include equipment, training, and locker rooms, as well as an infirmary).[40] Carver Senior, named by the school board after George Washington Carver, the black botanist who taught industrial education at the Tuskegee Institute, offered an education that spanned the trades and career preparation, and ultimately, college preparation.[41]

The Carver Junior-Senior complex was laid out on east-west and north-south axes (Figure 2.1). Carver Senior was located on the eastern side, and

FIGURE 2.1 Aerial photo of the Carver Complex, from the 1962 Carver yearbook[42]

Carver Junior on the western side; a library (4,000 square feet) stood in the middle with an entrance on each side. The two sides—Junior and Senior—were mirror images of one another. "Noisy" subjects (physical education, music, industrial arts) would be in separate buildings on the far ends east and west, connected by covered walkways to the main building where "quiet" subjects (English, math, science) were taught.[43]

Other areas shared by Carver Junior and Senior, which laid along the north-south axis, included a cafeteria with junior and senior sides (14,000 square feet); a gym on the north end (20,000 square feet); and an auditorium (24,000 square feet) with a stage, dressing area, orchestral area, and seating capacity of two thousand on the south end.[44] Edwards Elementary was on the far south side with an auditorium in the middle. The entire complex cost $4.3 million.[45]

Modern architectural concepts guided the Carver complex design, such as "less massive structures, more human scale, relationship between indoors and outdoors, and acknowledgement of [New Orleans'] climatic conditions with appropriate shade, cross ventilation, and open spaces."[46] Elevated classroom wings and covered walkways were featured throughout campus, offering relief from the day's heat and informal spaces for students to convene. Although built for the purpose of racial containment, teachers and students from Desire, the Upper and Lower Ninth Wards, and the Gentilly area just north would make this place their own.

STUDENTS AND THEIR EXPERIENCES

From the outset, those at Carver Senior sought community, consciously and proactively claiming the school as their own. Assuming ownership of place meant that teachers and students situated Carver and the surrounding neighborhood within a wider political context. Indeed, their experiences as black people, combined with historical knowledge, propelled them to embrace and navigate the school as a valued space and right of possession.

The very first year students and teachers published the *Carver Times*, a school newspaper highlighting clubs, events, accomplishments, and issues relevant to all RAMs. The May 1959 issue described the ceremony honoring the three-school complex: "On Sunday evening, December 7, 1958, at two-thirty, the Carver Site Dedication Program stimulated and impressed the people of this City."[47] School counselor Sterling Cincore opened the program by leading "The Star-Spangled Banner." Emile Wagner, president of the all-white Orleans Parish School Board, declared "how pleased he was to see [Carver] had become 'a reality instead of an architectural dream'" while acknowledging that "many more schools are needed."[48] A biographic portrait of George Washington Carver was presented and a list of first-year faculty—Yvonne Busch, Charles Hatfield, Enos Hicks, Lamar Smith, and others—who staked a claim and ultimately invested decades nurturing students appeared in the program (see chapter 3 for their teaching biographies). A photo of the school's much-loved breezeway, a covered outdoor walkway, is featured on the program's last page.[49] The formal ceremony was followed by an open house during which "parents and friends are invited to tour the buildings" with student guides.[50] In the same communal spirit, counselor Etheline Acox, writing in the *Carver Times*, declared the guidance department "an agent of the entire faculty in learning about and coordinating home, school, and community forces."[51] In this way, the hallways of Carver connected the community.

The same *Carver Times* issue included a commentary entitled "Carverites Are on the March," by graduating senior Alice Wilkerson. Situating the school in a broader historical and political context, she proffered, "Many of our friends have stereotyped our school, complaining about the location of the school and how the neighborhood exerts a bad influence upon the pupils." But she continued: "The first Negro public school in New Orleans was built in a run-down neighborhood, but that didn't interfere with its pupils getting an education and being among the outstanding men and women of today. Our great forefathers couldn't select the neighborhood for their schools. Instead, they had to go to school in the woods without proper books, shelter, etc."[52] Turning to the present moment, Wilkerson asked:

> Do these [critics] know how hard our Principal, Faculty, Staff, and Student Body are struggling to give our school that fine name it fully deserves? . . . How many schools can claim such progress as Carver has attained during the first three months of operation? The school has a football team, a basketball, and a baseball team. Full senior activities are being carried on, all types of clubs, choir, and a band have been organized. Trips as far as the National Capital are being planned.[53]

Wholeheartedly embracing Carver, she concluded: "We know that the road ahead is rugged and the obstacles are many. However, with the proper determination, . . . there is no height to which we cannot and will not be able to ascend."[54]

Such tenacity was demonstrated by the woodworking class its first year, not only embracing the school but literally building its infrastructure. The *Carver Times* reported, "The students of Carver walked into their woodworking shops to find [them] bare of chairs, desks and equipment needed for building of projects."[55] Industrial arts teacher Felix Provost reflected, "Now to show that where there's a will, there's a way, the boys took crates off the breezeway and salvaged boards that were used to make small projects," including bookcases and desks. Students also studied different kinds of furniture across various eras, turning the absence of material resources into a time and place to learn.

Althea Merricks, a member of Carver's first graduating class in 1959, was a typist for the *Carver Times* and participated in Carver's Arbor Day celebration on January 16, 1959.[56] Merricks and others honored Dillard University, a historically black college and university (HBCU) in New Orleans, with a gold plaque and a redbud tree planted in front of the Senior Building.[57] In this way, Carver was consciously situated—and physically rooted—in a lineage of schools dedicated to the struggle for black education. Merricks was aware of Carver's role in this struggle, and of race-place politics, sharing that she "couldn't go to [white] high schools," passing them on her way to the overcrowded all-black Joseph Clark Senior High School before transferring to Carver for her senior year.[58]

Theron Lewis, a 1962 Carver graduate and Olympic track star, remembered Carver was built to relieve overcrowding at Clark and McDonogh No. 35. He began at Carver Junior. According to Lewis, black students had "never seen anything like" the Carver campus: "Most of the [black] high schools in New Orleans during that time didn't have gymnasiums." "It was an exciting time," he said, "walking into this big, pretty school" and "we would look at the senior side and couldn't wait to be a sophomore."[59] White resistance to *Brown* resulted in containment but, not without irony, on a campus with facilities historically not available to black students. Carver teachers and students maximized the possibilities, with Lewis relishing that he was part of the generation "that started the legacy."[60]

Rhea Joseph, a 1963 graduate, reflected on the meaning of place, saying because Carver was near Desire, students "always . . . had to step up" and "prove to be the best and brightest."[61] Ernest Charles, who grew up in Desire, attended Carver, and graduated in 1965, identified strongly and positively with both places. In 1957, his family moved into Desire, which he described as a tight knit "isolated" community that believed "it was us against the world." He continued: "You from the Desire [Housing Project], that's one thing, but if you're from Carver, that's another thing. I don't care if you're staying in Pontchartrain Park, [a nearby] middle class [neighborhood], whatever, [if] you went to Carver . . . they had your back."[62] In this way, Carver was a place where black students from different neighborhoods formed a common identity as RAMs.

Willie Calhoun, a 1968 graduate, said there was "intent" behind Carver's placement "between two railroad tracks" in a "physical location" where the school board "really didn't wanna . . . send white children."[63] Yet the presence of so many black teachers in the locale translated into a seamless sense of community. Reflecting on Carver, Calhoun physically pointed in multiple directions as he spoke, recalling elementary and high school teachers who lived just blocks from where he grew up. "If you go to the square between Saint Maurice and Tupelo, between Galvez and Johnson [Streets], we had four coaches who lived there." Affirming that school was one touchpoint on a larger map, Calhoun stressed that his "family was known to those people, because they were part of the community. They were part of the neighborhood."[64]

Leonard Smith, who graduated from Carver in 1973, pointed out that the Carver buildings were "designed by the same architectural firm that built Angola," Louisiana's state penitentiary known for warehousing African Americans.[65] Indeed, Curtis and Davis, among other recognitions, acquired a national reputation for building prisons.[66] This fact sheds light on the complex racial-spatial politics at play. Further, Smith underscored, the area "was swamps originally" and "really not made for residential [living]."[67] The area was historically a Maroon colony, where enslaved Africans escaped to freedom and built a community linked to still-enslaved peoples as well as free blacks in New Orleans (Box 2.2). Later, it became industrialized with a public dump, train tracks, and canals in addition to a shipyard. Looking

---

BOX 2.2

PLACEMAKING IN CARVER'S PAST:

ST. MALO AND THE CHEF MENTEUR MAROON COLONY

Carver Senior High School was located in the backswamps of New Orleans, where a network of Maroon colonies once existed. Maroons were fugitive African slaves, and they contributed to the formation of Afro-Creole culture in New Orleans. Historian Gwendolyn Mildo Hall explains that "the ecology of the city and its surrounding cypress swamps and luxuriant waterways" facilitated "[M]aroon communities of escaped African and Indian slaves that began during the first half of the eighteenth century" during French rule and "evolved into permanent settlements under Spanish rule."[68] Notably, two-thirds of the slaves brought to Louisiana under the French were from Senegambia and included a strong contingent of Bambara.[69] By the 1780s, a cohesive community of once-enslaved Africans had built Maroon posts in the swampy outskirts of New Orleans.[70]

Early connections existed between African fugitives and Indigenous peoples of the region, including the Choctaw and Natchez, with both groups seeking to overthrow colonial rule through planned revolts.[71] Maroons cooperated with enslaved Africans in rural Louisiana and in New Orleans, establishing not only a shared culture of language, folklore, food, music, and religion but economic exchanges of various kinds.[72] These networks solidified a wider Afro-Creole culture throughout the plantations, backswamps, and city.

From the Maroon colonies rose a leader named Juan Malo, better known as St. Malo. St. Malo developed a headquarters in the swamps near New Orleans, which united a wider network of Maroon villages. One of the villages was located east of the city and called Chef Menteur, meaning "chief liar." It was likely named for a Choctaw leader exiled from his tribe for lying who settled there with his family.[73] Not far from where Carver stood almost two centuries later, a major thoroughfare developed called Chef Menteur Highway, connecting the Upper Ninth Ward with New Orleans East.

Historically, the site of the Chef Menteur Maroon village reflected Bambara culture. This culture was defined by concepts of "balance, duality, and the unity of opposites," which provided a "place for both the conformist and the innovator."[74] That is to say, the culture valued both discipline and defiance. St. Malo was ultimately captured by soldiers and executed, but he continued to be revered for his unyielding commitment to freedom and defiance of white power.[75] It is possible that St. Malo's name originated from *sans malo*, which means "without shame" in French and Bambara.[76]

New Orleans also developed the largest group of free people of color in the South. The city's free Afro-Creoles (*gen de couleur libres* in French) were highly skilled, self-reliant, and committed to Liberté, Égalité, and Fraternité. They were educated, owned property, occupied a range of professions—and many understood that their fragile position between whites and enslaved blacks required investment in the broader struggle for freedom that animated both brethren in chains and Maroons.[77]

These historic networks have a lineal connection to Carver and the very ground on which the school complex was built. Carver was established as an educational outpost in swampy terrain on the city's edge. There, despite the odds, teachers and students built a tight-knit, intergenerational community that continued the freedom struggle, initiated centuries earlier by Maroons on the same land. Reflecting these cultural roots and building on heritage knowledge, students were taught to be disciplined as well as daring.

Long after St. Malo and fellow Maroons peopled this place, Carver student Keiana Belton reflected on "Blacks and Our Nation." In 1992–93, she contributed to a school writing project, pondering, "As my life passes before my eyes, I think what a long road I have to go." She declared to fellow students, "We are letting the white men get the best of us." She continued, "But, if you go to school and get the best education you can get, then, you got them scared . . . because once you have that degree in your hand, you are very powerful!"[78]

Her analysis and declaration resonate with past ancestors who sought liberation there too.

In a similar vein, student Maxine Gives wrote about Carver as "a city" that hosted the summit Save Our Teens. Trouble was brewing in the Desire housing development and elsewhere, she explained, which could "spill over into our city." Principal Moore, who walked the "well-known streets of the city" would not be satisfied "until the teens of G. W. Carver were safe and protected."[79] Like the Maroon colony, Carver was a place of refuge where teachers and school leaders fought for students, tooth and nail, creating a space of safety, hope, and possibility in a world characterized by racism.

Carver counselor Percie Ann Rodney wrote alongside students and captured the tenor of many when she expressed that "accepting the 'status quo' is the antithesis of what education is all about. We are charged to 'Educate to Elevate.'"[80] Maroons once resided in Carver's place and sought to elevate the status and rights of racially oppressed peoples. The demand for equity that began centuries before on those grounds continued in the classrooms, hallways, and breezeways of Carver. It was a school erected in a place with a history ignored by the city's white school board and architects but not disconnected from those who made this place their own.

at a map of the area surrounding Carver, Smith pointed out: "This was Edna Boulevard at one time, and became Higgins Boulevard. It was named Higgins after the shipyard" near the Industrial Canal (an artificial waterway built in 1923 for commercial transit that divides the Upper Ninth Ward from the Lower Ninth Ward and connects Lake Pontchartrain to the Mississippi River).[81] Smith fiercely defended the school-neighborhood bonds that African Americans built despite racist efforts to isolate them. In fact, he produced an award-winning documentary film entitled *A Place Called Desire*, which chronicles the housing project's history through the eyes of longtime residents (Box 2.3).[82]

Trenesse Mosley, a RAM who graduated in 1981, recollected the Carver campus with great pleasure: "We would sit under the breezeway. . . . They had all these nice benches where we could sit . . . and wait for the bell to ring if you got to school early." "Then when we would have lunch," she recalled, "you could still come out to the breezeway." Mosley pondered: "Carver has so much land. That was the thing about it. . . . If you walked from the front of the school and walked all the way to the back of the gym, that was

BOX 2.3
A PLACE CALLED DESIRE

Most outside the community knew nothing of the
hard work, determination, and initiative it took to live in Desire.
If you research it, you'll find negative stories. But for those who
were there, Desire provided a strong sense of fellowship.
Desire was a thriving community.

—LEONARD SMITH'S
documentary film *A Place Called Desire*[83]

Carver alumnus Leonard Smith, class of 1973, grew up in the Desire area. He produced *A Place Called Desire*, an award-winning film that features the stories of residents from the Desire public housing development and Upper Ninth Ward of New Orleans. Their recollections of life in the Desire area provide a view of the community that is strikingly different from mainstream accounts, which portrayed it as a hopeless, crime-ridden neighborhood where little of value existed. The testimony of Desire community members—and the history of the Upper Ninth Ward—open a window with a courtyard view of the lives that were built there.

In the late 1940s, the streets in the Upper Ninth Ward were "mud and slush. . . . They had no drains," creating a challenge to reach newly built homes. Area resident Malvin Cavalier recollected that his children would sometimes catch crawfish in the waterlogged gutters.[84]

The first homes for black World War II veterans returning to New Orleans were constructed in this relatively undeveloped area. In 1955, Louisa Street homeowners each paid $500 for the street to be paved. The neighborhood thrived as community members built and nurtured local traditions and institutions. Voting rights campaigns, for example, focused on getting schools in the area. St. Philip's Catholic Church was built by residents using parts of a donated structure hauled from elsewhere in the city to the Desire area.

The Desire Housing Project would soon follow. Before it was built, however, the former cypress swamp was drained of excess water. Desire opened in 1956 with 260 buildings on one hundred acres of land, and the vast majority of residents were children; not by chance, the development for blacks was built on the cheap with brick veneer and floors that lacked a cement foundation, which soon caused structural problems. Two years later in 1958, the nearby Carver campus opened with an elementary, junior, and high school for many of Desire's youth. Outside of school, there were many enrichments. A Boy

Scout troop existed in the Upper Ninth Ward. Residents enjoyed a 25,000-square-foot Desire Community Center built after Hurricane Betsy in 1965; federal funds were secured by Carver graduate and community organizer Johnny Jackson, elected to the Louisiana legislature in 1971. A wide array of recreational activities occurred at the center, including sewing, exercise, boxing, tennis, basketball, choir, dancing, drama, and cultural events of all kinds. The Sons of Desire group, another community fixture, sold records, books, and Afro fashion, and utilized part of the profits to assist community members with rent and other needs.[85]

In the late 1960s, Desire was home to the Black Panthers, welcomed by residents for their breakfast and after-school tutoring programs and unapologetic stance on black self-determination. When the New Orleans police and National Guard came in 1971 to oust the Panthers using assault vehicles, the Desire community—especially youth—stood between the Panthers and the police like a human barricade.[86]

"The first time I ever heard the song, 'Young, Gifted, and Black,' [was at St. Philip's School and in the neighborhood]," said Tod Smith. "[Living in the area] really prepared you because you knew there was a self-identity—and you knew that you could compete with anyone, you didn't have to take a back seat to anyone, you weren't necessarily subject to anyone. I don't know if every neighborhood made you feel that way, but I certainly got that sense growing up in Desire."[87]

The "struggle was real" in the 1980s and '90s as the War on Drugs accelerated, targeting the Desire neighborhood, among other housing developments nationwide. One of President Richard Nixon's top advisors described the war as "a ploy to fight Blacks and Hippies."[88] During this period, the nearby Robert Moton Elementary School was built on the Agriculture Street landfill, which had been used as a dumping ground for city trash as early as 1909. The Environmental Protection Agency designated it as a Superfund site in 1994, identifying about fifty cancer-causing chemicals. Residents filed a class action lawsuit against the City of New Orleans, Housing Authority of New Orleans, and the Orleans Parish School Board.[89]

Between 1996 and 2001, under the federal Hope VI grant, the Desire housing development was razed. This initiative focused on deconcentrating poverty (and the dysfunctional "culture of poverty" said to exist) through mixed-income housing; no consideration was given to the cultural traditions and resilience of the community. Further destruction came when Hurricane Katrina struck in 2005. The still existent Carver school complex was inundated with floodwater.[90]

Tod Smith summarized the experience of Desire: "People would say, 'Oh, you from the Ninth Ward. Oh, you from Desire.' And it was like, 'Yeah, so what? It's a place to grow up.' It was, to me, the best of all worlds. . . . I think that some of the things that other people would thrust upon your community, maybe that was the 'ugly' of it. . . . The beauty of Desire [is that] people growing up at that time, they wanted a better life for the next generation."[91]

Desire residents built lives and community bonds against a backdrop of geographic marginalization and racially targeted policies. Not unlike the Carver school community and Upper Ninth Ward, Desire was a place where black people took ownership, built grassroots institutions, and created a home, despite the racism that characterized New Orleans. In contrast to negative depictions of Desire from those outside, Kirk Stevens spoke from the inside, making the point: "I didn't know that I lived in a ghetto until I started hearing about it on the news. But I tell you what, I wouldn't trade the experience for anything."[92]

probably a good mile. . . . You could be all over the campus engaging with your friends or just sitting out on the yard." The statue of a ram, she said, was displayed at the school's front entry. Like students who came before her, Mosley described Carver as "our own little enclave, 'cause everything was there. We lived together and we went to school together."[93]

Hasan Sparks, a Carver senior in 1993, grew up in Desire decades after Charles did. According to him, many felt a deep connection to Carver, even those not enrolled as students. Sparks recalled: "There was people who you'd see at Carver, just kick back and mellow, that did not go to Carver, that were not in school at all, but just to get away, they would come there. They would come to Carver. They would be there at lunchtime, and they blended in very well, but that was Carver. Carver was the place you can get away from everything."[94] In short, the walls that separated Carver from the surrounding community were permeable. At times, it was a place of comfort and refuge from problems that plagued neighborhood youth in the 1980s and '90s: neglect by public housing authorities, violence wrought by racial marginalization, police brutality and corruption, and a deadly epidemic spurred by crack cocaine and a racist War on Drugs (for more on these conditions as a function of racism in New Orleans, see chapter 9).[95]

Martaz Lynch was a senior at Carver when Hurricane Katrina struck in 2005. Like many students, he was displaced and attended his last year of high school elsewhere (in his case, Tennessee). Considering Carver and New Orleans as home, Lynch explained his graduation plan: "I talked to the Orleans Parish School Board. I talked to the Tennessee County Schools. They let me come down here. I wound up walking across the stage with the first [post-Katrina graduating] class at Joseph Clark [High School, since Carver had not yet reopened]." Said Lynch: "I started here. It was . . . best that I finished here in New Orleans, because of all the things that happened. All the trials and tribulations and losing everything. It was [imperative] for me to come back here in the city and graduate, even though I didn't have to."[96] Carver Senior High School was a place that mattered to generations of students. In part, it mattered to them because it was consciously embraced by their teachers, who nurtured a thriving school community "back in a corner someplace."

TEACHERS AND THEIR EXPERIENCES

Lenora Condoll Gray was a social studies teacher at Carver Senior High School from 1958 to 1996, almost forty years. She reflected on the placement of black public schools in New Orleans, pointing out: "They're all stuck back in a corner someplace where nobody could actually see them or know where they are. . . . In spite of that, so many of our kids succeeded."[97]

Her reflection on the geography of Carver and other African American schools speaks directly to the race-place politics of white supremacy in New Orleans. It also speaks to the steadfast commitment of black teachers to the achievement of students in their care, despite racially oppressive conditions.

Condoll said most students "had never been on the other side of Canal Street," which divides mostly white uptown neighborhoods from mostly black downtown ones, running adjacent to the city's well-known French Quarter. Condoll ultimately headed the Close Up program, part of a national initiative to introduce students to culturally and politically significant sites in the nation, at Carver.[98] Her cousin Carol Righteous, an English teacher and a drama club advisor who began at Carver in 1974 and stayed for nearly thirty years, likewise sought to connect Carver's hallways and breezeways to other places. "I did a lot of field trips with my students," recalled Righteous. She took the students to stage performances at Dillard University as well as cruises in the Caribbean.[99] Despite efforts to contain black students, teachers helped them succeed at Carver while purposefully situating them in wider spaces and places.

None of this was intended to disconnect students from their roots, however. "I'm gonna tell you," Righteous stressed, "this is no joke. We put our heart and soul into Carver Senior High School. Yes, we did." Righteous said Carver was "the best kept secret." She recollected, "I would go to [school district] meetings and around the table they'd say, 'Where are you?' Then I would say Carver. They'd say, 'Oh, Carver.' I'd say, 'Have you ever been to Carver?' 'No, I haven't been out.' I'd say, 'That's why you say that.' I said, 'I've been at Carver [for twenty years]. . . . You think I'd stay there for twenty years if it were that bad?'" Carver was a place that Righteous proudly embraced and she claimed the students without hesitation. In particular, she emphasized that students from Desire "wanted to learn" and "were ready to work." It did not matter that many Carver students resided "across the tracks."[100]

Vermon James applied to be a math teacher not long after Carver opened and was hired in 1961. During his twenty-seven-year tenure, he taught geometry, among other math courses, and advised the student council. From James's perspective, "Carver was one of the best schools they had in the city during those early years." Despite this, he says there was "resistance that some people may have had and didn't wanna go down there [in the Ninth Ward]."[101] Business education teacher Marilyn Pierre, who arrived at Carver one year after James and remained for almost a decade before accepting a district-level position, agreed: "Carver didn't have too good a reputation sometimes because it was in the Ninth Ward [but it was] reputation more than anything" and not the reality.[102] Pierre taught shorthand, typing, business English, business math, and accounting; headed the school's Future Business Leaders of America group; and coordinated the Cooperative Office Education program, which enabled students to work in business settings and occupations during part of their senior year. Although Pierre later worked in district administration and taught for short periods at two other public high schools in New Orleans, she expressed: "My best teaching years, I can say, were at Carver." It was a place, she felt, where there were "really good students."[103]

Clarence Righteous, who married Carol, arrived at Carver in 1972 and remained until 2005. He taught agricultural science, or horticulture, with a focus on plant science, landscape, and leadership skills. He worked with students to build the school's first greenhouse and led the horticulture club.[104] Righteous knew the school's landscape and the neighborhood from the ground up. "I had no car when I first took the job [at Carver]," he shared. He walked with students to school: "I would get off the bus at Desire. I would walk through the projects. I would hear the kids, 'Look at Mr. Righteous. Hey, Mr. Righteous.' . . . You hold a conversation with them. . . . They get to know you." This was part of getting to know the place and the young people, who Righteous came to regard as children of his own—and their kids, years later, as his "grandchildren."[105]

Avis James arrived from Minnesota and taught briefly at another New Orleans high school before the district moved her to Carver. This was in 1973, when Orleans Parish opted to racially desegregate faculty rather than students, recruiting white teachers from the North and elsewhere. James, a young, white, newly recruited teacher, taught math and accounting, then served as a school counselor. She deemed Carver a "great school" even though it "didn't have a good reputation" and recalled that just prior to her arrival, the Black Panthers—with a home base in the Desire housing development— had shaken things up.[106] Avis remained at Carver for thirty-two years until Hurricane Katrina struck in 2005, setting in motion the mass termination of veteran teachers and school closures, including Carver. She married math teacher Vermon James.

Unlike Avis James, most white teachers did not come to or remain at Carver. Danielle Foley arrived in 1971—around the same time as James—and taught health and physical education as one of the only black female coaches in Carver's athletic department. Foley attested: "A lot of the white teachers wouldn't touch Carver with a ten-foot pole. They would not go back there at all. [Once they] got there and saw what it was, the ones that really wanted to stay, they stayed [and] were dedicated." On the whole Carver was and remained an all-black school in the post-*Brown* years and after.

As for Foley, she was committed to Carver. After teaching for several years in Orleans Parish, she was invited by the district's head of physical education to start a girls' athletic program at Carver. However, Foley explained, Carver "was in the heart of Desire, and it was considered not a nice place to go." It had a reputation as a high-drug and high-crime area, but Foley explained, "Something was just pushing me to say, 'Go!'" In her first year there, she founded the girls' track team and "got to start knowing the kids."[107] Foley ultimately made Carver her home for thirty-four years and became the school's athletic director.[108] She retired in 2005, just before Katrina.

Carver was a place Lindsey Moore knew very well. A 1965 graduate of Carver, Moore returned as principal in fall 1984. Not long after he graduated, Hurricane Betsy struck New Orleans and "the school went under water." He remembered sitting out back with Carver's first principal, Milton Becnel, who told him that "they took all the records and spread 'em out across the yard to dry 'em out." Moore continued, "That's how they salvaged our records" because there were no computers at the time.[109] Some of his own past report cards dried there in the sun. On the grounds of Carver, school leaders and teachers made their way—no matter the weather or political climate. In fact, Moore recalled a storm during his principalship in the 1980s that necessitated roof and electrical repair. "We had classes under the breezeway," he said, "because my people didn't wanna go to the other schools that [the district] assigned us" during repairs. Moore elaborated, "I worked in my office 'til I couldn't see 'cause then, we didn't have electricity." Time and again, teachers and students demonstrated a passionate investment in placemaking.

For the school district, Carver was not just geographically marginal; education at Carver was a low priority. Moore was aghast: "When I first went there, my directive was not to educate the children—[it was to] keep the school out of the paper. What kind of charge it that?" "Keep the lid on the place," he was told. When Moore joined the leadership at Carver, "It had a reputation that it was a so-called bad [school]—nobody wanted to go, and they still can't figure out how did you stay there so long." More to the point, Moore says the district "looked down upon us." He readily understood the broader political context in which Carver was situated—one of racial marginalization and economic disinvestment—but he would not allow the school to be relegated in this way. Moore averred, "That's why I said, 'You know, we got to find some things that we are successful with and build.'" The girls' track team under Foley was one example. Moore shared, "The man from the state department came [to Carver] and said, 'How your girls do what they do? I been back there. Y'all are runnin' back there in the woods.'"

For Moore, there was one straightforward explanation: the teachers cared and made the most of things "back there," and so did he. "From the superintendent, [to] the board members on down, they knew what I stood for, and they knew what Carver was about," asserted Moore. He "never wanted to be" at any other school. The school "couldn't afford" much, but they, as a community, "made it work." In one such instance, Moore mentioned to Wilbur Young, a Carver history teacher, that the school needed air-conditioning in several classrooms for the computers to function properly. Moore asked the school board, but they offered no support. Thus, Young and other teachers raised funds by hosting school dances every other Friday night.

The 1986 Carver yearbook summarizes the place-making process at Carver and the ownership assumed by the school community based on personal experience and historical knowledge:

> Carver Sr. High is located in Eastern New Orleans on a [ninety] acre site, shared with Carver Middle School and Edwards Elementary School. Carver has a population of over 800, and boasts some of the best academic and trade courses in the area. The student body is a diverse community, made up of youngsters from the Desire and Florida Housing Complexes. We enjoy an ambitious group of students, whose goals are worthy of academic scholars anywhere. Our students are growing up in economically difficult times, but are determined to make things better.[110]

Carver teachers played a critical role in ensuring that students "back in a corner" would also be able to engage like scholars "anywhere." Like the ancestors who came before them, seeking freedom and building a Maroon colony in the swamps, Carver teachers and students dreamed from this very same place of a promising future.

Indeed, aspirations of high achievement and the development of social consciousness were set in motion by some of the school's earliest teachers, who came to Carver under Principal Becnel in 1958.

CHAPTER 3

"MAKING THINGS HAPPEN THAT WOULDN'T HAPPEN OTHERWISE"

Carver's First Teachers and the Culture They Created

I just followed the course of right as it came along. Of course, I tried
to make things happen that wouldn't happen otherwise.

—CHARLES HATFIELD, Carver Senior
High School language teacher and union leader[1]

We did not know about Ms. Busch, . . . Mr. Hatfield, . . . [or]
Coach Hicks. We didn't know anything about all of their histories. . . .
They all had done amazing things in their youth [despite racial
segregation]. . . . I remember one of the band members [said of the
music teacher]: "Ms. Busch told me, 'You better stop tryin' to chase
them little nickel gigs and try and learn some music.'" He said, "What
you know about nickel gigs?" Well, she knew about 'em. . . . [The
teachers] were very low-key, but you can tell when they spoke to you,
they spoke from wisdom. They had experience. They didn't just come
off the top of their head and say, "Oh, I read this." They had lived it.

—LEONARD SMITH,
a 1973 graduate of Carver Senior High School[2]

The all-black George Washington Carver Senior High School in New
Orleans was founded in 1958, just four years after *Brown v. Board of
Education*, the Supreme Court ruling against the racial segregation of public
schools. Thus, it is no small irony that, in New Orleans, white segregationist policymakers scrambled to build more black public schools during the
post-*Brown* era. They hoped that additional schools and new facilities for
blacks might curtail integrationist demands.[3] Carver was part of the plan,
and one of eight black schools opened in New Orleans that year.[4]

If all-black schools following *Brown* were consistent with segregationist
desires, they might seem antithetical to the Civil Rights Movement. For
many African Americans, however, racial integration was not the primary

aim; black self-determination was the deeper goal.[5] There were other ways to advance this goal, in the face of mass white resistance, and Carver educators embraced them, building on a long tradition of black power teaching that reached back to enslaved African peoples in the swamps of Louisiana and those who taught amid racist violence in Jim Crow New Orleans.[6]

This chapter profiles five founding teachers, veteran black educators who began at Carver in 1958 and taught there for three-plus decades. These profiles provide a glimpse into the lives and teachings of men and women who built a culture of self-determination and achievement against incredible odds. Carver was constructed on the geographic margin of the city, surrounded by train tracks, near a public dump, and adjacent to the Desire housing development. Although Carver was a state-of-the-art facility in comparison to other black schools of the period, once built, the school board did little to maintain, update, or resource it. It was the teachers who supported and advocated for students, nurturing intergenerational ties and embracing a dual commitment to academic achievement and the development of civic consciousness in the context of racially oppressive conditions.

While self-determination and civic consciousness were central to Carver's culture, these things were fostered organically as an outgrowth of who teachers were, what they experienced as black people in New Orleans, what they desired for the students in their care, and how they taught them. As Smith alluded in the opening quote, teachers' anti-racism was "low-key." In large part, it was woven into the microcosm of the science lab, social studies classroom, band room, and athletic field.

Although the day-to-day work of Carver teachers may seem distinct from the sit-ins and marches of the Civil Rights Movement—and Black Power politics—it was squarely in the ambit of pro-black activism. Each teacher's profile highlights the need for a more complex conception of activism, one that runs along a continuum from more obvious forms of protest, such as fighting court cases or organizing teachers, to behind-the-scenes work such as mentoring students for black excellence or ushering them into self and political consciousness.

Here, I profile five founding teachers—language instructor and teacher unionist Charles Hatfield, science teacher Lamar Smith, athletic coach Enos Hicks, music teacher Yvonne Busch, and social studies educator Lenora

Condoll Gray—by charting their early life histories and revealing how self-determination and consciousness were central to their educational advocacy. More specifically, I highlight three aspects of Carver's broader culture as exemplified by teachers' pedagogy, including an intergenerational network that fostered meaningful relationships among teachers and students across time and connected past, present, and future generations; an ethic of self-determination and achievement that nurtured students' intrinsic capacities through teacher commitment to high expectations and educational excellence; and a dual commitment to academic content and civic character in the context of racism, which meant that teachers taught more than traditional subjects, embracing a holistic approach that included development of students' critical consciousness and consideration of life circumstances shaped by race and class inequities. As the following portraits demonstrate, the RAM, or school mascot representing righteousness, achievement, and mastery, epitomized Carver's culture.

CHARLES HATFIELD: LANGUAGE TEACHER AND TEACHER UNION LEADER

Charles Hatfield was a scholarly man, political scientist, civil rights advocate, and labor organizer. He held multiple graduate degrees, taught Spanish and English for nearly three decades at Carver, acted as longtime yearbook advisor, and played a pivotal role in the history of the city's teacher union. He was also the first African American to apply, at great risk, to the law school at Louisiana State University (LSU), which resulted in litigation that opposed racial segregation.[7]

Hatfield was born in 1915, but his family roots in Louisiana go back much further. His grandfather fought in a Union regiment with free people of color during the Civil War. Hatfield came from a line of educators that included his mother.[8] During his youth, Hatfield lived in a house on Iberville Street in New Orleans. After his father died in 1931, the family lost the house and moved to the nearby Lafitte Housing Project. The Great Depression was in full force and Hatfield terminated his schooling to assist his mother and siblings. Despite the circumstances, he read philosophy, history, and political science intently—and later graduated from Gilbert Academy, a private black high school, in 1938.[9]

During this same period, Hatfield worked a range of jobs, building the Lake Pontchartrain seawall through the Depression-era Works Progress Administration (WPA) and laboring with ironworkers and longshoremen. "That was the time," he explained, "when I became interested in organized labor. [The Depression] made me even more conscious . . . of the necessity [of organizing]."[10] Only twenty-one years old, Hatfield was one of the few African Americans in Louisiana with a voter registration card.[11]

In 1940, Hatfield enrolled at Xavier University, a black institution in New Orleans, while he was a postal worker and WPA employee.[12] A newspaper article he penned during this period conveys his disgust with racial discrimination:

> Several days ago, I visited a certain park in this city. . . . There is a fine golf course, excellent tennis courts, [and] swimming pools. . . . About ten years ago, this same park was poorly developed. . . . [Then] plans were made to develop [it]. . . . As usual the labor had to come from the ranks of the Negroes. . . . As I walked through this place I saw . . . all other nationalities taking part in the amusements. . . . The Negro was the only person who was forbidden to use this public park. . . . This is one among the many instances where the colored man has been denied the right to enjoy the products of his toil. While his sons drown in bayous . . . others spend exciting moments in the fine public pools.[13]

In 1946, Hatfield graduated with a bachelor's degree, majoring in history, Spanish, and English and minoring in economics and political science. Just before graduation from Xavier, he requested an application for admission to the all-white LSU law school. Two weeks later, he sent a second request. Instead of receiving an application, he got a letter indicating that Louisiana maintained racially separate schools.[14]

Hatfield approached A. P. Tureaud, one of only two black attorneys in New Orleans, about a legal case. Tureaud, in turn, invited Thurgood Marshall, from the NAACP Legal Defense and Education Fund, and Louis Berry, a Howard University School of Law graduate from Louisiana, to act as cocounsel.[15] Hatfield soon learned that a special committee involving LSU had decided to advocate the establishment of a law school at the all-black Southern University. Tureaud filed a lawsuit (Figure 3.1).[16]

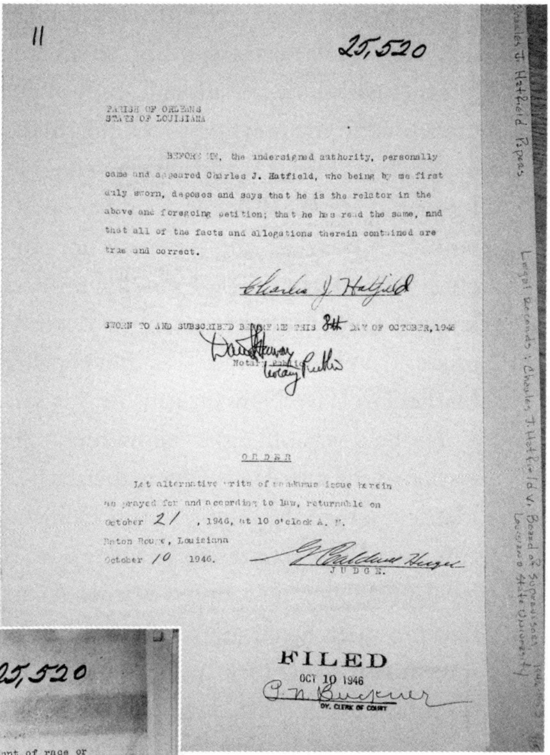

11

25,520

PARISH OF ORLEANS
STATE OF LOUISIANA

BEFORE ME, the undersigned authority, personally came and appeared Charles J. Hatfield, who being by me first duly sworn, deposes and says that he is the relator in the above and foregoing petition; that he has read the same, and that all of the facts and allegations therein contained are true and correct.

Charles J. Hatfield

SWORN TO AND SUBSCRIBED BEFORE ME THIS 8th DAY OF OCTOBER, 1946

Notary Public

O R D E R

Let alternative writs of mandamus issue herein as prayed for and according to law, returnable on October 21, 1946, at 10 o'clock A. M.

Baton Rouge, Louisiana
October 10 1946.

JUDGE.

FILED
OCT 10 1946
DY. CLERK OF COURT

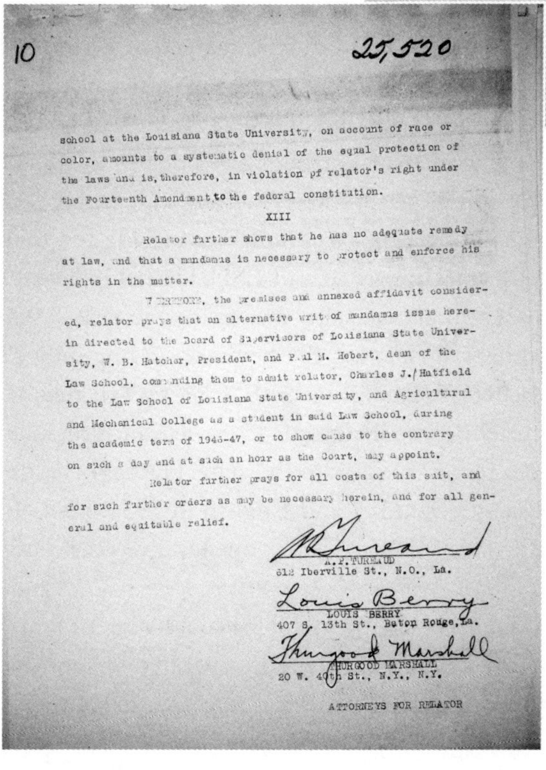

10

25,520

school at the Louisiana State University, on account of race or color, amounts to a systematic denial of the equal protection of the laws and is, therefore, in violation of relator's right under the Fourteenth Amendment to the federal constitution.

XIII

Relator further shows that he has no adequate remedy at law, and that a mandamus is necessary to protect and enforce his rights in the matter.

WHEREFORE, the premises and annexed affidavit considered, relator prays that an alternative writ of mandamus issue herein directed to the Board of Supervisors of Louisiana State University, W. B. Hatcher, President, and Paul M. Hebert, dean of the Law School, commanding them to admit relator, Charles J. Hatfield to the Law School of Louisiana State University, and Agricultural and Mechanical College as a student in said Law School, during the academic term of 1946-47, or to show cause to the contrary on such a day and at such an hour as the Court, may appoint.

Relator further prays for all costs of this suit, and for such further orders as may be necessary herein, and for all general and equitable relief.

A. P. TUREAUD
612 Iberville St., N.O., La.

LOUIS BERRY
407 S. 13th St., Baton Rouge, La.

THURGOOD MARSHALL
20 W. 40th St., N.Y., N.Y.

ATTORNEYS FOR RELATOR

FIGURE 3.1 Hatfield's lawsuit, filed October 10, 1946, signed by New Orleans attorney A. P. Tureaud, with cooperating attorneys Louis Berry, a Louisiana native and Howard University law school graduate, and Thurgood Marshall, NAACP attorney (and later US Supreme Court justice) (bottom left) and by Hatfield (top right)[17]

Hatfield faced a wave of threats after filing his lawsuit. In one instance, he received a letter asking him to meet at the Pythian Temple to discuss funds to withdraw his suit and study elsewhere. Hatfield was infuriated and proceeded to the meeting to tell the solicitor he planned to attend LSU. He recollected, "I went there and walked up to the sixth or seventh floor. When I got up there, the elevator door was open, and the elevator was down at the bottom. It was dark and there was nobody around, and you can believe I got out of there right quick. I ran down the stairs as fast as I could. . . . I don't know if they wanted to push me down the shaft or not, but I didn't wait to see."[18] While the case was moving through the courts, Tureaud advised Hatfield to leave New Orleans for his safety.[19]

Hatfield was offered a fellowship at Atlanta University in 1947, and he was pursuing a master's degree there when Southern's law program opened. Hatfield joined the Alpha Kappa Delta national honor sociology fraternity, completed his master's in sociology in 1948, and was invited to join the faculty.[20] However, he opted to leave Atlanta because of threats from a racist hate group on Spelman's campus, where he supervised student teachers. On returning to New Orleans, he had trouble finding employment because of fears surrounding his lawsuit. Thus, he returned to the post office, while he taught religion, history, Spanish, and English at Gilbert Academy.[21]

Hatfield continued graduate work, receiving a master's degree in education from Xavier in 1950. He completed student teaching at Joseph Clark Senior High School, where he received an "exceptional" rating. He also took courses at Southern, New Orleans University, and LSU. Hatfield's lawyers appealed his case, but the program at Southern was opened with $40,000 in appropriations.[22] Meanwhile, even though Hatfield was among only 13 percent of public school teachers in Louisiana with a master's degree, he faced challenges getting his teaching certificate due to retaliation, ultimately requiring Tureaud to submit a formal request to the state. Hatfield's certificate was issued for social science, Spanish, and English in 1952. Hatfield joined the faculty at Clark in 1953. When Carver opened five years later, he transferred there.[23]

Hatfield headed Carver's language department.[24] He could often be found in the school's foreign language laboratory, where he operated the console that controlled thirty-five student listening stations. Ten years into his tenure, eight hundred students were enrolled in Russian, Latin, French, and Spanish courses.[25] Ella Shaw, a student who graduated in 1974, said Hatfield would tell "class clowns . . . 'You can do better.'" She added, "He was a very good teacher" who "tried his best to work with us." After forty-seven years, she remarked, "I still remember the Spanish."[26] But Hatfield envisaged more than just students' language mastery. He was concerned about "the poor unfortunate Negro who is infected with the idea of white superiority" and thankful for those "who have never nor will [ever] permit our children to become infected by this dreadful ideology."[27]

Not long after Hatfield began teaching, he found himself "amazed" at the challenges teachers faced; not only did these challenges shape their work lives, "but it affected the child in the classroom."[28] He became active with the teacher union, Local 527 of the American Federation of Teachers (later United Teachers of New Orleans). He was the building representative at Clark and Carver, and as an organizer, he brought in two thousand new members. He also served as secretary-treasurer, was elected vice president, and worked as a legislative lobbyist. In 1966, Hatfield and Local 527 began a campaign for the school board to grant collective bargaining, which was rejected. This led to a three-day strike, the first teachers' strike in the South; efforts persisted, and in 1974, the board agreed.[29] For Hatfield, collective bargaining was a critical component of respecting teachers' labor, which did not, in any way, compromise their commitment to students or the understanding of teaching as a distinctly human profession. Hatfield believed, "Teaching is not just an ordinary thing. . . . You're dealing with human beings and human lives, and especially little young lives. . . . I've given hours of my time and I've seen other teachers give hours of their time, even weekends. . . . But they did it voluntarily, they weren't doing it under a demand. And that's the difference."[30] Union organizing enabled Hatfield to shift power imbalances that affected black teachers and address the intergenerational needs of "children and teachers," not just teachers, as anti-union forces liked to suggest.[31] Marilyn Pierre, a business education teacher at Carver during the 1960s, described Hatfield as a "union guy," noting, "If we had a strike, Hatfield organized it." Hatfield, she said, was "large and in charge."[32] Finally, under Hatfield's initiative in 1972, the teacher union established a federal credit union, with $20 million in assets by 1999.[33]

Hatfield seamlessly wove his organizing with his teaching and extracurricular activities. For years, he acted as advisor for Carver's yearbook.[34] The 1973 yearbook staff included the tribute: "Hatfield has worked untiringly with us. He has given unaccountable [countless] hours [of] advice, criticism, and legwork in helping us to realize the completion of the project. We salute you, 'Mr. Hat.'" Above the tribute is a photo of Hatfield, wearing what appears to be a union pin on his jacket.[35]

Hatfield retired in 1979, saying he "spent thirty years trying to help young minds improve."[36] He received a certificate of merit from Ernest "Dutch" Morial, the city's first black mayor, in 1978, and the union's Pioneer Award in 1983 for "untiring efforts . . . in helping to build a viable teacher union movement" in New Orleans.[37] In 2002, Southern University Law Center bestowed its first honorary doctorate on Hatfield in a hooding ceremony—one month before he passed.[38] Regarding his activism and teaching, Hatfield concluded, "I just followed the course of right as it came along. Of course, I tried to make things happen that wouldn't happen otherwise."[39]

LAMAR SMITH: SCIENCE TEACHER
AND CARVER COMMUNITY SCHOOL PRINCIPAL

Lamar Smith was a Lower Ninth Ward resident in New Orleans for over sixty years. A Navy veteran of World War II and the Korean War, Smith later became a beloved science educator, with a bachelor of science in chemistry and biology from Xavier University and a master's degree in educational leadership from the University of New Orleans. Smith worked first at Samuel Green Junior High, then at Clark High School from 1952 to 1958. He transferred to Carver its opening year, where he headed the science department and taught chemistry and physics until his retirement in 1986.[40]

Theron Lewis, the student-athlete who graduated from Carver in 1962, said Smith inspired an interest in science. "I wanted to be a biologist," said Lewis. Thinking back to science class with Smith, Lewis said, "He taught chemistry, but he always had this life lesson." Students would explore "what would happen if you mixed this with that," but whatever the scientific content of the day, "Smith almost always ended his class with a life lesson" that addressed broader issues (Figure 3.2). "He was very majestic in his speech and

FIGURE 3.2 Lamar Smith (middle, in black jacket) with students in the science lab, from the 1962 Carver yearbook[41]

in his classes," concluded Lewis.[42] It is important to note Smith's teaching emphasized both content mastery and social consciousness.

In addition to his high school teaching, in 1972, Smith became the founding principal of the G. W. Carver Community School, an evening program open to neighborhood residents. In its inaugural year, Smith described the school as a "human development center," explaining:

> It provides opportunities for education, the development of vocational skills, cultural enrichment, special interest, and recreation for all citizens. It makes available . . . services such as educational guidance, testing, vocational counseling, job information [and] welfare and social security information. The community school cuts across all ages, racial lines, religious, and economic interest[s], needs, and abilities.[43]

As the Carver Community School's "backbone," Smith employed at least fifty workers through the Comprehensive Employment and Training Act (CETA), passed in the 1970s to prepare low-income communities for public service positions. In doing so, he enabled students with economic challenges to remain in school while assisting their families.[44] He served in this capacity until his retirement, providing critical social and educational supports across multiple generations.

Like Hatfield, Smith was an active member of the city's teacher union. He acted as chair of the union's human relations committee and sat on its executive board. Following a 1969 strike, he wrote:

> The [New Orleans] School board was forced to give some token recognition to the Teacher Union. The strike witnessed a group of predominantly black teachers starting at 1,200 and dwindling to [269], who for ten hectic days with sore feet, wet eyes, and fallen hopes courageously endured threats and fear tactics of every conceivable denomination. The question is: why did they persevere? Was this the beginning of something new—the prime step in demonstrating to the white power structure that black teachers are determined to solve their own problems and, moreover, plan, shape, and direct their own destiny?[45]

Smith declared that "the double-standard educational system in [New Orleans] has been far more productive than its white designers had originally planned, for it has been more than successful in keeping the races separated and relegating to a position of near serfdom the black protagonist of the classroom."[46] He hoped the "gears of the system" could be reversed, urging, "Who would be free themselves must strike the blow."[47] Self-determination for teachers and students was central to his work.

Smith was a respected community activist, not only affiliated with the teacher union but also the NAACP, the political organization SOUL (Southern Organization for Unified Leadership), and the neighborhood-based Black Club, which monitored the "economic and political changes that affect the community" and sought "solutions for these ills."[48] Along these same lines, Smith was a member of St. David's Holy Name Society, a Catholic organization that "spreads the teaching of the church through examples in the community."[49]

His son, Lamar Smith Jr., and former student Douglas Haywood described Smith as an "astute theologian" who knew the Bible "in and out" and was constantly reading books. After high school, Haywood operated a barbershop, where Smith came for haircuts and often discussed politics. Haywood recollects: "He'd come to the shop. He would sit three or four hours. He always had a book in his hand."[50] Married to Shirley Guidry Smith, Smith had nine children, two boys and seven girls, all of whom obtained college degrees, with several in the education field. At church, the Smith family took up "the whole bench."[51]

Smith received various awards during his life, including the NAACP Jessie Vickman Special Teacher Award and the Outstanding Science Teacher of the Year Award from New Orleans public schools. He was recognized by Ernest "Dutch" Morial and Sydney Barthelemy, both black mayors, for his teaching and was named an honorary state senator as well.[52]

After Smith died in 2003, the Louisiana state senate passed Senate Resolution No. 41 to honor his legacy of encouraging "students to further their education," with "many becoming influential members of the community."[53] Smith Jr. said that his father's students were successful, among them state legislators, members of Congress, and mayors. He shared, "I meet so many people and they tell me, 'Man, your daddy was just an inspiration to me.'"[54] Ultimately, Smith "encouraged his students to be self-disciplined and to help light the torch for another individual."[55]

Haywood remembers when this "little guy, Ray" came to the barbershop. He checked Ray's homework and noticed spelling problems, which he showed Smith. Smith told Ray to come back the next evening to the shop. In the meantime, Smith brought Haywood flash cards to assist Ray. Years later, when Haywood and Ray crossed paths, Ray expressed gratitude: "Tell Mr. Smith, 'Thank you,' and I want to thank you too. Because if it wasn't for you and him, I wouldn't have graduated [from college]."[56]

"My dad would always iron his shirt in the morning," said Smith Jr. "I mean, white shirt with the tie. That was his thing."[57] Smith picked up Coach Enos Hicks each morning, and they rode together to Carver.[58]

ENOS HICKS: PHYSICAL EDUCATION TEACHER AND HEAD COACH

Coach Enos Hicks was five feet, six inches tall and weighed 160 pounds, but he was "mighty in presence to most." He was a world-class athlete: the fastest sprinter in the South during his college years at Xavier, winner of the 60-yard dash in Madison Square Garden, runner in the Penn and Drake Relays, and participant in the Olympic trials.[59] He began his teaching and coaching career at Clark, and when Carver opened, became head coach of track and football and athletic director there. His mentorship of student-athletes spanned nearly four decades, from 1939 to 1976. Hicks held bachelor's and master's degrees from Xavier.[60]

Hicks had ten children of his own, seven boys and three girls, with nearly all earning college degrees.[61] Enos Hicks Jr., also a coach for forty-plus years in New Orleans, attests that his father was a guidepost for most students he encountered. Hicks was soon regarded as one of the state's best track coaches.

Lewis, who ran track in the 1964 Olympics, reminisced about Coach Hicks. He had "heard about the legendary Enos 'Hoopy' Hicks," so it was phenomenal "to finally be in the man's presence" at Carver. Hicks was not only an excellent mentor but also "a near-world's record runner." Lewis noted that Hicks "was coached by Ralph Metcalfe at Xavier, who ran with Jesse Owens in the 1936 Olympics, so Coach Hicks came through that lineage."[62] Lewis remembered Hicks receiving Carver's Teacher of the Year award in 1961 and seeing "the bag of medals that he won in track and field," which were visible during the ceremony. "We thought . . . we could win a bag full of medals [too]," said Lewis.[63] In describing Hicks's legacy, Lewis referenced the movie *Camelot*, in which King Arthur asked a young man why he wanted to be a knight of the Round Table: "Because of the stories people tell." "It was the stories people told about Coach Hicks," Lewis passionately conveyed. "He was larger than life to us."[64]

Lewis recalled being nervous about a race in the city championships. "I went to talk to Hicks. . . . I can't remember what he said to me, but it calmed me because . . . he said he had confidence that I would pull it off. . . . He just helped me work through it."[65] Lewis remembered that Hicks was "high on trying to secure scholarships for his top athletes" and "was always talking to athletic directors."[66] (Figure 3.3) Lewis won a scholarship to Southern University and held multiple world records.[67]

Hicks Jr. recalled that Carver coaches were always together at his house. "When we would be home and all the other coaches would come over there socializing," he said, "it was always about sports and who was gonna get a scholarship." Along with his father, he explained, the coaches were "preparing students" years in advance. He contends, "These cats always wanted the betterment of the students. I'm not just saying athletes—other students [too]. [My dad] was always trying to make them better and prepare them for the future."[68]

Hicks was also a disciplinarian, as "that was a part of coaching." "His whole thing was respect . . . If you had any sense, you immediately knew who was in charge" conveyed Hicks Jr.[69] Former student Lloyd Wills, who ranked nationally in the 400-meter dash and became a coach himself, reflected on Hicks's can-do philosophy, which pushed students to new heights. Wills remembers a challenging time as a Carver athlete:

FIGURE 3.3 Coach Enos Hicks (left) discussing athletic scholarships with Coach R. Lee of Southern University in 1973[70]

> I had just finished a hard-won race and felt sick to my stomach and drained of all energy. I told Coach [Hicks] that I couldn't go anymore—I was exhausted. He put his hand around the back of my neck and calmly walked me off to a semi-secluded spot. He imparted to me in very colorful language that I was the best runner in the next event and I could defeat anyone, even if I was sick. Coach was right. I ran the next race and was victorious. Coach Hicks never gave up on his athletes—even when we wanted to give up on ourselves.[71]

Herman Gray, a Clark student, remembered when, in 1955, Hicks disciplined him because he "was too smart to be a damned hoodlum." Hicks had heard Gray was doing things that would lead to trouble. After speaking for an hour and coming to an agreement that "I was about to throw my life away," Hicks brought Gray to his next class. Gray credits Hicks: "I am firmly convinced that if he had not gotten my attention, I would be either in jail, or dead." Gray went on to earn a bachelor's degree in physical education from Dillard University.[72]

Hicks was committed to supporting and developing students fully, not only as disciplined athletes. His son recollected, "When a kid have a problem, they would come to the gym. You're a coach, you're a counselor. He was mama, he was daddy, he was parent." Perhaps most important, Hicks Jr. recalled that his father

> set . . . in a kid's mind that there is a lot of ways to be successful. . . . You gotta have what he would call the safety net. What you gonna be when you grow up? Can't play football forever. Can't run track. . . . They're [Carver coaches] not trying to make you the athlete they was, they trying to make you the person they want you to be and they just using sports as a vehicle to get you there. That was his philosophy.[73]

Hicks Jr. was recruited as an athlete by McNeese State University, where he desegregated the track team.[74] But track was not at the forefront of his father's mind as he prepared him for his future. When the McNeese coach came to recruit Hicks Jr., he told Coach Hicks, "I'm gonna do all I can for your kid to graduate." He remembered his father's response with clarity: "My dad told [the coach], 'A lot of coaches have come here to talk to me and my wife about recruiting my kid.' He said, 'But you one of the first ones to talk about education.' He said, 'I like that, Coach. I'm gonna see if you a man of your word.' [The McNeese] Coach said, 'What that mean?' [My dad] say, 'He'll sign with you.'" For all his children—his own and those at Carver—Hicks emphasized the importance of educational achievement and personhood before anything.

Ernest Charles, a 1965 graduate, similarly reflected on Hicks and other Carver coaches: "As a young black man who didn't have a father, these guys talked to you about being a man." Of Hicks's influence five decades later, Charles attested:

> Coach Hicks was just there. . . . Different things, dealing with ladies and stuff like that, different little things that I still hold to right now. He used to tell us: Look fellows, if y'all gonna court [date] . . . get you a mint and put it in your mouth. . . . If anybody know me, they say, "Damn, why you got those two mints in there?" I'll be seventy years old, and I still do the same thing now [that Hicks taught me then].[75]

It is important to note that Hicks attended to the full range of matters relevant to students' coming of age. Hicks died one year after his retirement in 1976.[76]

YVONNE BUSCH: MUSIC TEACHER AND BAND DIRECTOR

Yvonne Busch, a legendary music teacher and band director, spent most of her career at Carver. Although short in stature, her talents, commitment, and command were unrivaled. She trained and influenced countless musicians in New Orleans, many of whom built not only local and national but international reputations.

Born in 1929, Busch grew up in New Orleans' Tremé neighborhood, where brass bands and second lines (processions that follow the brass band) often passed her way. From a young age, Busch exhibited a passion for music, even though her parents could not afford an instrument for her to join the band at Joseph Craig Elementary School. Her cousin, James Clifton Polite, however, was a student at Piney Woods Country Life School in Mississippi, known for its instrumental music program, and persuaded the school's founder to admit fifth-grader Busch in 1940. There, Busch learned multiple instruments, including alto horn and trumpet, and traveled nationally with student singers as part of the Swinging Rays of Rhythm to raise school funds. This included performing in states throughout the South and beyond.[77]

Busch returned to New Orleans in 1943 and played trumpet in the band at Albert Wicker School during eighth grade. She next attended Gilbert Academy, Hatfield's alma mater. Under band leader T. LeRoy Davis, she mastered additional instruments—baritone horn and trombone. In 1947, she won first place in the Tristate Music Festival in Arkansas. By twelfth grade, Busch aspired to be a music teacher.[78]

Busch followed Davis to Baton Rouge's Southern University, where he became director of bands. She majored in trombone and joined the teacher-training program in instrumental music.[79] Her freshman year, Busch was named student conductor of the Southern University Concert Band, and it became "routine for [her] to organize, teach, and discipline students who were several years older."[80] In addition to the instruments that she already played, she learned bass clarinet, bassoon, and oboe and took classes in woodwinds, percussion, and arranging. She also assumed first seat in trombone in what had been, up to that point, the all-male Southern Jazz Band. When the jazz band traveled throughout the South, Busch "was making contacts that would help her students obtain music scholarships in the future."[81] She graduated in 1951.

After graduating, Busch interviewed with New Orleans public schools and was hired for a short-term position at Booker T. Washington High School. She discovered a band program in which "many of the instruments were too old or damaged to be used, little or no sheet music was available, and methods books . . . had fallen apart."[82] Relying on personal funds, she had instruments repaired and obtained sheet music for students. Impressed with her capacity to play an astonishing number of instruments, students "instantly understood that Yvonne Busch meant business."[83] Although somewhat ragged, Washington's band uniforms became a symbol of pride and Busch's precise half-time shows set a new performance standard. Student Tony Bazley later participated in poetry and jazz recitals with Langston Hughes.[84]

When Washington's band director returned, Busch was assigned to teach at three schools—Clark High School, McDonogh No. 41 Junior High School, and Craig Elementary School.[85] Busch spent a half day at Clark and divided afternoons at Craig and McDonogh No. 41. Moving from one underfunded school to another required lugging music stands and books to the afternoon school and returning them to Clark. For a time, Busch's parents even paid a gentleman to assist her. Busch invested additional time on weekends to prepare students for football games, parades, and competitions. At the same time, she initiated work on a master's degree in instrumental music at the VanderCook College of Music in Chicago over the summers.[86]

When Carver opened in 1958, Busch was assigned with Hatfield, Smith, and Hicks.[87] There, she kept students practicing half-time shows until nine o'clock at night. In 1961, *Louisiana Weekly* named Carver the Band of the Year. Other awards followed, with the marching band repeatedly winning first place. Busch also received Carver's Teacher of the Year award in 1962.[88] Student teachers sought her mentorship, including Cynthia Sheeler Perkins, who ultimately taught music for twenty-one years in the city's public schools.[89] Jazz pianist Ellis Marsalis was a student teacher under Busch.[90] Herlin Riley, one of the top drummers in the world, also studied with Busch at Carver.[91]

Herlin Riley spoke to the precision of Busch's teaching and her demanding standards. Recalling Busch and his junior high band teacher, Lloyd Harris, Riley stressed: "Those two teachers, they really, really instilled a sense of discipline in me as far as music is concerned. [Busch, in particular,] taught me about paying attention to details because the small details will make something that's good great." He went on: "They taught me the method of how to count and how to figure out . . . the rhythm, [which] served me so well playing with the Lincoln Center Jazz Orchestra [as well as the New York Philharmonic]." Under Busch's direction, the band did not march until the music was perfected. On a Monday, according to Riley, she would tell students to "go out on your porch and know [a song] by heart by Friday," and on Friday, she would "go down the line to each and every person, 'Let me hear you.'" Riley emphasized it was not about "just going on the field and putting on a show [rather,] you had to have some substance [first learning the music, then the steps.]" (Figure 3.4). In this way, Riley secured the "solid foundation" for future achievements.[92]

Providing students with a foundation for future achievements was central to Busch. Student Leonard Smith recollected Busch telling students they "better stop tryin' to chase them little nickel gigs" and instead refine their musical knowledge and skills. Students were steered away from easy-to-get, low-paying work toward higher pursuits that required double the effort in a racist system. Such admonitions "were very low key," said Smith, but they came from teachers' experience of racism.[93] Highly accomplished and disciplined herself, Busch offered students "detailed instructions about every instrument in the band room," said Paul Batiste, once a student teacher under Busch.[94] Beyond the band room, Busch offered music lessons free of charge

FIGURE 3.4 Yvonne Busch with band students, from the 1973 Carver yearbook[95]

to students during summers.[96] Former students and student teachers went on to become veteran music teachers and musicians of the next generation.

In 1983, Busch retired after thirty-two years of teaching her musical repertoire. To honor her, Leonard Smith, also a former band member, produced the documentary, *A Legend in the Classroom: The Life Story of Miss Yvonne Busch*.[97] In the film, student Diane Jackson Hunt emphasized, "[Busch] taught us discipline and respect. . . . The entire band was a family."[98] Eddie King concurred: "This lady knew some things and she was trying to give it to us. You are our mama. You took care of us."[99] In the film, Clyde Kerr portrays Busch as member of a pantheon of black women leaders, asserting: "A woman like that in our midst to me is like being around a Mary Bethune or a Harriet Tubman or a Phillis Wheatley."[100]

When Busch died in 2014, 1963 Carver graduate Rhea Joseph saw many former students and musicians at her funeral. "They played some music before the service, and then after," she explained, everyone did "what we do in New Orleans, we have the second line—it was just beautiful."[101]

LENORA CONDOLL: SOCIAL STUDIES TEACHER AND CLOSE UP ADVISOR

Lenora Condoll Gray taught social studies at Carver from 1958 to 1996, nearly four decades. She said she was a "little cutie pie" when she first began—and she still is. This descriptor, however, does not describe Condoll's untiring efforts as an incubator of young citizens. After majoring in social studies and minoring in library science at Southern University, Condoll accepted a post at Carver, teaching civics, US history, world history, free enterprise, and applied economics during her career. She also traveled annually with students to Washington, DC, and other sites of political importance.[102]

Condoll grew up in New Orleans' Seventh Ward and graduated from McDonogh No. 35. Her father worked on plantations outside of New Orleans and was later employed on the city's railroads; her mother was a seamstress. Although her family was poor, her mother bought her books about places around the world, fueling an interest in human geography, world cultures, and travel. Growing up, Condoll was discriminated against, experiencing racism from whites and colorism in parts of the black community.[103] These life experiences shaped how she taught: she wanted students to see the world and recognize that they could exercise influence as politically engaged citizens.

Condoll was aware of the ways that racism affected black students at Carver and other New Orleans schools: "One of the things you may notice is the location of all the black schools. . . . They're all stuck back in a corner someplace. . . . In spite of that, so many of our kids succeeded."[104] Her commentary on Carver's geography speaks directly to white supremacy and the steadfast commitment of black teachers to the achievement of students, despite racially oppressive conditions.

For Condoll, teaching social studies meant more than engaging students in traditional study; she sought to ignite political consciousness and foster agency. To accomplish this, Condoll focused mostly on local government. She said she "always loved" teaching civics and "used to take kids out to work in campaigns." They would stand on corners, hand out fliers, and learn the work of organizing. Then came a letter from the white school board: "Teachers are not allowed to involve their students in political activities." Condoll became emotional recollecting her effort: "In the black community, this is . . . the only exposure [students] had." Condoll sought to develop civic consciousness through active participation, but, she explained, "[The board] found a way . . . to take away from our kids the ability to work in politics and learn." This pained Condoll, who believed in engaging young people on the ground.[105]

Dwan Julien, a student of Condoll's in the 1980s, credits her as "the one who kinda convinced me to become a registered voter when I turned eighteen." By Julien's account:

Condoll always talked about having your voice heard and it's not always something you have to say [verbally], but it can be something as simple as a . . . check on the paper in the voting booth. She said, there are so many ways our youth don't get their voices heard and it would be a good way to exercise your right after so many have fought for you to have it. It was one of the reasons that I registered to vote.[106]

Hasan Sparks, who grew up in Desire and attended Carver in the 1990s, also had Condoll as a teacher. He said that students "read a lot, and we did a lot of essays, but it wasn't dull though. We learned in that class."[107] Condoll helped turn on a light.

Condoll says she also "exposed [students] to the world of economics." She took them to neighborhood businesses to "find out what they did, how did they want us to advertise." Students would then create ads for them. Some businesses found it so helpful that they "wanted us to work during the summer," with one class generating substantial income. Condoll reflected, "Those are the kinds of things I did that did not look [traditional]—was not down on a lesson plan." In short, Condoll says she focused on "entrepreneurship," to "find out whatever your passion is and try to make it work for you."[108] It was a strategy of self-determination.

Beyond local politics, Condoll introduced students to national politics through Close Up, a Washington, DC–based program initiated in 1971 to advance students' knowledge of government and social issues. Under Condoll's direction, students took annual trips to political sites.[109] Condoll reports: "Each year for about twenty-three years, I would take a group of students to Washington, DC, so that they would get firsthand knowledge of the government as it worked from the ground up. . . . They would spend a week there. I mean, literally sitting on the floor of the House of Representatives, interacting with our Congress people. . . . It opened their world."[110] While in DC, Condoll planned visits to nearby universities, including Howard University, an HBCU, where students later applied. One such student was Clarence Nero, a youth from Desire who studied with Condoll, then received a bachelor of science from Howard and a master of fine arts from LSU.[111] Condoll had spoken with Nero the weekend prior to our first interview, revealing lifelong connections between students and teachers.[112]

Getting students to Washington, DC, required funds, and Condoll never balked. In 1982—one of many instances in which Condoll secured resources for students—she organized a French Quarter flea market to raise funds.[113] Not surprisingly, in 1983, she was recognized by the *Times Picayune/States Item* for her "dedication to students."[114] In 1985, Condoll was designated by students as the Best All-Around Teacher and described as a "beacon light" for Carver youth.[115] The very next year, Condoll was again among their "favorite" teachers, noted for her service as "senior class advisor, student council and Close Up advisor, coordinator of Teacher Appreciation Week, and one thousand other student related activities."[116] Commendations such as this came when Condoll was thirty years deep in teaching, demonstrating her unwavering desire to make things happen, as Hatfield described.

Condoll taught more than subject matter. Condoll recalled an "expensive black cashmere skirt," which she wore "to school four days a week." One day she would wear it long, and the next day, she rolled it up; sometimes she would wear it with a sweater, and at other times a blouse. She overhead students talking about clothing costs and mentioned that she wore her skirt frequently. In disbelief, the students observed the next week. "You told the truth," they said, conceding, "Now we know we don't have to always spend all that money." Condoll summed up the lesson, "It's not about how much or how many. It's what you do with what you have."[117] She taught students to maneuver around barriers.

Condoll "taught the person," not only the academic content, and supported students holistically. In cases where girls' mothers could not assist, Condoll stepped in. She recollected students who asked her to help them pick their dresses for prom. Condoll explained:

Not only did I do it, I said, "Okay, we're gonna run to the bridal shops. You're gonna try on some dresses and see which ones look good on you." Then they said, "Well, we can't afford it." A former student of mine who was in homemaking, now a teacher at Clark, made those dresses, but we wanted to bead 'em up. . . . Laid out some paper in the library . . . [and] I taught them how to bead the easy way. When they walked in that prom . . . they were fabulous. These are the things that our kids [needed]—it was like a family.[118]

Condoll wanted black youth to know that "they are important people." When students wrote names on papers that included initials, such as "Jon B.," she returned the papers and demanded their full names. "Who are you?" she asked. "This is not your name." It may have been "something simple," Condoll reflected, but it taught students: "Be proud of who you are." When marijuana came on the scene, she instructed students that drugs were "a form of slavery."[119]

Condoll's radiant smile in yearbooks (Figure 3.5) belies the rigorous work required to teach as she did, especially over a forty-year time span as post-*Brown* disinvestment took its toll on black public schools. Speaking of such neglect, Condoll shared, "I can recall one year, I had sixty-six students in every class. No place to sit. No books. Those are the kinds of things we put up with [from the 1970s onward]." She recalled problems with the auditorium, which propelled her "for a solid year" to request repairs from the school board. They wanted Condoll to take students to another high school for senior

FIGURE 3.5 Lenora Condoll in a social studies classroom with students, from the 1982 Carver yearbook[120]

events. Condoll put down her foot, conveying, "It would not happen." She personally met with someone at headquarters, making clear, "This is totally unacceptable. These things will have to be repaired."[121] Repairs were made and seniors convened in Carver's auditorium. This kind of steadfast advocacy defined Condoll's day-to-day work.

Despite the challenges, Condoll conveyed with deep sincerity, "I loved that school. That's the only place I ever wanted to [teach]."[122]

"THOUGH LIFE BE PERILOUS, CARVER WILL GUIDE THE WAY"

Reflecting on teachers during the Civil Rights Movement, Riley emphasized that their pedagogy went beyond academic content to address the life circumstances and prospects of black youth. He said teachers were guided by a desire: "I really want them to go further than we are." "[Teachers] saw some glimpse of light [in the 1970s]," attested Riley, and "[wanted students to] get outta that dark hole we were in socially and economically." He believed students were not fully aware of how this sensibility drove the small things teachers did, teaching not just school subjects but ways for students to successfully prevail, given the racial and political climate: "Looking back on it, we can see why they were like that."[123]

Whether organizing teachers like Hatfield, teaching life lessons in science class like Smith, inspiring student-athletes and seeking scholarships like

Hicks, providing disciplined music instruction on school nights like Busch, or taking students to DC to develop political consciousness like Condoll, Carver educators did deeply challenging work. Yet they did it with determination and vision for the next generation. Carver's culture, shaped by teachers' practices along a continuum of organized interventions to everyday interactions, is best characterized by Hatfield's invocation of trying to "make things happen that wouldn't happen otherwise." Despite the challenges of racism, teachers taught students to inhabit a world that did not yet exist—one in which they could thrive as fully human beings.

Grasping the depth of racism in New Orleans may have been what prompted Busch and choral teacher Zenobia Stewart to pen the words of Carver's school song:

Hail to Carver, Alma Mater Forever aye.
Though life be perilous
Carver will guide the way. . . .[124]

Things were happening that otherwise would not *because* experienced teachers wisely and proactively showed students the way. The next several chapters examine in-depth the culture that teachers created at Carver to guide the way for students.

CHAPTER 4

"THEN I HAD MY GRANDCHILDREN"

The Intergenerational Network That Shaped Carver

> As time went on, then I had my grandchildren.
> I called them grandchildren, because some of my students
> had children. Now I'm teaching their children.
>
> —CLARENCE RIGHTEOUS,
> Carver Senior High School horticulture teacher[1]

The sense of place evident in the Carver community was one aspect of a wider school culture. It was linked to other dimensions of culture, including an intergenerational network developed over time in a particular place. Carver meant something to students because of the people who inhabited the school and surrounding neighborhoods—veteran teachers who taught multiple generations within families and were also neighbors and fellow church members. Classroom teachers were encountered daily in the community and often acted as lifelong mentors. In sum, sustained relationships between teachers and students—and the belief that past, present, and future generations were vitally connected—defined the Carver experience. Teachers also fostered lifelong friendships with one another, as did students who stayed connected long after graduation while continuing to support Carver students behind them. Parents, too, were a part of Carver's enduring collective.

STUDENT EXPERIENCES

Most of Althea Merricks's brothers, and her sister, attended Carver after her.[2] Irvin Blackburn, a 1968 graduate, had relatives at Carver before him and with him; a cousin who lived next door attended Carver, played football, and received a scholarship.[3] Leonard Smith shared that his mother had an uncle at Carver, a class president and football star who "talked me into going."

Smith also "had a lot of friends there already" and "two cousins that actually graduated with me . . . in '73."[4] Trenesse Mosley's mother attended in 1958, plus her mother's brother and two sisters. She explained, "I would hear stories about how great the school was, [which made me] excited to keep the tradition going." On the importance of Carver in connecting generations, Mosley shared: "[In] other cities your college that you went to was real big. In New Orleans your high school was real big. . . . It doesn't matter that I graduated from Tulane University. I only get, 'You went to Carver' [when talking to people]. That's what matters."[5]

Kenneth Royal, a RAM who walked the stage in 1980, said, "You had a lot of families that had attended Carver . . . mamas and kids too. Some of the teachers that had been around for a while knew generations."[6] Lenora Condoll, as one example, taught social studies almost half a century there. Nearly all the veteran teachers from Carver interviewed for this book taught for three-plus decades. Almost thirty years after Carver opened, a 1987 review of Carver by the Southern Association of Colleges and Schools (SACS), which accredits educational institutions, noted that "teacher turnover is very low."[7]

Kelly O'Guinn, a 1986 graduate, said four of her five siblings attended Carver and recalled that Thomas Hoover, an industrial arts teacher and vice principal who taught for decades, "could tell you who you were." She elaborated: "He would tell you, 'Oh, you're an O'Guinn.' Mr. Hoover knew everybody's family. He could tell you, 'Oh, you're Christine's sister,' or 'You're Terry's little sister.' Yeah. . . . He knew exactly who you were because he had been there so long. He knew generations of children. That was it with a lot of teachers."[8]

Kelly O'Guinn, a student-athlete, remained in close touch with her high school coach, Danielle Foley, who taught at Carver from 1971 to 2005.[9] Martaz Lynch, who said "my whole family is Carver alum," appreciated that band director Wilbert Rawlins already knew his mother and "made it a priority to know all parents." Adrienne Gladney, Lynch's wife and a student at Carver from 2002 to 2004, emphasized that Sergeant Major Simpson, and many other teachers, "thought they were family," saying: "They would call your mom and talk to 'em like they've known 'em their whole life. [This included calls] to see why you aren't in school."[10]

Like a family photo album that spans generations, Carver yearbooks reflect rich kinship networks. In just one example, a 1962 yearbook photo shows a PTA meeting in the auditorium, standing room only as Principal Milton Becnel addresses the parents of seniors. Another photo, entitled "House of Doubles," features several sets of twins at Carver during this period. Ads in the yearbook demonstrate broader community support for the school, with sponsorship from "our friends," including black-owned businesses such as laundromats, supermarkets, drugstores, churches, barbershops, restaurants, and funeral homes.[11] A culture that connected "me" to "we" situated students as part of a lineal tradition.

For students, this intergenerational network included classroom teachers in addition to past figures of note in the African American community. The 1964 Olympian Theron Lewis recollected Coach Enos Hicks. He had "heard about the legendary [teacher]" at Carver. Significantly, he underscored that Hicks was not only a valued mentor but "a near-world's record runner." Hick's past accomplishments inspired Lewis, who likewise noted that Hicks had lineal connections to eminent black athletes. Lewis understood himself as a part of this intergenerational pipeline.[12]

Mary Polk, a 1968 graduate, remembered with great fondness Martha Francis, her choir and voice teacher. Ms. Francis "was my music teacher from sixth to twelfth grade," she reflected, as Francis had taught earlier at Polk's junior high. It was Francis who Polk says "taught me how to read a lot [of] the music that I sung," and the "importance of how I sit and how I stand [for projecting the voice]." "That was my mentor," proclaimed Polk almost fifty years later. Polk emphasized that Francis "knew my family" and "communicated with my parents, and she assured them that I would be okay whenever I was in her care." Now a minister with a master's degree in theology, Polk says her choir teacher was "very instrumental" in her singing—and Polk still sings today at concerts, weddings, and funerals.[13] Polk also noted that Principal Becnel "was a wonderful person" who would "talk to my father at length," always making time for students and parents.[14] Polk and her family were surrounded by a network of educators and caregivers with whom they had built trusting relationships over many years.

Herlin Riley, a 1974 Carver graduate and world-renowned drummer, learned music under Yvonne Busch, who taught for more than thirty years. Riley shared: "In my formative years, as a child growing up, my uncles were musicians. My mother is a musician. . . . They were all students of Ms. Busch. . . . I was hearing the name Yvonne Busch from the time I was in elementary school."[15] By the time Riley made his way to Carver's music class-room, he was primed to learn from this respected elder. Equally significant, he remained in touch with Busch throughout her life. Riley's emotions were evident as he shared a memory: "I still love Ms. Busch to this day. Anyway, I was in touch with her until she passed away a couple of years ago. . . . In her last years, I went to see her. . . . It was her birthday—[she was born on] October 18, 1929. . . . She was, maybe, now eighty-five. . . . This particular day I went to her house . . . I had a trumpet, and I had some flowers, and I played happy birthday to her. She welled up in tears."

Riley recollected that Busch said, "Boy, give me that horn," and, though too old to play it, "she was just holding it and just feeling it." A photo from that day shows Busch snuggled in a chair with a blanket and trumpet, while Riley, Smith, and fellow Carver graduate John Lewis huddled behind her with big smiles (Figure 4.1). "We stayed in touch her whole life, from the time I met her in '71 until she passed away [in 2014]," said Riley.[16] Riley still possessed the program for Busch's funeral, where both he and Smith were honorary pallbearers.[17] Musicians from across the city, trained by Busch, played at her jazz memorial. Smith, who worked for Kodak and is now a documentarian and producer, made a film on Busch and her contributions to generations of students in New Orleans.[18]

Ella Shaw, who graduated the same year as Riley, conveyed with pleasure having recently crossed paths with Marilyn Pierre, her Cooperative Office Education (COE) teacher at Carver (COE was a program designed to give juniors and seniors on-the-job experience in various professions). Shaw obtained a civil service job in her senior year and ultimately worked in the New Orleans shipyard industry, handling imports and exports. Shaw detailed their encounter: "She looked at me, and I looked at her, and she just smiled at me. I said, 'Are you Ms. Pierre?' She said, 'I know you, I know you, but I just'—I said, 'I'm Ella, your sweet child.' She say, 'That's you?' She gave me a big ol' hug." Shaw concluded, "It

FIGURE 4.1 Yvonne Busch celebrates her birthday with former students John Lewis (past drum major), Herlin Riley, and Leonard Smith (standing left to right).[19]

feels beautiful to still see a teacher . . . and they remember you."[20] Even years later, heartfelt connections remained between student and teacher.

Carver students also nurtured networks among themselves, maintaining relationships with those of their generation through lifelong friendships and class reunions—and across generations through the RAM Jam, a festive annual gathering of Carver graduates. Most Carver alumni shared stories of friendships with classmates, urging me to interview countless other alums with whom they remained in touch. Blackburn reported that his first high school reunion occurred ten years after graduation, then "Twenty, and then we did twenty-five, thirty, thirty-five, forty, forty-five, and now fifty."[21] Smith runs a private Carver Facebook group to keep alumni informed and connected, and said, "I [sometimes] throw in some tidbit history that a lot of people don't know." For example, connecting his Carver experiences to a longer struggle for black education, he shared: "Our original staff, Ms. [Zenobia] Stewart, which was our choir teacher, [and] Ms. Busch, they wrote the alma mater. They put a lot of thought into even the [school] colors [orange, green, and gold]. That came from Florida A&M [an HBCU]. That's where they got the colors from."[22]

Mosley reported that to this day, she talks with at least ten fellow RAMs weekly. "We are still just that close," she affirmed, "'cause we more than just went to school. We lived amongst each other."[23] In this way segregated schools and neighborhoods, created through racist practices and policies, nonetheless fostered close knit communities, where multigenerational networks thrived and connected people in ways that were personal and meaningful, even as the broader political climate marginalized African Americans.

In fact, Carver alumni consistently returned to the school, years after graduation, to develop supportive relationships with Carver students who came after them. Even though Blackburn graduated in 1968, he was featured in a Carver Middle School career day program in 1989, returning to discuss his work as an accountant and his service in the Navy.[24] Shaw detailed how the class of 1974 sponsored a banquet for juniors and seniors. She recollected that one classmate, an owner of several Subway sandwich shops, "did the inspirational speech" and "assured [students] if they try to better themselves and graduate, she'll try to look out for 'em."[25] Mosley spoke of what was called Alumni Return Day in the 1990s: "They wanted alum that was successful to come back and . . . try to motivate the kids. To try to tell them about their years at Carver and how it was. . . . They wanted the kids to see that these people came from the neighborhood . . . and they made it."[26]

Similarly, Kelly O'Guinn, who attended Southern University in New Orleans and played basketball, made a point of returning to Carver. She stressed, "Even then I came back . . . and would actually come in and practice with some of the younger girls, helped scrimmage them to improve myself and also to help them." In fact, she said, there was a long history "of alumni that would come in and help out and cheer you on." During her time as a student, Carver's gym was called "the dungeon" because alumni would "come in there with their drums and their beating. [They even] had chants." It was intimidating to visiting teams and "even if you weren't the best player," said O'Guinn, "you felt very comfortable because you had that sense of community [and] people there that had your back."[27] Resonant with O'Guinn, Dwan Julien said she attended homecoming games and alumni picnics after graduating.[28] Adrienne Gladney, too, recollected alumni returning to support students: "If they were in band when they were in school, they came back and helped Rawlins. . . . Cheerleaders, majorettes, everybody came back."[29] Smith said, "I became the president of the PTA, even though I didn't have any children here, but as an alumni, I felt we needed to give back."[30]

Finally, Mosley has been integral in planning the RAM Jam, which began in the 1990s as an annual alumni celebration (described later in greater detail). Here, it is relevant to note that this multigenerational gathering of Carver graduates is "not just to come together and have a party," said Mosley. "[Rather] from day one, our focus has been to raise money and to give back to the students."[31] From the 1980s onward, Carver had an on-site nursery, which enabled students with children to continue their education. Mosley and other RAM Jammers bought the first washer and dryer for Carver's daycare center.[32] Bridge building among past and current students created and sustained a robust and supportive community around the Carver identity.

TEACHER EXPERIENCES

When Clarence Righteous first began teaching horticulture in 1972, teachers with years of experience at Carver mentored him. At the time, he guessed, about five new teachers were hired, "but you had all those veteran teachers who were already in place." "If you needed help," he expounded, "they would take you under their wing."[33] Much as veteran teachers made Righteous a part of the Carver lineage during his first year, he built connections with students in the years to come.

Indeed, Righteous harvested more than plants at Carver. He was a part of growing families. Righteous described the school's intergenerational network in this way:

> As time went on, then I had my grandchildren. I called them grandchildren, because some of my students had children. Now I'm teaching their children. The first day of school I'd have them stand up and introduce themselves. "Who are you?" I might ask you, "What's your parent's name?" They'd tell me, and I'd say, "Oh, did they go to school here? Was it so and so?" "That was, oh yeah, Mr. Righteous."[34]

Righteous told a similar story about a teacher who taught brick masonry at Carver: "The guy that taught masonry was a graduate of Carver himself." After graduation, he "worked in the field for a while." Then, when "his teacher got ready to retire," he stepped into the classroom at Carver.[35] This is the kind of continuity that existed across past, present, and future generations at Carver.

Similarly, Vermon James taught math to Lindsey Moore when he was a Carver student in the mid-1960s. James said Moore "was a good student . . . studious in everything." James was still teaching math when Moore returned as school principal in the mid-1980s. James was "proud to see that [Moore] had come back" and said it "was an encouraging thing for me to continue doing what I was [doing]."[36] Pierre recalled that as a student, Moore "used to like to imitate" assistant principal Thomas Hoover. Pierre narrated the storyline:

> Moore would stand . . . [by] the lockers where [students] put their books. . . . [He] would stand right there where the kids couldn't see him. He would sound just like Mr. Hoover. "Alright, boys and girls, to your class!" and the kids would go flying because they were afraid. I can remember Moore when he became principal, and I saw him. I was at central office and he got there.

Then, I said [jokingly], "Damn, they don't care who becomes principal," and he fell out [laughing].[37]

Avis James concluded, "Later on, Dr. Moore was principal, and Mr. Hoover was assistant principal under him."[38] Moore's trajectory illustrates a living culture connected at a deep tissue level.

Moore recalled learning math as a student under James. He also drew inspiration from science teacher Lamar Smith: "In the yearbook, where you put down your intended vocation, I had physicist." In fact, said Moore, "Ms. Busch wrote a letter and got me a band scholarship at Southern."[39] The same caring disposition of teachers during Moore's time as a student was present two decades later when he returned as principal. He pondered the interconnections that spanned generations:

[The teachers] all cared. We didn't have bad teachers at Carver. I can't think of one bad teacher at Carver because when I was there, as principal, I saw the same thing. They worked together. [There were] some things I said we needed to do, and they'll come and . . . [tell me] that's not gonna work. That's the teachers tellin' the principal. Luckily, I had enough sense to listen because I trusted them. A lotta folks say, "Well, you stayed there so long." It wasn't me. It was my people. I had good people.[40]

Moore, of course, was one of those people who cared for students—and their children. During Moore's tenure as principal, Carver's childcare center was established. Just as Mosley and fellow students raised money through the RAM Jam for the center's laundry machines, Moore plotted the educational future of Carver's youngest by insisting that they wear school colors. He detailed his thinking about students and their little ones:

It wasn't just you bring your baby and leave 'em and go to class. It wasn't like that. Everything was centered on education—making a difference in the lives of children. They said, "Well, why you make it where the children have to wear the same uniforms as their parents?" . . . What I was trying to do—the closest person to those babies were their young mothers. I wanted them to be role models for their babies. . . . I said, "Even if the mamas fall short,

that baby knows about coming to school. That baby is in the environment."
I think that's gonna make a difference down the road, and I think it did.

Moore was tearful as he shared, "I would find out girls were pregnant before their moms would. They would come and tell me." He said students would give him photos of the babies, which he kept "right under that glass on my desk." Moore said he would "play with the babies" and "used to fuss" at students about how to feed them properly. He was always intent on supporting students' well-being in the present as well as the future. This intergenerational lens was a critical part of his mentorship.

As a school counselor, Avis James connected students with elder mentors in the community. For years, she arranged to have Sally Ann Roberts, a local black television news reporter, visit with students every Thursday.[41] Over the school's history, teachers and school leaders sought ways to network with students' parents. In 1971, for example, Carver principal Willie LeBeau was asked to serve as a member of the school district's Principals School-Community Relations Advisory Board and invited to think "about ideas and problems" for the board committee to consider.[42] Two days before the first meeting, the district director released a memo on possible topics, including methods to achieve "better attendance at PTA meetings."[43] In 1982, teacher Lenora Condoll was featured as the lead organizer of a parent social deemed a "smashing success." Parents enjoyed a buffet and were able "to meet their children's teachers in a relaxed atmosphere."[44]

In 1991, parents were a part of the school improvement plan for Carver Junior-Senior High School when the junior and senior sides combined due to enrollment and resource concerns.[45] In the plan, home-school relations were outlined as critical, fostered through the PTA, report card conferences, newsletters, seminars, and other means. Moore hosted a "Parents as Partners in Education" seminar, which addressed issues such as improving school attendance and creating a drug-free school.[46] Avis James introduced parent participants to various "I Can" efforts—or ways to be involved—from parent-teacher conferences to meeting the school nurse, librarian, and social worker.[47] Coach Foley addressed AIDS and safe sex.[48] A sign-up sheet enabled parents to help in the classroom, from working with individual students to acting as room parent, chaperoning a field trip, or raising funds. A pledge that included the school principal, as well as teachers, parents, counselors, secretaries, and custodians, was circulated and signed.[49]

OVER THE COURSE OF TIME

In the Carver tradition, intergenerational relationships stretched beyond high school mentorship and graduation. Clarence Righteous was knowledgeable about students' life work after their time at Carver. His horticulture students, some of whom were placed in jobs through the Cooperative Agricultural Education program, "used to work at Smith Florist and . . . nurseries around the city," he said. Some remained until those places "went out of business." Righteous noted that one student had recently retired from the Public Parks Commission, and another, who worked for a florist, retired but still delivers flowers "just to get out of the house." Others "have their own lawn and garden care businesses." Righteous said that former students "pass by [his house] sometimes and say, 'How you doing, Mr. Righteous?' They find out where I live. I've got three or four of 'em pass by here. They stop. One stopped the other day out there. He saw me on the street, and he hollered at me. They're everywhere with their lawn and garden-care businesses."[50]

Marilyn Pierre has also continued to see her students. "I see my students all over the place," she emphasized, again demonstrating the shared geography of teachers and students in downtown neighborhoods. Pierre crossed paths with former COE students, "who worked out in industry." She reported that a majority stayed in industry or went on to higher education. "When I go down to City Hall, I see them still working there," Pierre noted. She also corresponds with "some who have retired already." Seeing their lives unfold in this way has been "rewarding" to her.[51]

Carol Righteous indicated, "We always go to [students' class] reunions [because] they invite us all the time."[52] Condoll echoed: "I actually cried because, not only did [this] let me realize the effect I had on them, but when you have former students tell you what they are doing for their children, and their grandchildren, you know it worked."[53]

Moore believes Carver "had the best alumni association in the city." He said he had been asked by many people: "What did you do to get all your alumni [so connected]?" He emphasized that he "didn't do anything" formal to foster such a network. It was the outgrowth of Carver's entire culture, much like the RAM Jam in City Park, where graduates of all classes gather annually to celebrate their connection to one another and Carver. Regarding the mass reunion, Moore declared, "They'll contact me and say, 'Dr. Moore, come out.'" More to the point, he said: "They remember us. . . . There's just something about that bonding [across the generations]."[54]

Foley evacuated and moved to Texas after Hurricane Katrina, but it did not disrupt her correspondence with past students. "I'm in touch with a lot of them," stated Foley, including those in Texas. She went on, "Danielle lives up here. I see Kelly. There's two others, Lamika and Wendy—Lisa, and then . . ." These women were once girls on Foley's track team. Foley also gets "emails from a bunch of [former students]" and others befriend her on Facebook. This teacher, still connected to her students, took pride in one "little lady" who attended college, discontinued her studies, and then returned. Foley disclosed: "I went to her graduation. She came and got me, and I went to her graduation. She lives up here in my area."[55] From Carver's graduation to the pomp and circumstance of receiving a college diploma, Foley was an ongoing part of students' lives.

Even those who passed away remained an ever-present part of the Carver community. Foley described the late Charles Hatfield as "dedicated," someone who "worked hard with those kids" and "made beautiful yearbooks" as advisor. Lamar Smith, she said, worked with the after-school program and helped students find jobs, likely through the Comprehensive Employment and Training Act (CETA) program, which was tied to the Carver Community School that Smith directed.[56] As past athletic director, Foley attested that Enos Hicks was "a good coach and a good teacher." As for Yvonne Busch, Foley giggled: "She was a little woman, but she could handle those boys, honey. Ain't nobody mess with Ms. Busch. She was tough, rough, but she was doggone good. I mean it. She was an excellent musician [in her own right]."[57]

THE INTERGENERATIONAL NETWORK IN REAL TIME

From the school's breezeway to the basketball court, from neighborhood street corners to class reunions and beyond, Carver teachers and students maintained relationships with one another over the course of their lives. In completing alumni interviews, I was consistently offered the names of other RAMs to potentially interview. Phone numbers and contact information were readily available, revealing deep connections among those in the Carver network. Merricks offered to host a get-together with a large inner circle of friends from her graduating class of 1959, whom she sees regularly, for a large group interview.

Further, reaching out to teachers revealed ongoing connections between Carver faculty. Individual teacher interviews sometimes evolved into small groups, as still-in-touch teachers invited others to the table for discussion and recollection. Informal references by teachers regarding the whereabouts and well-being of former students were common. In one case, a teacher reached out to me by phone; a student that I had interviewed contacted and encouraged her to speak with me. I was also added to the private Carver alumni Facebook group. Possibilities for connecting with those in Carver's network were abundant.

A memorable moment, which affirmed these connections, occurred when I was departing from the interview with Merricks. I asked her if she had taken any courses with science teacher Lamar Smith, as I was trying to assemble biographies of several deceased teachers whose work occurred during Carver's early years. Merricks said she had not but informed me that her husband, Reverend Douglass Haywood, a Carver graduate, not only learned science from Smith but cut Smith's hair for years in his barbershop. She pointed to the house across the street where Lamar Smith Jr. lived. Within minutes, I was speaking to Lamar Smith's son, who gave me a quick tour of his house, showed me some pictures of Fats Domino on his wall, and invited me to return for an interview with him and Reverend Haywood. Such were the connections between a teacher like Smith, a former Carver student, and his own son. Moments like this crystallize the meaning and role of the intergenerational network as part of Carver's culture and history.

CHAPTER 5

"DETERMINED TO EDUCATE OUR KIDS"

Carver's Ethic of Self-Determination and Achievement

> We didn't have a lot. We knew we didn't have a lot,
> but that didn't stop us. It wasn't gonna stop us.
> We were determined to educate our kids.
>
> —DANIELLE FOLEY,
> Carver Senior High School
> physical education teacher and athletic director[1]

Carver students were immersed in a culture that expected and supported excellence. Students attested that their teachers imparted an ethic of self-determination, sought to develop their sense of inner authority, and held only the highest expectations for them. Principal Milton Becnel, in the 1962 yearbook, wrote a foreword that conveyed Carver's commitment to righteousness, achievement, and mastery, proclaiming: "We, the faculty . . . dedicate ourselves to the principle of INTELLIGENT SELF-DIRECTION on the part of each and every 'Carver student.'" Significantly, he went on clarify:

Discipline, to us as a faculty, [is] . . . deeply rooted in the term DISCIPLE (one who adopts the standards and values of another person who is admired and respected). Discipline, to each "Carverite" connotes . . . a type of internal self-control, self-reliance, [and] self-assurance. (To us as a faculty, discipline does not necessarily mean punishment, nor does it denote the various techniques and devices by which a teacher maintains an orderly situation.)[2]

Self-direction, said Becnel, "is not commanded or forced," rather it is "a product of the individual student's WHOLESOME INTERACTION WITH HIS TOTAL ENVIRONMENT."[3] The total environment at Carver was characterized by the expert teaching, high expectations, and caregiving of educators who were part of the community's daily life. It was not about discipline and punishment; the development of youth in reaching their full potential, despite the odds against them, was the goal.

In 1968, Carver was featured in *Louisiana Weekly*, a black newspaper. This ten-year progress report, issued a decade after the school's founding, included Becnel's statement on "intelligent self-direction," along with photos and programmatic highlights of student and teacher work: A photo on "new science innovations" shows youth in a lab, where physics was "taught to Carver students who demonstrate the ability to do college work in science."[4] Another lab photo highlights a biology course that "replaces student 'memorization' by student 'participation and student application' [of knowledge]." Carver's language library is also applauded for the "effective use of hundreds of tapes and records" to assist students in learning either Russian, Latin, French, or Spanish "taught at all levels to the 800 students enrolled." Charles Hatfield operates the language lab's control panel in another picture.

Programs in the industrial arts are featured, including mechanical drawing (with Thomas Hoover), auto mechanics, and small gas engine shop, as are programs that allow students to explore the "world of work" through salesmanship and secretarial training.[5] One caption underscores that Carver is a national charter member of Future Business Leaders of America. Carver's 1966–67 SACS accreditation certificate appears in print too.

This spotlight revealed the academic range that Carver sought, supporting achievement in the trades, career education, and college preparatory work. The same was captured in an undated, typed statement of the school's philosophy and objectives, which read, in part: "to have a smooth articulation between senior high school, college, and high levels of learning: and to provide opportunities for economic achievement upon completion of high school by providing a sound general education emphasizing basic skills required in various occupations and on-the-job training."[6]

STUDENT EXPERIENCES

No matter the course of study at Carver, self-determination and achievement were central. Graduating only five years after *Brown*, Althea Merricks aspired to be a secretary: "During that time, because of us being black people, there was limited things that you could do."[7] The only alternatives, she elaborated, were working in a shrimp factory and performing domestic labor for whites. However, as a part of Carver's business education program, Merricks learned typing and shorthand; she was proud of her participation in state rallies, where she "came in first place . . . as a stenographer."[8] After graduation, she enrolled in a two-year stenographic program at Southern University and earned a certificate. During her college program and the beginning of what she called "token integration," Kaiser Aluminum came to Southern University to interview "young ladies . . . and they chose me to work."[9] Merricks began in 1965 and worked there for thirty-seven years and five months, retiring in 2002. During that time, she moved up the ladder, operating as a statistical clerk for higher pay.[10] For her, Carver set this career path in motion; she was one of the first three blacks hired by Kaiser.

Theron Lewis shared the story behind his initial interest in track. When he first participated in track at Carver Junior, he "couldn't outrun anyone," although at home he jumped wooden hurdles that he built with his brother.[11] During tenth grade at Carver Senior, Lewis was at home practicing guitar—he loved his Jamaican grandfather's calypso music—and the Olympics came on television. Dashing to the living room to watch, he hit his knee and broke the guitar. He explained: "Sitting there with my mother, my father, sister, and brothers, [I blurted,] 'I'm going to the Olympics!'"[12] He also discovered a book in Carver's library called *The Story of the Olympic Games*. But his real motivation was fostered by Coach Hicks: "I remember being nervous and he would always say something to encourage you. The main thing about Coach Hicks—he'd always say, 'Listen, you're not running for me; you're running for yourself and your family name.' Then the school."[13] Hicks aimed to bolster students' inner drive. By junior year, Lewis was the best quarter miler in New Orleans, and by senior year, he won state. In 1962, Carver's track team was "public school, district and city champions," with Lewis serving as team captain.[14] Lewis recalled that Hicks was committed to obtaining scholarships for student athletes and in frequent contact with university athletic directors.[15] Lewis got a scholarship to Southern University and went to the 1964 Olympics in Tokyo.[16]

True to form, Becnel was writing letters to school district officials about the accomplishments of Carver graduates. He wrote assistant superintendent John Monie on February 16, 1967, indicating that Lewis, "a 1962 Carver graduate" had "set a world indoor record for the quarter mile" and "will represent the United States at the Olympics in Mexico City, Mexico, next year."[17] An appended news clipping indicates Lewis also earned special recognition during a Carver assembly.[18] Valuing all student accomplishments, Becnel alerted Monie in a separate letter on April 5, 1967, of Carver graduate Hannah Brown's position as New Orleans' first female mail carrier.[19] An attached news article has Brown reporting: "I took the Civil Service exam, passed it, got the job, and started to work [after waiting] two months to get my uniform for they had to order the blouses and women's slacks from Ohio."[20] Monie wrote back, thanking Becnel for the news releases, as "it is always good to hear nice things connected with our schools."[21]

Similarly, on May 22, 1969, Becnel enclosed for Superintendent Carl Dolce a notice promoting Shell Oil Company as an equal opportunity employer. Pictured is Thomas Bennett, "a graduate of Carver High School in New Orleans," working near a microscope. The caption read: "I am employed with Shell . . . as a Junior Laboratory Technician. My job is to prepare surface samples and drilling cuttings for examination in our geological process. You can get a good job too if you prepare yourself now." The ad states in bold below: "THINGS ARE CHANGING."[22] Over a single decade, through both trade and college preparatory education, Carver was responsible for many firsts in the African American community.

Rhea Joseph, class of 1962, recalled her English teacher, Alvirda Gaspard, who held a master's degree. She was "prim and proper," Joseph giggled, and "one of those teachers that never wore anything that showed the clavicle in her neck." Gaspard was "very hard" and "very meticulous" when students did their writing. Specifically, Joseph remembered her teacher having students read a poem that ended with the line, "I am the captain of my ship." Students "looked up to her" and she inspired them to take command of not only their writing but their destinies.[23] When asked whether Carver students had been well educated, Joseph replied:

> Oh, very well! We had scores of folks who were . . . honors students. I was an honor student. We had so many folks that came from Carver who produced. . . . We had doctors, we have lawyers. . . . Our first fire chief came from Carver, [a] black fire chief. . . . Not everybody were doctors and lawyers, but they came out to be [successful]. . . . Nurses, laborers. . . . We had the trades [at Carver too].[24]

In short, Joseph believed Carver's ethic of achievement inspired students in a range of professions and trades, many of whom she called out by name for their accomplishments.

Irvin Blackburn explained his expectations about Carver: "I was gonna go to a school that was gonna give me an opportunity to enrich my life and make things better, because there were several different programs that existed," including auto mechanics, carpentry, and industrial arts. "Then they had the academic side of it," he said, "if you were interested in going to college." It was like the television sitcom theme song of *The Jeffersons* about black upward mobility, quipped Blackburn: students were "movin' on up." "That's exactly what happened to me," he shared. He testified: "All of the teachers that I encountered, I found to be encouraging and helpful, and they had lasting impressions on my life. [They instilled the notion] if I tried my very best, then good things would happen, [but] I have to work hard in order for it to happen."[25]

Blackburn participated in Carver's DECA (Distributive Education Clubs of America), a program that introduced students to various business professions through a combination of high school coursework, projects, and experience in applied job settings. Charles Brown was Blackburn's DECA teacher, a "positive person, strong," who ensured that students "participated in city and state competitions where we would write papers" in addition to working in business settings. Blackburn planned to attend college and says Carver "provided me with what it was that I needed to go to Xavier."[26]

During his time at Xavier University, Blackburn participated in a summer program where he worked in Philadelphia. Due to "the exposure that I had from my experiences at high school with working through the [DECA] program, going away . . . wasn't a biggie," he reported. He also did an internship with the Internal Revenue Service, which led to a job offer before college graduation in 1973, and where he ultimately worked as an accountant and manager for thirty-nine years, with several promotions along the way. "What happened to me in high school prepared me for the rest of my life," he said. This was the case for many Carver friends too. Blackburn, having recently attended his fifty-year high school reunion, mentioned alums who were ministers, pharmacists, and business owners, what he called "a club of successful people."[27]

Mary Polk expressed appreciation for the contributions of Martha Francis to the development of her musical knowledge. This choir teacher offered to teach her piano in addition to singing, and "asked my parents if I could stay with her" to learn during the family's summer travel.[28] Polk's father, a Baptist minister, preferred that she join the family for vacation and religious conventions, while Francis continued to open doors on learning. "She would ask me to come early to school," Polk reminisced, "and she . . . helped develop my singing voice [and] taught me how to read the music that I sung." Polk underscored Francis's level of dedication and support: "She invested a lot of time that she didn't have to, because she had a family, [but] if you wanted to learn, she was right there to do what needed to be done."[29] With high hopes for Polk's future, Francis "was instrumental in getting me two scholarships: a partial scholarship for Xavier and a four-year scholarship for Dillard," which she presented to Polk at graduation. Although Francis had encouraged Polk to audition at Xavier, the Dillard scholarship was orchestrated by Francis alone.[30]

Leonard Smith was vice president of his senior class.[31] Smith elaborated on his experiences at Carver: "You can either decide you want to do a trade or be college prep." He "rode the fence," wanting at first to be an attorney, then taking an interest in drafting.[32] Hoover, his industrial arts teacher, was pivotal to his development. He recalled a photo of a friend and him drawing in Hoover's class and fondly shared, "If you didn't understand, he would take the time, as if you the only one in the class, and come over and talk to you."[33] Smith recollected that "everyone looked up to him" even though "we coulda knocked him down—but you respected him [because] he was one that would bend over backwards."[34] Hoover, a relatively short man with a hunched back, also functioned as a disciplinarian, known for admonishing students: "Young man, get out the hall!"[35] Hoover submitted Smith's name for a scholarship in architecture at Howard University, accompanied by an apprenticeship at General Electric. Smith was awarded the Howard scholarship, among others (Figure 5.1).

Ella Shaw focused on Cooperative Office Education (COE) during her Carver years. She never attended college but has "always been [fortunate] to have good jobs." "All the teachers back then was very inspirational [as] far as trying to get you to better yourself," she attested. "They didn't talk down to nobody. . . . The teachers, they always inspired."[36] Of the same generation,

Smith spoke to the achievements wrought by teacher support, recalling one RAM who studied nursing at Carver, became a registered nurse (RN), and then completed graduate work; another RAM, he said, owns a mechanics shop not far from Carver (Figure 5.2).[37]

Herlin Riley was influenced by the exacting standards in Yvonne Busch's music classroom. He reminisced about the "sense of discipline" that defined her teaching and the lessons he learned about attending to "small details" in striving for excellence.[38] Only the highest expectations were communicated by Busch and fellow teachers.

Trenesse Mosley described Gwendolyn Tate-Smith as "one of the best English teachers ever." She was "notorious" and "carried a big stick." Says Mosley: "She was loud, but she was very educated. She wanted her students to be phenomenal. She just didn't want average."[40] When she and other honors students arrived in Tate-Smith's class in ninth grade—Carver Senior had absorbed grade nine almost ten years earlier—the teacher warned: "If any of you are thinking about going to your counselor and getting your schedule changed, don't. I'm gonna have you for the

FIGURE 5.1 Leonard Smith as "most likely to succeed," from the 1972 Carver yearbook[39]

FIGURE 5.2 Certified nursing assistants at Carver Senior High School, from the 2001 school yearbook[41]

next four years. I'm gonna be your English I, English II, English III, and your English IV teacher."[42] Mosley did indeed have Tate-Smith for four years.

Mosley remembered that Tate-Smith would have students read a book, with "a test every morning." Every two weeks, students received a new book. Mosley noted her teacher's rigor: "You would read the book, then you would have to stand up. She would randomly pick you and ask you a question about the book or ask you about a character." This was a way of "making us think," says Mosley. Tate-Smith would often say, "Take your time. Think about it. Don't speak too soon. . . . Think about what you read." She would also "throw words at us," without giving the definition, and it was "your job to go back and find a definition—that's how she always challenged us." In fact, "she had us writing theme papers before we knew what they were," ultimately inspiring a love of journalism in Mosley.[43] Tate-Smith, the yearbook and newspaper advisor, encouraged Mosley to join the staff of both. Not without significance, Mosley described the ethic at the heart of Tate-Smith's teaching:

> She made us want to do better. She made us challenge ourself. . . . Those teach-ers, they saw in you what you didn't see in yourself. They applauded that and they always told you to think outside the box, that you can do this, you're better than this. The world was yours if you listened to those teachers. I really started thinking, "I'm really smart 'cause they're saying I am. Because they say I am."[44]

Mosley also spoke highly of Benny Pullum, one of only a few white teachers who taught for decades at Carver.[45] He taught Algebra I, II, and III, and geometry. He was "a very good teacher" who "made it very challenging." Importantly, "if you didn't understand, he would sit there with you after class if he had time."[46] After graduation, Mosley got into Dillard. She pointed out that she had "no remedial classes in math or English," noting, "I knew that Carver had—I was prepared."[47] In later years, Mosley completed paralegal studies and a human resources management degree at Tulane.

Kelly O'Guinn credited Coach Danielle Foley for supporting her growth. Under Foley, O'Guinn played volleyball as well as shot put and discus for track, not to mention her participation in softball and basketball. "I was a heavyset girl," O'Guinn reflected, "and was very insecure at that age about my appear-ance in the clothes, the uniforms." Foley, however, would "pull you to the side and let you know that—just encourage you, 'Hey, you can do this. Hey, get out there, perform, don't worry about how you perceive yourself looking.'"[48] Specifically, O'Guinn recollected a time when athletes had to jump over a pole, prompting her to think, "Oh, my God, I don't wanna do this." Foley "pulled me to the side and said, 'You're just as light on your feet and athletic as the rest of these girls. Get out there and show 'em what you can do.'"[49] O'Guinn made the deeper point: "That's the type of teachers we had. They wanted the best for us."[50] Foley truly cared about her—and her success as a student-athlete.

Denise O'Guinn arrived at Carver the same year that her sister Kelly was graduating. She participated in an out-of-state summer program recommended by her science teacher at the end of her junior year. "I think I would like you to do this," the teacher urged.[51] O'Guinn thus spent her summer at the University of Minnesota, where youth of color were exposed to science. "It changed my life," she proclaimed, "[as I] wound up going there for my undergraduate [degree]."[52] She explained that student aspirations were bolstered by "motivational speakers that would come" to Carver. She recollected school-wide assemblies in the auditorium: "They would pound us with 'You have to do better.'" Black speakers "came to inspire and they came to prepare us and give us information." One thing was for sure, she said: "I got those messages."[53] With a master's degree in social work, O'Guinn has supported families navigating the education system.

Dwan Julien attended Carver ten years after Mosley studied under Pullum. She likewise pondered Pullum, who taught her trigonometry and calculus: "The way he would teach . . . was just amazing." Julien continued:

> He drew me into math 'cause he made math feel like poetry to me. . . . The way my mind works, it didn't go from step one to step two to three. I process things very different than some of my peers. . . . Instead of telling me my answer was wrong because I didn't work out every step the way that he did it, he started to understand how I processed it. . . . He took the time to understand me. When we worked through it together, he was like, "I see where you're going." . . . I just really loved how he didn't say . . . "This is wrong."[54]

Like so many Carver teachers, Pullum nurtured students' capacities and supported achievement by recognizing strengths and building on them.

Hasan Sparks reflected on how various teachers compelled students to reach new heights. Of Lenora Condoll's teaching, he says students "read a lot," "did a lot of essays," and "learned in that class."[55] Of Clarence Righteous, his horticulture teacher, Sparks said his class was "way more than the act of just seeding and sowing." Righteous taught students "what makes [plants] die, what makes the color" and the importance of "chlorophyll to them pollinating." Righteous and students even maintained a greenhouse "right there by the classroom." Sparks was enamored when one time "we came early in the morning, and we found an owl stuck in there."[56] Regarding Lindsey Moore, the Carver graduate-turned-principal, Sparks reported, "Dr. Moore and Mr. [John] Thompson would be on these walkie-talkies chasing students. I mean they made sure that we went to class."[57]

Martaz Lynch was also chased by a teacher, so to speak. He credits band director Wilbert Rawlins for getting him back in school. He explained:

> [Mr. Rawlins] was there for us anytime we needed him, no matter what the case was, no matter how hard the situation. You as a band member, as a Carver student, you can always count on [him]. I can say if it wasn't for Mr. Rawlins and the band, I probably wouldn't have graduated. . . . I think I was going through a rebellious point in my life, as most of us kids will do. Mr. Rawlins was the man. He came and talked to me. He told me this wasn't the path that I need to go.[58]

Catherine White, a student and band member at Carver with Lynch, felt that Rawlins taught "discipline." As one of the best bands in the city, Lynch says it was "hard work" and "we used to call ourself Carver University." "That's what we sounded like," White weighed in.[59] "Like a college band," affirmed Adrienne Gladney.[60] Lynch said Rawlins was the first to introduce seven to nine drum majors, a trendsetting move, far from a bunch of kids beating on tin. "This was serious," underscored Lynch. The band practiced mornings and evenings, at least four hours after school, and headed home after dark. Nothing but excellence would suffice.

TEACHER EXPERIENCES

During Carver's early years, the school's curriculum council consisted of teachers, department heads, counselors, and a principal who worked "to improve the learning situation for children in the New Orleans public schools."[61] Many of the teachers mentioned by students—Hatfield, Smith, Hicks, Hoover—participated. Advancing student achievement was a top priority at Carver. Heading the council was Principal Becnel, who Vermon James said was "there for business." James said Becnel made clear: "If you were to come to that school, you're gonna be involved in teaching the students. Everything was you were there for these students."[62]

Clarence Righteous exemplified this ethic. He wanted his students to shine as scientists and leaders and explained:

> Horticulture played a great role within the school. Kids were expected to learn it well, as they did in other academic subjects. I had to explain how it fit into the curriculum. As it went on, they saw how it fit into the curriculum because we had math. We had the science. We had the reading. We had the writing as well and maybe some other things. You had leadership skills too because they had to participate in various activities. We competed locally . . . then we went [to] state.[63]

Righteous said Carver had a range of vocational training programs. "Some students got jobs over summer months," he recalled. "Some of them, when they graduated, they retained those jobs."[64] Importantly, Righteous stressed that vocational education was not conceived as a low-level endeavor that would undermine students' futures. It was taken seriously and connected to interdisciplinary content that linked hand and head and assisted students in seeing themselves as groundbreakers, or leaders, in the widest sense. Notably, this endeavor included both boys and girls.[65]

Moreover, for those who planned to pursue higher education, Righteous ran an after-school program in urban forestry in collaboration with nearby Delgado Community College. All the students in the after-school program "were college-bound."[66] They earned minimum wage and worked two to three hours every evening. They were enrolled simultaneously in courses with Righteous. Many went on to study and ultimately opened their own businesses.

Righteous's pedagogic approach, and the aspirations behind it, resonated with the teaching of Carver faculty. Recall Condoll, who emphasized entrepreneurship as well as citizenship in her social studies courses, who wanted students to find their passion and mold promising futures for themselves and the broader community. For her, Junior Achievement and Close

Up were not simply programs, but reflected her commitment to fostering self-determination, consciousness, and a sense of self in students. She wanted full names on papers because she wanted fully developed people.[67]

Avis James, who moved from math to guidance counseling, shared: "We were trying to prepare the students for their future knowing that some of these kids are going to go to college and some of these kids are going to go into a trade. We wanted everybody to be prepared to go into something and so [we pursued] the idea of exploring different things [with students]."[68] Career Days in the 1990s, for example, featured people in "all kinds of occupations," from dentists to auto mechanics who ran their own shops. Marilyn Pierre headed the COE program as well as a high school executive internship program. The first offered opportunities in business and office settings; the second offered the chance to shadow individuals in specific professions, such as engineering.[69]

Organized by Avis James, Career Day 2001 consisted of professionals convening at Carver "for a day of guidance and information" in fields such as accounting, marketing, education, and the Navy. In this way, explained James, students "gained insight into future career choices."[70] The Dillard University Educational Talent Search was also part of such annual events at Carver, as was College Recruiter Day with Southern University, Nunez Community College, and Sidney Collier Vocational College.[71]

James also hosted a College Fair for juniors and seniors at the Carver library. She explained that students "would come for half an hour and talk to all these recruiters."[72] Recruiters came from a range of institutions across Louisiana, from Collier's beauty school across the street to Delgado and beyond. At the same time, the school had a long history of teachers who advocated for students and networked with college recruiters—Coach Hicks and Ms. Busch, for example. Teachers did their best to support students in diverse pathways.

This was not always easy work considering the broader racial climate of New Orleans in the 1960s and '70s. Pierre "had to go find the jobs for the kids." She explained:

I experienced a lot of discrimination when I tried to go out and place the students in employment. Two things were working against me. Number one, I was from Carver in the Ninth Ward. Number two, because these are black students. I decided, hey, I gotta figure out . . . how am I gonna go around this crap? That's what I called it. I had friends who were in government jobs and who were multiracial. They were [in programs] designed to help students to rise above and to place 'em out in industry. . . . I worked with others in the community who I found were more receptive.[73]

In the end, Pierre delineated a "really strategic" plan about where she placed students: "I didn't want them to experience that kind of negative stuff." The ethic that Pierre implanted was: "You got to be read. You gotta be double equipped. You've got to be bilingual [and able to speak black English and so-called standard English]." Most important, she urged students: "Operate from the point of view that you're just as good or better than a lot of people."[74]

Pierre also knew that for many positions, students would be required to pass a pre-employment or civil service exam. She asked the school board and companies to show her sample tests. With the content in mind, she then prepared students to take such exams. She knew her students "had to compete with [John F.] Kennedy [High School]. They're all white. I had to compete with John McDonogh [High School], which [was] still all white and [Alcee] Fortier [High School], which is still all white."[75] Students already knew the material, she reminded them, because Carver teachers had been teaching them fractions, English, and other important subjects. She thus marshalled students' knowledge, telling them: "Let's use it."[76] During her tenure at Carver, Pierre also led and advised a chapter of the Future Business Leaders of America.[77]

Foley supported the achievements of her student-athletes in a similar way. When she began coaching at Carver in the early 1970s, she didn't realize "how gifted these kids were." But it didn't take her long to discover it. The girls' track team "made it to a competition out of state" and later set records that still stand; Foley thought her team's four-by-four relay record set in the 1980s still stands in Louisiana.[78] Her "main goal" was to open opportunities to higher education. She told students, "If you run for me and you do what I ask you to do, I'm gonna get you in [college]."[79] Through travel, for example, "the girls started making names for themselves. . . . Then more people started looking at them once they started setting records." She says most of her student-athletes received scholarships. Foley also took pride that her special needs kids were supported in finding job opportunities: "I got them to be successful [even when college attendance was not part of the plan]." Foley remembered that she and Hicks advocated for one such student, who became "manager of one of the food chains."[80]

Like most Carver teachers, Foley was highly accomplished despite existing barriers. She told the story of Coach Johnny Harris, athletic director at Carver during her early years, who brought her to a Louisiana High School Athletic Association (LHSAA) convening not long after it had racially integrated.[81] The 1982 Carver yearbook dedicated a full page to Foley as a female athletic coach. Below her photo are her reflections on being "a female in a male dominated department." Foley wrote, in part:

> Since 1980, I have been the only female in the Physical Education Department. It has been hard in that role because I have to supervise all females who may be enrolled in a co-education class under a male teacher. . . . Male teachers are off-limits in female dressing rooms. My job has also expanded to include [supervising] girls' athletics. . . .

Although Foley wanted "another female for companionship," she noted the advantage of having "lots of big brothers."[82]

When Harris became ill in the 1980s, he asked Foley to oversee the entire Carver athletic program, which included golf, tennis, gymnastics, football, basketball, baseball, softball, swimming, track, and volleyball.[83] Ultimately, Foley was elected LHSAA vice president, the first black woman to serve in this position, but she recalled an early meeting in which "there was only one other woman in the room" among all-white male athletic directors.[84] Both teachers and students in the Carver community sought to break new ground and achieve at new heights.

Just as racism created hurdles for Pierre in finding student internships, racism shaped the financial resources available to Foley (and other teachers) at Carver. Chronic disinvestment by white policymakers in black public schools (see chapter 9) meant that things needed for athletic training were not always available. This did not dissuade Foley and her student-athletes. Foley explained: "[When visitors] saw the track that we practiced our kids on, and the conditions . . . they said, 'How could y'all do what y'all did?'" Foley said, "[I] ran children on the railroad track 'cause we didn't have a track." She even relied on "old automobile tires to use as weights to train the kids."[85] This approach revealed not only the tenacity to achieve but an orientation toward place that leveraged the limitations of the school's geographic location as assets. Foley put it this way: "We didn't have a lot. We knew we didn't have a lot, but that didn't stop us. It wasn't gonna stop us. We were determined to educate our kids. We were determined to make these children succeed, so that's what we were all about. We took those difficulties in stride. . . . We just went on and did what we had to do. We stuck together." Never did she or other teachers allow a lack of resources or racism to undermine high expectations.

Moore experienced the same ethos as a Carver student and advanced this culture of achievement as principal. During his high school years, Moore had Lamar Smith for chemistry and physics. He opined on Smith's classroom and others: "You worked. There wasn't no play. You worked in everybody's classroom back then. Mr. Smith—nice fellow. Nobody ever failed Mr. Smith's class. He used to always tell us he could've worked at [a local chemical plant], but he loved—he'd say, 'I love you kids.'"[86] Moore also said that Vermon James taught him math, though due to school overcrowding, "class was held in a closet, a storeroom." Nonetheless, Moore remembers, "[James] used to wear that black suit and it'd be full of chalk."[87] A teacher wearing a suit—full of chalk—in a closet just about says it all. This was the serious business that James said Becnel, he, and teachers were engaged in, despite the odds against them. In fact, Moore said he still remembers his "geometry book, and it have F. T. Nicholls [inside the cover], and I always wondered, 'What was F. T. Nicholls?'"[88] Francis T. Nicholls was a white public high school that fiercely resisted racial desegregation and bore the name of the Confederate general and Louisiana governor.[89] Moore realized that Carver had "hand-me-down books" no longer useful to a white school. Dressed in his Sunday best, James made every use and no excuse.

Moore did the same as principal. He professed: "I wanted every kid to be the best he could be. I took it personal. In fact, there's people at the school board [who] thought I was crazy because I used to fight so hard. I would go to school board meetings . . . for those kids."[90] Moore took seriously his own ongoing education and strived in all things. When he was hired as Carver's principal, he regularly attended school district meetings with principals from across the city. He noted that many white principals had doctorates, which propelled him to say, "I got to go get [one]." This way, Moore thought, "Carver could have the same kinda principal that these so-called goody-goody schools

FIGURE 5.3 Principal Lindsey Moore receiving his doctoral degree from the University of Southern Mississippi (photo appeared with a brief biography in the 1992 Carver yearbook)[94]

had."[91] Over the course of several years, after full days of work as principal of Carver, Moore would drive to evening classes at the University of Southern Mississippi. He completed his doctorate in 1991, the only black male to receive a terminal degree in the graduating class that August (Figure 5.3). Not surprisingly, his dissertation focused on "the relationship between organizational climate and student academic achievement, student attendance, and student needs" through a study of seven urban high schools.[92] He, too, was now Dr. Moore, all for his kids.

Dr. Moore worked tirelessly at Carver with teachers, students, and parents. He made clear to students that "you have to work twice as hard" to compete because he knew the deck was stacked against them.[93] He trusted his teachers and knew his parents shared their goals. "If I called a group of parents together, they were there," Moore pronounced with assurance. Although parents had not always completed their own formal education, they wanted "the best thing for their kids." To be precise, Moore said he'd "seen parents not pay their light bill so kids could graduate [and cover associated fees]."

When asked about the standardized test scores of Carver students during his tenure in the 1980s and '90s—and mainstream explanations that low scores reflected a lack of teacher care and school leadership—Moore did not hesitate. He detailed his determined approach:

What I did, as principal, I dug out the test scores. If you could read, that was half the battle. I had to get the board to allow me to—I wanted to buy a reading lab, and [hire] an excellent reading teacher. . . . The first thing I do is . . . go over everybody's scores, and I didn't want over fifteen kids in the lab, so I would pull 'em based on their test scores. . . . They did two years. We called it Reading I and Reading II. . . . You still had to take those courses [required] for graduation, but instead of an elective that you wanted, you had to take Dr. Moore's elective.[95]

Moore saved up Title I funds for an entire year to pay for the lab. He explained: "[I] had to go argue with them knuckleheads [at the school board who said], 'Oh, we don't do it that way, Dr. Moore.'" In response, Moore queried: "Why? Why? You got to think out the box. You got me down here, and you got my hands tied."[96] Due to his unrelenting advocacy, they finally let him build the reading lab. His hands were indeed tied, and only he, teachers, and parents cared to challenge this reality. In the spirit of the Carver Community School spearheaded by Lamar Smith years before Moore's principalship, the reading lab's resources were made available to parents after school to enhance community literacy.

CARVER'S ACCOMPLISHED FACULTY

Carver's teachers and school leaders expected and supported excellence from students. Not surprisingly, they lived out the same ethic of achievement that they infused throughout school culture. Becnel, Carver's first principal, pursued a doctoral degree in later years. Nearly all the teachers in this book's study held graduate degrees. Over decades, in fact, Carver yearbooks denoted the educational attainment of faculty, many of whom held master's degrees and had done thirty hours of additional graduate coursework. Clarence Righteous, for example, held a master's degree and completed forty-five hours of additional graduate coursework.[97] The counseling staff in 1971–72 included three women with a master's plus thirty—Gladys Stevens, senior counselor; Shirley Washington, junior counselor; and Mrs. Blackmore, sophomore and freshmen counselor. Two additional counselors, Mr. Romaine Maurice and Mrs. R. Forte, held master's degrees.[98] That year, 25 percent of faculty members held advanced degrees.[99]

MORE THAN ACADEMICS

Almost twenty years deep into teaching at Carver, Carol Righteous showed a commitment and enthusiasm that remained strong. Among her many contributions, Righteous organized and directed class night for seniors. Under her guidance, the class of 1992 marched into the school's auditorium in "Kente attire . . . symbolizing their unity to the Motherland, Africa, and to express their own Black pride and dignity."[100] Learning at Carver entailed more than academics. It involved students' identity formation as black people in a wider social and historical context.

This same year, seniors enjoyed an annual awards breakfast, where Dr. Moore addressed the graduates and students who received honors.[101] Holistic mentorship of students was a critical component of Carver's culture. While students were supported and honored for traditional academic achievement, they were likewise applauded for a wide range of interests and contributions. Seniors in 1993–94 were applauded for awards in science, math, history, and English as well as diverse extracurriculars. Whether students were giving a media interview on "how to abstain from sex," working in the mayor's re-election campaign, or being involved at Guste Nursing Home and Charity Hospital, their development was defined broadly.[102]

CHAPTER 6

"KNOWING HOW TO MANEUVER THROUGH THE SYSTEM"

The Dual Commitment to Academics
and Consciousness in the Context of Racism

When you left Carver, you feel you were ready for the world. . . .
You had street sense and you had book sense. You knew
how to maneuver through the system.

—ERNEST CHARLES,
a 1965 graduate of Carver Senior High School[1]

As Carver teachers fostered an ethic of achievement, they were equally committed to developing students as citizens—human beings able to navigate personally and politically. Teachers' pedagogy focused on the whole person, not simply traditional academic measures like content mastery and test performance. Students reported that teachers were sensitive to challenges related to coming-of-age, their life circumstances, and the larger political context that would shape their destinies as black people. In ways that were often subtle but consequential, teachers made the personal development, character, and civic consciousness of students central to Carver's school culture.

STUDENT EXPERIENCES

At a personal level, teachers guided students in transitioning from adolescence to adulthood. Rhea Joseph first encountered Juanita Bonifice at Carver Junior. "She was like a mom," recalled Joseph. As a physical education teacher, Bonifice taught students about self-care and health. Joseph shared: "At that time . . . a lot of us young ladies, we're now [having] menstrual cycles and everything. . . . She taught us all of that. Even some of the girls who may have been sexually active, she talked about that also. She was just a jewel."[2] Joseph graduated high school in 1963, and she attended Bonifice's funeral in 2012, remaining ever grateful for her teacher's mothering.[3] In a comparable vein, Trenesse Mosley reported that Trudi Haney-Dyer, her Fancy RAM dance team teacher, "wasn't just our dance teacher [but] taught us about life skills, about how to be a young lady." According to Mosley, Haney-Dyer conveyed to dancers: "I don't want y'all to be fast little girls. Don't let those little boys talk anything into your head." This, says Mosley, was a "life lesson."[4]

Ernest Charles similarly reflected on industrial arts teacher Felix Provost, Coach Thomas Priestley, and Coach Enos Hicks, emphasizing, "As a young black man who didn't have a father, these guys talked to you about being a man."[5] Charles attested that Hicks's guidance remained with him. Now seventy years old, he said there are "different little things that I still hold to right now." This included advice on social interactions, health, and how to be a "complete person."

Outside of the developmental matters of adolescence, teachers ushered students through major political events. Charles remembered when President John F. Kennedy was assassinated: "Coach Priestley said, 'Gentlemen! Gentlemen!' That's how he talked. 'Gentlemen! Gentlemen! The president's been shot. Let's say a prayer.'"[6] Next, said Charles, students reported to civics class, where the teacher "brought a TV in there and we watched . . . when they pronounced him dead." From personal concerns to politics, teacher pedagogy addressed a broad range of issues not limited to reading, writing, and arithmetic.

Theron Lewis thought back to science class with Lamar Smith. In addition to teaching chemistry, "Smith almost always ended his class with a life lesson" that addressed wider issues.[7] Mary Polk said teachers "poured" into students at every turn, even when they "changed classes" in the hallway. "They knew their students," Polk stressed. "There are teachers that get up, and they teach because they know the material," said Polk, but at Carver, she "didn't feel that way." Teaching was about investing in students fully—mind, body, and spirit. Now, as a minister—and like the teachers at Carver—she preaches and tries to "pour into others" and "pull out what [people] have within them."[8]

Teachers also attended to the wider political context in which students were situated. This included de facto segregation and associated racial injustices. Joseph believed it was Manuel Foy, a counselor at Carver, who convened assemblies and "would tell us certain things on how to act, how to respond on buses, on public transportation, 'cause a lot of us . . . had gotten to be part of the junior NAACP" during the civil rights era.[9] Joseph told the story of an interracial scuffle on the bus route to school and how it was handled by Foy:

We [students] would catch the St. Claude bus and transfer to the Desire bus. . . . That particular day when we got off [to board] . . . the Desire bus, one of the girls tripped. [The involved students] began to fight and the bus driver closed the door so we couldn't get back on. . . . That same morning we were called to the [school] office, [and Foy] spoke to us about how to act [and handle such incidents].[10]

Additionally, "because they were so concerned about us," Foy spent the next week "at [the] bus stop when we were transferring, reading a newspaper, watching."[11] In other words, teachers looked out for students' safety and well-being in a racially hostile world, not simply the grades they received in the classroom. Race consciousness was a central part of teaching and learning.

Irvin Blackburn, who participated in Carver's Distributive Education Clubs of America (DECA), remembers his teacher's frustration with finding student placements in white-owned businesses during the mid-1960s. Through the program, students learned about business and how businesses operated, first by going to school in the morning, then at a job site in the afternoon or evening. According to Blackburn, DECA teacher Charles Brown shared with students "that it was difficult to get us into various places [and some] initially probably wouldn't let us do some of the things that . . . our white counterparts would probably be doing."[12]

Blackburn detailed his experience working at the A&P grocery, where management prohibited him from operating the cash register, assigning him other tasks instead. One task was walking the neighborhood to gather carts that people used to roll their groceries home—hardly an exercise in business operation. Following the way of the RAM, however, Blackburn saw a way forward and took it. He recollected:

The store became very, very crowded. We were stock clerks but . . . when the store was crowded, they'd call us up to bag the groceries. . . . The manager called me and asked me if I could operate the register. They would make an express line where people could only have five items to make it real simple for me. [Blackburn laughed] . . . I knew how to work the register just by observing as I was bagging groceries. . . . I got on the [register]. I became so proficient at it, that that's what they wanted me to do all the time—operate the register and close out the other registers in the evening, to check people to make sure that their balances [were accurate]. I started doing things that related to what . . . the [DECA] program was designed for.[13]

Blackburn's DECA placement at A&P turned into a job he worked until graduation from Xavier University in 1973. But he never bowed down. Occasionally called to work at other A&P locations during college, he was asked to mop floors and declined. "Then you can't work at this location" and "We'll never call you back again," the store manager would tell him. Blackburn clocked out, responding, "You don't have to worry about calling me, because I'll never come back again."[14] He concluded:

> I think what Carver did for me more than anything else, it just provided me with self-confidence and understanding that a lot of time, some of the things that you're gonna encounter, they're gonna be extremely difficult . . . but you just need to take advantage of what it is you already know. You will be able to work something out to get you through whatever it is that you find yourself faced with.[15]

These were life lessons learned through experiences at Carver, and they assisted Blackburn in moving from an A&P cash register to a college degree to a career as an IRS accountant and auditor.

Teaching students how to navigate racial barriers took subtle and not-so-subtle forms. Leonard Smith said Yvonne Busch would tell her music students they'd "better stop tryin' to chase them little nickel gigs" and master instrumental skills that would better serve their futures.[16] In this way, students were guided toward greater possibilities, which may have been realized only through purposeful effort in a racist climate. Such admonitions were "low-key," says Smith, but it was clear that teachers had firsthand knowledge of the challenges students would face.[17] Herlin Riley shared Smith's memory of teachers' pedagogy, which went beyond academic performance to the life prospects of black youth. Says Riley:

> During the Civil Rights Movement . . . as black people, we were more unified and more cohesive . . . because of . . . the social and political climate of the time. . . . As a result of that . . . teachers were more hands on, more about [student] development. "I really wanna see the students develop and

strive." . . . That was the general climate with the teachers back then. . . . They were so passionate because they actually lived through [racial segregation].[18]

They "saw some glimpse of light" in the 1970s, attested Riley, and wanted students to "get outta that dark hole" where the black community had been historically. He believes students were not cognizant of how much this shaped teachers' approach in the classroom. "Looking back on it, we can see why they were like that," teaching more than subject matter but also how students might successfully navigate an unequal terrain.[19]

Sometimes the political instruction was more explicit. Ernest Charles reminisced about the time his English teacher told the class that white New Orleans district attorney Jim Garrison said he did not want James Baldwin's *The Fire Next Time* sold in New Orleans. Charles recalled her message was "I guess if somebody told me I couldn't see nothing, I sure would wanna know what it was about." Students "rode down to Canal Street" and bought every copy available at the bookstore "so we could come back and talk about the book."[20] He ultimately concluded: "When you left Carver, you feel you were ready for the world. . . . You had street sense and you had book sense. You knew how to maneuver through the system."[21]

Mosley remembers Ms. Huntley, who "didn't just open a book and say, 'This is it.'" Rather, she "would give you the story behind the history."[22] In the late 1970s, this included Alex Haley's *Roots*, a novel about Kunta Kinte, who was forced from Africa into slavery in the United States, and the generations that followed him. According to Mosley, Huntley and "those teachers at Carver, they took that *Roots* and they ran with it."[23] Both Huntley and Gwendolyn Tate-Smith, she said, "did more than just textbooks. . . . It was a lot of critical thinking."[24] At the local level, Huntley engaged students in discussions about the city's first black mayor, Dutch Morial. "Before we even got a chance to vote," Mosley said, "[this] brought a lotta real-life stuff [into] history." Huntley showed students that they and their elders were a "part of history," addressing the integration of buses and water fountains, the politics of why Carver was built, and more.[25] In this way, teachers addressed students as citizens, focusing on political consciousness as opposed to facts for a history test.

Beyond classrooms like Huntley's, Carver's library also had an "especially strong . . . collection of black literature."[26] Notable black figures were brought to students' attention in school yearbooks as well. The 1982 compendium featured various "heroes," including Mayor Morial; Dr. Charles Drew, "a black physician who discovered the use of blood plasma"; black boxer Muhammad Ali, who has "turned his activities to civic and social endeavors"; Jesse Jackson, "founder of Operation PUSH"; and Marva Collins, a "teacher who defied the system and started her own school for inner city blacks."[27]

As mentioned earlier, Dwan Julien had memories of Lenora Condoll teaching civic consciousness when she attended Carver in the 1990s. She credits Condoll for having "convinced me to become a registered voter when I turned eighteen."[28] By her account, Condoll urged students to be engaged voters because "so many have fought" to secure the rights of citizenship for African Americans.[29] Under Condoll, students participated in Close Up, taking annual trips to sites of political significance across the nation, from the US Supreme Court to Williamsburg, Virginia.[30]

At Carver, teachers aided students in developing the consciousness necessary to push forward despite existing racial structures—and to challenge them. At the same time, students were taught concrete skills and offered strategic support responsive to existing racial and economic realities. For instance, Kenneth Royal recalled Coach Johnny Harris "would give us a lot of mimeographed little tests." He told students, said Royal: "These are the kinds of things you're gonna find on a civil service test. . . . You take this and learn it, and go get yourself a city job, or go get a job with the state government, and you'll have a retirement down the road 'cause he knew a lot of folks, they would just end up drifting."[31] This also meant institutionalizing student support by establishing a school-based health clinic as well as a childcare center. Both were pioneered by Dr. Moore as principal in the late 1980s. The clinic provided "a holistic approach to healthcare, addressing all high-risk behaviors, family concerns and environment factors which may have a negative impact on the students' physical and psychological well-being."[32] Along these lines, clinic staff offered workshops, rap sessions, and health fairs.[33] Hasan Sparks recalled a dental van coming to the school in the 1990s, a "big, long RV [recreational vehicle]," he laughed. Additionally, Sparks explained, "They even brought a daycare in there for the students. . . . It was very helpful for the girls who had babies."[34] Sparks said that pregnant girls "were disappearing" and "their chairs were empty for weeks and weeks." The school nursery allowed them to go to class and complete their schooling.[35] In this way, Carver accommodated students' life circumstances, no matter how complex or challenging they may be.

Attentive to the context of students' lives, the Carver curriculum consisted of college preparatory academics as well as training in various trades. Teachers recognized that some students "will not continue in formal education or higher education, but will proceed to the work world."[36] Alongside the university, other pathways to a viable future were considered critical, a prime reason the school offered training in an array of trades, from drafting to auto mechanics. Asking "What's Your Claim to Fame?" the school's 1986 yearbook featured a range of students, including Joseph Lucian, a top-ten honors student in his senior class; Kevin Almore, a horticulturalist; Walter Curry, a brickmason; and Tammy Davis, Chantel Anderson, Beatrice Booker, and Trenice Banks, nurses in training.[37] Similarly, in 1993–94, senior class profiles did not focus singularly on academic performance but highlighted extracurricular involvement and community service. One was an outstanding English student in the University of New Orleans Upward Bound program, another won a world history certificate for an essay, yet another had been president of the National Honor Society. Students were featured for participating in the church choir, tutoring at the Desire Community Center, working at Charity Hospital, supporting a city clean-up program, contributing to a political campaign, providing food for the homeless, and volunteering at the Carver nursery.[38]

Over the course of Carver's history, academic pursuits and accomplishments mattered, but so did the political context that shaped students' lives and the way their lives might shape the nation's political future. Principal Herbert McCullum penned the following farewell to the class of 1978: "Many of our graduates have acquired positions of prominence as productive citizens of the New Orleans community. . . . The graduating seniors . . . carry the responsibility to follow in the tradition of those Carverites who have preceded them. . . . Let this responsibility translate itself into productive activity *regardless of future educational plans*."[39]

Thus, a Carver education did not boil down to school performance or self-interested advancement without reference to community. What students did with their education, or contributed as citizens, made a difference. During this time, for example, Junior Achievement operated as a student organization focused on work and entrepreneurship. A student chapter of the American Foundation for Negro Affairs (AFNA), founded in 1968 with headquarters in Philadelphia and New Orleans, existed at Carver in the 1970s as well.[40] AFNA sought to document and support black achievement in all areas— education, housing, health, civil rights, science, commerce, and more—and sustain Afro-American heritage.[41]

Carver teachers consistently adopted a wide lens. A philosophy statement that opens the 1986 yearbook illustrates ongoing recognition of students' political-economic marginalization and a corresponding commitment to changing this reality: "The student body is made up of youngster[s] from the Desire and Florida Housing Complexes. . . . Our students are growing up in economically difficult times but are determined to make things better."[42] Carver's nursing students, pictured in uniforms, are depicted as more than future health professionals; they are "preparing to render service to mankind" as good citizens are apt to do.[43] Other student changemakers included Linda Ellis and Veronica Swaing, highlighted as scholars who traveled to Washington, DC, for a week-long youth leadership conference, where they represented Carver and the New Orleans area, met with lawmakers, and convened with the president's staff.[44] Senior Tanya Perrier is pictured with Congresswoman Lindy Boggs and the Reverend Jesse Jackson; Perrier was selected by Boggs (as one of only sixty-six students nationwide) to serve as a page for the House of Representatives, which meant beginning her day in the Library of Congress, then working at the Capitol.[45]

At all levels, Carver students were encouraged to be civic-minded and conscious of the larger racial and political world that shaped their lives, and their capacity to shape it. Teachers did indeed want the world to be theirs.

TEACHER EXPERIENCES

As students attested, teachers embraced a broad definition of schooling, one that encompassed not only traditional measures of education but development of the whole person. This meant addressing a host of needs arising from students' life circumstances in New Orleans, a Deep South city with a history of racially targeted policies and structural neglect of black communities. Parents and family elders worked hard, but economic struggle and marginalization were a reality for those who had themselves attended historically underfunded schools and confronted limited opportunity in the city's racialized political economy.

To teach well, the basic needs of students had to be met. Teachers knew this and did what they could. Carol Righteous did more than teach English and drama, more than organize and host senior night, more than plan field trips focused on the arts. She brought "bags, bags, bags of clothes" to students living in Desire. "I used to bring in the project . . . bags to the ceiling of my car," she reiterated.[46] Condoll likewise alluded to "clothes that we bought" for students over the years.[47] After Katrina, for example, Righteous learned that a student needed shoes and spent eighty-five dollars getting her a pair.[48] In the same way, Clarence Righteous did not teach horticulture in isolation but gave away "veggies" that students brought home to nourish family members. He recalled telling kids to "take the okra [from the school garden] home to the parent." Growing "edible plants"—from mustard greens to collard greens—was a part of Carver's agri-science program for good reason.[49]

Similarly, Moore stressed: "I used to tell my cafeteria managers, 'Don't throw away no food. If the kid comes there and wanna eat twice, let him eat twice because you don't see what I see in these projects.'"[50] Despite many challenges, Moore emphasized, students still came to school. He fostered a climate at Carver: "[There] is something we got that they want, is something we got that feels important to them."[51] Carver offered sustenance on many levels.

The curriculum taught by teachers at Carver took into account the complex circumstances that students faced. College preparatory and honors coursework were offered, but so were various trades in an unapologetic way. There was dignity in planning a future that did not include higher education, and as Clarence Righteous emphasized, a chance for leadership as well. It is difficult to overstate the pride and intellect that characterized teaching of the trades at Carver. Mr. Righteous was intent, with a master's degree plus forty-five additional hours of graduate coursework—the virtual equivalent of a doctorate.[52] Student Willie Calhoun remembered Ruffin Dawson, his auto mechanics teacher. Dawson's presence in the industrial classroom did not undermine his self-presentation as a "very clean mechanic." "He dressed extremely well," Calhoun pointed out.[53] Hoover, who taught drafting, was also a religious minister and served as assistant principal for many years.[54] The trades and industrial arts at Carver were serious business (Box 6.1).

BOX 6.1
HISTORICAL NOTE ON INDUSTRIAL ARTS AND TRADE EDUCATION

By the early 1900s, white policymakers and philanthropists advocated an industrial model of education for blacks in the South. They hoped schooling centered on agriculture and low-skilled trades would sustain the caste system established after Emancipation and Reconstruction.[55] African Americans such as Booker T. Washington, who founded the Tuskegee Institute in Alabama, likewise advocated industrial education as part of a self-help strategy for racial uplift.[56] In contrast, W. E. B. Du Bois favored a classical academic curriculum and the training of African Americans for higher posts, including a select group called the Talented Tenth. Du Bois argued this group would advance the interests of the race and demand civil rights.[57]

Most African American communities during the first half of the twentieth century appreciated the value and necessity of both approaches. Reflecting on educational advocacy in New Orleans, historian Donald DeVore notes:

> African American leaders and parents also embraced vocational education but wanted a full range of educational options. They knew that even in a race-neutral society varied intellectual abilities and vocational interests necessitated a diverse school curriculum. . . . So the struggle for industrial and vocational education remained an integral part of the overall strategy to improve the lives of individuals and develop the black community.[58]

McDonogh No. 35, the first publicly funded black high school in New Orleans, opened in 1917 with a traditional academic, or college preparatory, curriculum. By 1927, it offered manual and domestic training, including sewing, cooking, printing, carpentry, and bricklaying,[59] which did not compromise the school's commitment to academic instruction.[60]

It is essential to understand that although white school officials "consistently expressed the belief that African Americans should receive, almost exclusively, manual, industrial, and domestic training," they nonetheless "refused to adequately fund vocational training for black students."[61] School officials did not want to allocate monies for black education of any kind. At the same time, they delegated funds for white industrial education. In 1907–08, for example, whites in New Orleans protested what they perceived as the large number of African Americans in the federal civil service. Warren Easton, the white school superintendent, responded by establishing evening schools, but none of them enrolled black students.[62] As DeVore points out, most local skilled labor unions excluded blacks, and thus "white workers had a vested interest in suppressing the development of black skilled workers."[63]

In 1920, more foreign-born white males than African American males had trade jobs, even though blacks outnumbered foreign-born whites nearly four to one. In 1944, black median income was half that of whites.[64] In one *Louisiana Weekly* editorial, in fact, the paper pointed out if trade schools were such a bad idea, whites would not have more of them than blacks.[65] Thus, the struggle to include trade education alongside a traditional academic curriculum was part and parcel of the African American struggle for education in New Orleans.

Two examples reveal the level of white resistance to funding black education, including trade programs. In 1916, the school board contemplated an addition to accommodate industrial classes at the Thomy Lafon School. However, the plan was scrapped as being too costly at $2,250; meanwhile, the board allocated $100,000 for the vocational education of white students. Monies were finally disbursed in 1918 to build a three-room annex for manual training at Lafon.[66]

Further, in 1930, the board issued $3 million in bonds for school construction and pledged $275,000 from the bonds to build a black trade school. The Julius Rosenwald Fund committed $125,000 to the same project.[67] The board decided to instead purchase a building to serve as its central office, paid for using monies originally designated for the trade school, which was not built.[68]

During the Great Depression of the 1930s, the New Orleans chapter of the NAACP and other African American advocacy groups continued to pressure the school board. Through funding provided by the Depression-era Works Progress Administration, the construction of a black trade school in New Orleans began in 1940.[69] It opened in 1942, named after Booker T. Washington.

Carver Senior High School, which opened in 1958, was named by the school board after George Washington Carver, a black botanist, teacher, researcher, and inventor at Booker T. Washington's Tuskegee Institute.[70] Reflecting the full range of options desired by black families and leaders in New Orleans, Carver offered both trade and college preparatory education, with self-determination as a guiding principle. Cooperative Office Education (COE), drafting, automotive mechanics, carpentry, bricklaying, horticulture, and other trade courses existed alongside academic courses in language arts, history, mathematics, and science. As horticulture teacher Clarence Righteous explained, Carver's educational model was interdisciplinary and focused on leadership no matter the students' aspirations.[71] All students, college- and career-focused, were taught to maneuver the endemic racism that characterized New Orleans through a combination of excellence, advocacy, and strategic resistance. The hybrid curricular model at Carver, which included industrial arts education, should be understood within its appropriate historical context and in the context of Carver's dynamic, achievement-oriented culture.

In March 1973, under the federal Elementary and Secondary Education Act, Carver teachers in the Upper Ninth Ward joined with those at Alfred Lawless High School in the Lower Ninth Ward to submit a funding proposal for the Carver/Lawless Career Development Program.[72] The proposal's statement of needs and objectives reveals the astute reading of political context by teachers who envisioned the program. They wrote that many residents of the Desire and Lower Ninth Ward areas were:

> socially, economically, and physically isolated. . . . Cut off from the remainder of the city by railroads, canals, and a corridor of industrial uses, the Desire sections encompass the city's largest public housing project. . . . Nearly three-fourths of the employed males and four-fifths of the employed females work in low-paying, unskilled jobs. The situation is illustrated by the fact that 61 percent of the families in these areas earn less than $3,000 annually.[73]

They went on to clarify that outside the Desire area in the Lower Ninth Ward, "the majority of the residents . . . are homeowners." However, they specified, "these homes are not to be compared with those owned by lower middle class Blacks" because "people in the Lower Ninth Ward have a serious economic problem." This included not only "huge areas of abandoned and poorly kept homes," but "poor streets, drainage, lighting, and recreational and educational facilities."[74] These, of course, were the result of conscious decisions by white policymakers to enable discrimination in the job sector and neglect investment in the infrastructure of black communities.

The statement goes on, indicating that children at the elementary level "know nothing about vocational options open to them, as they experience little but . . . hand-to-mouth existence supported by a parent who works on a day-to-day basis, if at all." Further, at the middle and secondary levels, students in these areas have "the highest reported rates of dropouts." In sum, the program aimed to "prepare low-income students . . . for a responsible and productive life by providing . . . knowledge concerning possible vocational choices and . . . skills salable on the New Orleans job market."[75] The project director was Carver teacher Richard Theodore, who held a bachelor's degree in math and a master's in educational administration, and coordinated the existing Exemplary Program for Occupational Preparation (EPOP) initiative in Desire-area schools.[76]

To be clear, teachers were trying to secure resources to compensate for the systematic lack of investment on all levels. "The New Orleans Public School System," they wrote, "is still badly underfinanced." The proposed program, therefore, "must depend, at least, on the availability of such supplemental funds" as those requested.[77] EPOP's federal funding was due to expire on June 30, 1973.[78] The proposal would enable the Desire program to continue and expand to Lower Ninth Ward schools as well. The general design of the program would focus on a range of occupations from childcare and food handling to the building trades, industrial arts, clerical work, and health occupations, including practical nursing.[79]

Fortunately, the career development program received funding. A program continuation proposal submitted in May 1975 addressed the overall effect of "a comprehensive K–12 Career Education model via curriculum, field trips, career days, career displays and exhibits, audiovisuals, on-the-job training, simulation, and use of resource persons."[80] Students had visited the Bunny Bread plant, the US Post Office, City Hall, the New Orleans Public Library, Avondale Shipyard, the *Times-Picayune* Publishing Company, IBM, the radio station WYLD, Delgado Community College, New Orleans Art Museum, American Telephone and Telegraph Company, Charity Hospital, and Meadow's Draughon Fashion and Merchandising.[81] Speakers came from the radio and television industries, the US Marines, South Central Bell Telephone Company, the police, the Free Southern Theater, New Orleans Mosquito Control, and elsewhere.[82]

Danielle Foley began teaching at Carver around the same time that the Carver/Lawless Career Development Program took shape. She explained the duality of the Carver curriculum: "When I first got there, those kids had . . . a whole world of opportunities outside of college. We had barber and we had beauty girls. We had nurses. We had bricklaying. We had drafting. We had auto mechanics. We had—let me see what else they had. Woodworking. . . . Art, ooh, the art department was fabulous. Let's see, I'm missing some stuff. You name it, we had it back then."[83] In sum, Foley explained, "If we knew they weren't college bound, we put them in a craft where we knew they could succeed."[84] In later decades, Dr. Moore contended that it continued to be "important for my kids to see people in the business world."[85] COE, DECA, and Career Day remained a conscious and strategic part of the school culture. Even if students did not plan on college, contended Moore, "they had skills. They could work with their hands, so I always made sure I fought for my trade and industry programs."[86]

Marilyn Pierre, in addition to teaching business education and overseeing COE, led the Future Business Leaders of America (FBLA), which competed at the local and state level and beyond. This work also occurred in a wider political context that required conscious navigation. Pierre told the story of Carver students "integrat[ing] the FBLA."[87] One of the competitions brought the students to the capital city of Baton Rouge:

> We applied . . . and were accepted . . . for the hotel. We got there. They didn't have any rooms for us. Well, [it was decided that] "We're gonna stay in the lobby tonight, kiddos," so we all stayed in the lobby. . . . Right before you knew it, they found some rooms for us. Well, the rooms were outside. You had to go through the inclement weather, so we sat back down in the lobby until [they] found some rooms inside the hotel because we had applied and sent our money early, so they should've prepared a place for us.[88]

It was part of the difficult education that students received in the reality of racism and the necessity of challenging it. Pierre continued: "The kids learned a heck of a lot. We told 'em there'll be no hoopla. We're not makin' a whole bunch of noise. Nobody's fussin' and cussin' and carryin' on. We're gonna sit right here quietly. They listened. Then . . . they were all so excited when they got into their rooms. 'Oh, Ms. Pierre, we got our rooms.'"[89] They had learned an important lesson in civil disobedience and participated firsthand in demanding equitable treatment. At the same time, Pierre simultaneously attended to the work of the FBLA team. "I wanted them to concentrate on their contest," she said, "I didn't want 'em to get upset."[90] The team did very well, despite the fact that the shorthand test administered at the competition utilized a new shorthand system.

The FBLA Baton Rouge trip was only one experience that characterized students' multilayered education at Carver. Condoll traveled with students to Washington, DC, and elsewhere through Close Up. Dr. Moore joined the students one year on their trip, but acknowledged such travel was Condoll's "claim to fame."[91] He thought it was a good experience and "made him fight even more" for Close Up. "That's how my kids met kids from all over the country. We exposed 'em to that," professed Moore.[92] This was another way Carver teachers and administrators sought to expand students' horizons.

Vermon and Avis James sought to do the same. Mr. James was in charge of student council for a long time. He pondered, "We took our students out of town to Washington, DC" and "used to take 'em to Xavier University for meetings" in New Orleans.[93] Mrs. James said he was also "part of the first group that went on a field trip out of state."[94] Sadly, she recalled one of the teachers saying they "wouldn't take these kids across the [Mississippi] River." According to her, Mr. James's response was "What? I'm gonna tell you [otherwise]." "He said, 'I'm gonna show you. I'm gonna take these kids out of the state,'" recalled Mrs. James.[95] This included not only DC but trips to New York City and Chicago, a Florida cruise, and time in Toronto, Ontario. Mrs. James also joined Close Up for their trips to DC.

Back at Carver, teachers addressed more than traditional subject matter. Some of these efforts connected pedagogy and school programs to the problems students faced. Principal Willie LeBeau wrote in 1972:

> It is truly a long day when you are the principal. As a matter of fact the day never ends. Many of the problems encountered in the course of the school day find a place in your mind long after the sun has disappeared. . . . So be it. The tasks of trying to help young people solve the many problems that beset them along their way is an unending one—one that never leaves one at ease until a solution is found.[96]

This explains why Coach Danielle Foley taught basic health and sex education, "because we had a high rate of sexually transmitted diseases."[97] Foley was also "working on alcoholism and how many kids were affected by it." She ran a program on the topic for almost three years "until the state defunded it."[98] In the early 1990s, in fact, a Carver school improvement and accountability plan included a parent engagement seminar that addressed the school's drug-free program, nonviolent behavior, and AIDS/Safe Sex.[99] Goals included a safe school environment with less "class cutting [and] suspensions involving fighting or weapons."[100] Time and again, teachers had to do for students what the state refused to do: support their education in all respects.

These complexities, and concerns for student well-being, are what propelled Moore to establish the school's first health clinic and childcare center in the 1980s.[101] Moore reported: "I ride around in the project, and I would see these kids. . . . I see my kids sittin' on the porch. I stopped and get outta my car. I'd say, 'Why aren't you in school?' 'I don't have nobody to watch my baby.'"[102] Another pivotal moment occurred when he saw a cheerleader and a little baby with her. He explained: "I'd say, 'Why is your baby here?' Ms. Foley was over the cheerleaders. 'I don't have nobody to watch my baby.' Ms. Foley [said], 'You wanna watch him for me?' I watched a baby out there, after school."[103] This is when Moore recognized the importance of a daycare center, which would address the challenges of students who became parents at a young age.

In investigating "why attendance is so bad," Moore learned two things. First, he saw students did not have childcare for their babies. Second, he discovered when students got sick, "they used to have to go to Charity Hospital for [free] medical service. Sometimes, they would stay so long at Charity [the school day was over]."[104] Both instances highlighted the racial and economic position of students and their families; they had little access to childcare and healthcare.

Moore, in collaboration with Dr. Shelia Webb, a Carver graduate who worked in the city's health department, wrote a foundation grant and secured funds for a school-based health clinic and daycare. Moore said he received a phone call from the education superintendent about his effort to establish a clinic. He recalled his response to the superintendent: "You know, y'all told me to increase my enrollment, so I went out looking for—it's what I found [students needed]."[105] The superintendent gave his approval; Moore did the work. It was a comprehensive educational effort. Moore shared: "If I find out who the [baby's father] was—we used to make 'em go and feed their babies and you'd learn childcare skills." He continued: "It wasn't just you bring your baby and leave 'em and go to class. It wasn't like that. Everything was centered on education—makin' a difference in the lives of children."[106]

Both the Carver spirit of self-determination and attention to the context of students' lives permeated the daycare under Moore's leadership. Avis James raised this point: "The students who had their babies there . . . had to be passing their classes." You could not "drop off your child" and then "disappear off campus."[107] The student-parent was expected to visit the baby, help feed them, change diapers, and assist when possible. Meanwhile, home economics teachers taught parenting classes.[108] Even when circumstances proved challenging, students were supported in completing their high school education. In the best of circumstances, Moore hoped the babies would one day be Carver RAMs themselves.[109] Toddler Troynel Brown, a "future Carver RAM," is featured in the 1996 yearbook, along with other children learning their "first lessons." Connecting school and community, grandparent volunteers assisted in caring for the youngest RAMs at Carver (Figure 6.2).[110]

In line with this holistic approach, the 1992 yearbook commemorates Coach Thomas Priestly, at Carver from 1961 to 1991, who "coached kids for life instead of just for a single game or season."[111] Such was the dual focus of Carver teachers. An undated statement on Carver's philosophy and objectives perhaps speaks for itself. The school was dedicated to "having a smooth articulation between senior high school [and] college" and offering "opportunities for economic achievement upon completion of high school by providing . . . skills required in various occupations."[112] Significantly, teachers were committed to the following:

- Making activities available for students to participate in the democratic process
- Helping each student . . . develop a positive self-concept and a concern for his total environment
- Developing an educational program that has as objectives human relationship . . . and civic responsibility
- Continuing to make adequate provisions for youth who possess hindrances that may interfere with their potential success
- Fostering critical thinking and the ability to do self-directed study[113]

From the very beginning, Principal Milton Becnel wanted Carver teachers and students to do more than teach and learn. He wanted a community of thinkers engaged in the classroom and with the world around them.[114] Whether Carver students were benefiting from Condoll's voting rights and citizenship education or Moore's advocacy of parenting education; learning life lessons in Lamar Smith's science lab or exploring the wider world

FIGURE 6.2 Photos of Carver's child daycare center, from the 1996 Carver yearbook[115]

through fieldtrips, Student Council, and Close Up; preparing for college or taking a civil service exam and learning a trade, they were growing in myriad ways. They were treated holistically as young people situated in a broader sociopolitical milieu, characterized in part by racial and economic inequities that required purposeful thinking and action.

CHAPTER 7

"ALL OF ONE ACCORD"

The Community-Building Traditions of Carver

Most of the teachers [at Carver]—and I'm really saying most of them—we were all of one accord. . . . We'd all get together: "OK, this student needs this." . . . We'd get them after school and tutor them. We never left school before 7:00 . . . in the evening. Even the cafeteria lady, she would leave sandwiches for us to feed the kids . . . after school.

—DANIELLE FOLEY,
Carver Senior High School physical education
teacher and athletic director[1]

Under contract with Curtis and Davis Architects, the Orleans Parish School Board built the Carver complex. Principals, teachers, students, and families built the Carver community. In part, the community was built by instituting practices and programs that generated mutual association and a shared mission as RAMs. Students were offered countless ways to come together, learn together, accomplish together, and experience joy together. Most developed lifelong friendships in the process, as did the teachers who taught them. At Carver, community-building traditions contributed to school culture and were often rooted as well in the culture of black New Orleans.

STUDENT EXPERIENCES

More than fifty years after graduation, Althea Merricks retained a mimeographed copy of Carver's alma mater. She said it often appeared on the back of the programs for students to sing at events. Written by choral teacher Zenobia Stewart and band director Yvonne Busch, the song went:

Hail to Carver, Alma Mater Forever aye.
Though life be perilous
Carver will guide the way[2]

Rhea Joseph recalled singing the alma mater at various school assemblies in the early 1960s.[3] Mary Polk fondly remembered the voice training she received from her choral teacher Martha Francis and sang the school's song as part of her oral history for this book.[4] She said the band would play while the entire school sang. This ritual solidified community among students and invoked deep feelings. As Polk described it, "It wasn't just words. It was a feeling. It was how you felt about what Carver was doing for you in life, not just present, not past, but in your future."[5] Significantly, the song itself was connected to the fight for black educational progress; as Leonard Smith noted, composers Busch and Stewart chose orange and green as Carver's colors—the same as those of the HBCU Florida A&M.[6]

The alma mater was the most obvious manifestation of community-building traditions at Carver. Students were given a striking range of opportunities to learn and grow together as they pursued the school's mission of righteousness, achievement, and mastery. The *Carver Times* queried not long after the school's opening:

> How many schools can claim such progress as Carver has attained during the first three months of operation? The school has a football team, a basketball, and a baseball team. Full senior activities are being carried on, all types of clubs, choirs, and a band have been organized. Trips (as far as the National Capital) are being planned and anticipated. Other activities, in which new talent will be discovered or developed, are in the making.[7]

This was no exaggeration. Just four years after its founding, Carver boasted more than twenty-five extracurricular organizations of all kinds and purposes (Figure 7.1).

Students shared fond memories of their participation together in such activities and after-school programs. Ernest Charles first played baseball at Sampson playground with kids from Desire. When he got to Carver, he shared: "[I] met some of the guys that were still playing. [But] I was a skinny little kid, so I had no confidence." He tried out for baseball and recalled Coach Thomas Priestley's affirmative words, "Hey man, if you want to, you can play on my team." Although Charles did not play that much, he traveled with the team, which, he explained, "felt pretty good."[8] For Priestley, sport was about more than athleticism; it was about team building in the

EXTRACURRICULAR ACTIVITIES AND CLUBS, 1961–1962[9]		
Art Club	Ewettes	Red Cross
Audiovisual Aids Club	Football	Student Council
Band	French Club	Tennis Club
Baseball	Industrial Arts Club	Track Team
Basketball	Journalism	Yearbook
Business Education Club	Library Club	Y-Teens
Cheerleading	Majorettes	
Choir	New Homemakers of America	
Drama	Opera Club	
Electricity Club	Parent-Teacher Association	

FIGURE 7.1

broadest sense. As a part of the team, Charles attended sporting events at Carver even after graduation because "you go back there and you support those kids."[10] Priestley welcomed him into the sporting community as a student, but Charles embraced the communal spirit long after.

Graduating a few years after Charles, Willie Calhoun had memories of football, basketball, baseball, track, and even tennis and golf. "We beat everybody," he asserted. "If you talk to anyone now," he continued, "they will tell you one of the most energetic alumni is the Carver RAMs."[11] Supporting the school's sports teams brought together players, fellow students, and alumni.

Trenesse Mosley participated on the flag team and the Fancy RAMs dance team at Carver Senior, but she started on the drill and dance teams at Carver Middle School. "By the time you get to the senior side, you gotta have chops," she stressed. "[Busch] would run us so you just couldn't go no more [and tell us,] 'It needs to be right at practice. We're not waiting until it's time for the game to get it right.'"[12] Wilhelmina Hogan was right there corralling the flag team.[13] By the time the band and flag team hit the field for games, they were a disciplined, cohesive group. Dwan Julien was a cheerleader—pom-poms and all—and recalled: "We would do football games, basketball games, and [Mardi Gras] parade season. [Performing at games is] where the school spirit actually started to come in."[14] Julien emphasized: "It was just really cool to be in the stands and gettin' everybody involved and tellin' 'em it doesn't matter if we lose, let's just cheer 'em on because they worked hard. . . . When things were going on [around the school] we would cheer."[15] Such traditions helped build community. Kenneth Royal said he "loved to go" to the football and basketball games on Tuesday and Friday in the gym, where there were "always a lot of alums" supporting the teams.[16]

From the first year, there was the Carver Day Classic, also known as Homecoming. " On Friday, November 7, 1958, as reported in the *Carver Times*, the first-ever motorcade "which consisted of some thirty-five beautifully decorated cars, began to move from the school campus."[17] Homecoming queen Ruth Cooper rode in the first car, while "Green, Orange, and Gold ribbons with silver trimming adorned each vehicle" along with "paper RAMS." The procession ended at Pontchartrain Park Stadium, where "hundreds of students were thrilled that afternoon by the gala gridiron event" (Figure 7.2).[18]

FIGURE 7.2 Carver students at the 1971 Homecoming football game[19]

Yet at Carver, community building was accomplished through more than sports-related activities. During the school's first year, the Dramatics Club, known as Carver's Little Broadway, presented a play, placed fourth in the district rally, and performed on stage in the Carver auditorium.[20] In the years to come, students joined a wide range of extracurricular activities and after-school clubs. Merricks was a typist for the *Carver Times*.[21] Joseph was a part of Y-Teens, a Young Women's Christian Association (YWCA) program hosted at Carver for girls, and president of her junior class in 1961–62. In 2017, fifty-six years later, her association with the Carver community remained strong. Joseph then provided a heartfelt oral history of her high school experience wearing a new bright-white shirt embroidered with her name, the Carver RAM in green, and the notation "Class of 1963" in orange (Figure 7.3).[22] Irvin Blackburn explained that in the mid-1960s, he participated in Distributive Education Clubs of America competitions in which "there might be a theme where you would write a paper" or do "a trifold" presentation related to "operating businesses." He enjoyed meeting

FIGURE 7.3 Photo, top: Junior class officers, 1961–62 (left to right): Thaddeus Marshall, chaplain; Beverly Wilson, vice president; Rhea Joseph, president; Estella Fleming, secretary, Wilmer Johnson, treasurer.[23] Photo, right: Rhea Joseph, age seventy-two, in a Carver shirt at her oral history interview on April 10, 2017[24]

students from other schools, such as Booker T. Washington, and explained: "Those who were most engaging and friendly to us were people that looked like us."[25] Carver students built a community not only among themselves but with black students from other high schools.

Leonard Smith was vice president of his senior class in 1973 and played in the band during his time at Carver.[26] In the early 1980s, Mosley enjoyed time on the yearbook staff and newspaper staff. This, too, generated community because for yearbook and newspaper, she explained, "You get to know everybody 'cause you're going to different classes, you're taking pictures."[27] These publications highlighted all aspects of the Carver community. In fact, Carver yearbooks from 1962 to 2001 feature an impressive number of student groups, from Close Up and the American Foundation for Negro Affairs to Horticulture and Chess, all of which gave students the chance to be part of something larger.[28]

In addition to student organizations, numerous events were institutionalized at Carver. They offered shared experiences and a treasure trove of memories across generations of students. The Carver Talent Show, for example, spanned decades and brought joy to the faces of all who recollected it. Polk described the "big event" where "students would display their own musical talents [and I won] first place in the gospel category [one year.]" The talent show was "a packed house" and "like a real *Night at the Apollo*," said Polk. She continued, "Anybody will tell you that was one of the highlights of the year."[29] Royal said the talent show built community, "because people would come from all over to see that show," which affirmed for him that there was "a lot of talented people at the school."[30]

Mosley had attended the high school's talent show since her time at Carver Middle School. With everyone in the auditorium and excited, she said it was "like going to a concert."[31] Performance requires planning, and on this account, Mosley explained: "You had to prepare. [Students] had their outfits ready. They prepare[d] like a year before." She also spoke about how talent show performances were culturally rooted: "Since we were all such a close community—we had our churches and we had our neighborhoods—you always knew who could sing. You knew who was gonna try to be outsinging who. . . . Some of 'em performed as a group. You had a family that was good as a group and then you had some single performers that did their thing singing." There was a panel of judges too. Meanwhile, Mosley said, the audience "would be howling and screaming and clapping," and as a community-building tradition, the talent show "was the best thing in the world." In fact, according to Mosley, the event was so popular that the Desire Community Center started its own series of talent shows because "the Carver Talent Show had just gotten too big. . . . That's how it branched off." Hasan Sparks also remembered the talent show as a "neighborhood event," stressing, "it wouldn't just be the school" because the school "would run out of space." The shows were "family oriented," he added, and followed by "a big feast for everybody, more like a reunion."[32]

Some events were specific to Carver, while other Carver traditions blended with those of the neighborhood, such as church or the community center, or fed into citywide traditions distinct to New Orleans, such as Mardi Gras. This was partly the case with the band. Band concerts were memorable events and brought together the school and community. Polk recollected, "The band and choir concert would be during the Christmas holiday."[33] The choir donned green robes with orange trim, Carver colors. Former band member Smith reported, "We had so many people from the community that we had to have the band concert two nights. . . . [This was the real deal; people wore] tuxedos and everything."[34]

Another band-related event, deeply rooted in New Orleans cultural traditions, involved marching and performing in Mardi Gras parades. During Carver's first year of operation, in fact, Carnival came to the school. "On February 6, 1959," the *Carver Times* announced, "we celebrated our very first 'Carnival Season' with a Jamboree 'Sock Hop.' Our beautiful and spacious gym was opened to capacity for the occasion. . . . More than one thousand Carverites danced and applauded to the entertainment of personalities from radio station WYLD."[35] In later years, Carver came to carnival, and the school band marched as part of the Mardi Gras parades. The record shows that in 1982, for example, the band participated in at least five parades under Busch's guidance: Babylon, Bacchus, Mecca, Okeanos, and Pegasus.[36]

Herlin Riley, another band member, noted that students also "form[ed] funk bands that would be a spin-off from the large marching bands."[37] Beyond the concerts and Mardi Gras parades, young musicians "would get together in garages or people's living rooms" to produce and perform their own music, Riley revealed.[38] Band events were part of a wider array of community-building traditions centered around music and the arts. Denise

O'Guinn fondly recalled parties and dances in Carver's gym: "[They were] not like a prom . . . not dressed up, just DJs show up, person taking pictures, and everybody go there."[39]

Senior class night was a capstone event that occurred annually for decades. On her senior class night during Carver's first year, Merricks said, she enjoyed seeing classmates "showing off their various talents."[40] At Carver decades later, Mosley celebrated senior class night in the auditorium, where she explained, "they bring the seniors all together and we wear our cap and gown, [enabling students] to wear it more than once."[41] Aside from granting senior awards on class night—Mosley received awards in English, history, free enterprise, and dance—there was, she described, "a little skit that the seniors perform, and we do a dedication to our teachers."[42] All in good fun, the skit poked at various teachers and caused much laughter. Class night was emotional for Mosley, who said it was not only fun, but made her "full [of emotion] because that was it, that was our going out ceremony. [In some ways, it was] more personal [and] better for us than graduation was."[43] Denise O'Guinn named class night as one of her favorite events: "It was a good time, lot of laughs at that."[44] Through joy as well as heartfelt tears, class night cemented students' mutual association and friendships as Carver students.

Graduation served a similar purpose in perpetuating the Carver community and legacy. Merricks recalled Carver's first graduation held in the auditorium, where she says over one hundred students walked the stage.[45] Recalling her graduation in 1968, Polk marveled at Ms. Trish, who ensured she could march on stage with her best friend Cynthia, even with a graduating class of six-hundred-plus students:

> Some kind of way, 'cause [my friend] was a [last name starting with] "C" and I was "P," but she [still] ended up next to me. When we marched up—I don't know how Ms. Trish did this. . . . [My friend] Cynthia was able to march next to me instead of with the Cs where she was supposed to be. . . . For all those diplomas to be put in the students' hand[s], and it was your name on it when you received it, [was amazing].[46]

Each graduate mattered, evidenced by Trish's perfectly orchestrated procession that delivered diplomas to hundreds of students. Smith recalled that Maxine Copelin, a graduate of Carver Senior, principal at Carver Middle, and deputy superintendent for New Orleans public schools, gave the commencement address at his graduation; in this way, the continuity of community continued across generations. Smith says he "cried too [because he graduated with] people who you had been with not just four years. . . . Some . . . had been together since kindergarten."[47]

After graduation, class reunions served the role of sustaining the community that Carver built. With consistency and across decades, Carver alumni planned and attended such gatherings—at the ten-year mark, twenty-year mark, thirty-year mark, forty-year mark, and beyond. For example, Joseph, wearing a Carver shirt during her interview, shared a keepsake booklet from her fifty-year reunion, which listed participants from reunions occurring every five years from 1963 to 2013. Past reunion artifacts were featured in the booklet as well.[48] A reflection from the class of 1963's twenty-year reunion read:

> Unlike the graduates of the Class of 1983 who have the world at their disposal, their counterparts in the Class of 1963 were faced with a tremendous amount of responsibility when they embarked in the world. . . . Even though James Brown, Gladys Knight and the Pips . . . [and] the Temptations . . . sang to sell-out concerts they still led the life of a second-class citizen. . . . Carver was only five years old in 1963. The students believed in school spirit and pride. A beehive of activities at the school found all students engaged in one or two extra-curricular activities. . . . The graduates in 1963 dined at Dooky Chase, Mule's and Hunt's, all predominately black restaurants. . . . The Class of 1963 realized that success would only come through hard work, determination, and perseverance.[49]

Here again, a shared history of racial struggle, political consciousness, and cultural experiences created unbreakable bonds.

Rhea Joseph's fifty-year reunion opened with a dinner and dance on a Friday evening. On Saturday, Joseph explained, the class "chartered a bus and we went on a tour. We toured the site where the school was. . . . We took a tour . . . through places where people grew up, the Lower Ninth Ward, Gentilly. . . . Then we had a church service" on Sunday, followed by brunch. Four months later, class members took a Caribbean cruise together.[50] Polk shared the booklet from her forty-five-year reunion, which featured Lucille Simms, a Carver English teacher, as a guest speaker.[51] Among other mementos, the booklet contained a letter from Blackburn, who also graduated in 1968. He wrote, in part: "We had the good fortune of attending a great school with teachers and administrators who sincerely cared about us. Contrary to what others may have thought, we received a first-rate education that enabled us to be very productive citizens."[52] He continued, acknowledging that he was "thankful for EVERYTHING I received at Carver, including lifelong friendships." Blackburn signed his letter, "RAMS FOREVER."[53] Polk sang the alma mater for their forty-fifth reunion.[54]

As for Riley, a 1974 graduate, he stressed that the "Carver school spirit is very, very strong" and noted his participation in a Carver alumni cruise, picnics, and attendance at homecoming games.[55] Like others, he also mentioned the RAM Jam, an annual event—held at City Park or a ballroom—where alumni from across the decades gather for a big party: "The DJ . . . will play music from 1958 up until present times, saying 'All right, all right, all my people from '58 come on out and get on the [dance] floor. Okay, now '59, get on the floor,' '60 and . . .'"[56] Riley described Carver as "a network," with the RAM Jam being the most obvious instantiation of "a bond" that many share.[57] Sparks, a 1993 graduate, said he headed to City Park for the RAM Jam one year but "couldn't make my way through" because "it was so crowded."[58]

TEACHER EXPERIENCES

Students built community with one another and with teachers through various school traditions. Not without significance, teachers established their own ways of working together, which fostered and deepened their shared commitment to student well-being. Through day-to-day practices at school, actions that demonstrated mutual concern and cooperation, and informal gatherings, Carver educators built a family-like community. They had neighboring classrooms but were also neighbors off campus and shared cultural connections at many levels. Further, the community at Carver was all-inclusive, including hall monitors, custodians, and cafeteria workers, not to mention parents.

Foley explained, "Most of the teachers there—and I'm really saying most of them—we were all of one accord," with a common goal to help students "make something of themselves."[59] Thus, teachers operated, she said, as a collective: "The English teachers, the math teachers, we'd all get together.

'OK, this student needs this.' We'd get tutoring for them. We'd get them after school and tutor them. . . . Even the cafeteria lady, she would leave sandwiches for us to feed the kids . . . after school."[60] Foley also told the story of a student that everyone called Preacher because "he carried his Bible around."[61] She relied on the well-established practice of working closely with colleagues to assist Preacher. Foley elaborated: "His mother was incarcerated. His father was incarcerated. He was left with three younger siblings, and he had to take care of them, get them to school and try to get himself to school. Then he was trying to support these kids, all on his own."[62] Preacher approached Foley and pleaded, "I don't wanna sell drugs. What can I do? How can I support my [siblings]? I wanna finish school." Foley responded immediately, "OK, baby, we gonna work on this."[63]

First, Foley went to the teacher who headed the school's job program, who replied, "Let me see what I can find." The teacher found a job for Preacher working at a grocery store, which allowed him to be home during the evening with his brothers and sisters. Next, she went to the counselor and said, "Look, we gotta get this boy out of school. What can we do? What classes [does] he need?" The counselor "sat down there and worked up a curriculum for him," said Foley, which charted a pathway to graduation with one more semester of courses.[64] In short, Foley strategically coalesced with supportive colleagues commanding the knowledge and resources to help Preacher graduate. When his mother got out of jail and was able to take care of her younger children, Preacher went on to study at Delgado Community College. Foley reminisced with great emotion: "He sent me [a] card thanking me. I cried when I saw that boy's card, thanking me for saving his life."[65] No doubt, the tradition of school faculty working together made this possible for Preacher, and it only served to deepen the mutual respect felt by Carver's faculty.

In a reciprocal way, this respect fostered ongoing cooperation on behalf of students as well as fellow teachers. Regarding faculty, Foley said, "We made do, and we helped each other. If this one needed [something], we'd get together and do it."[66] Foley spoke from personal experience as the recipient of teachers' strategic planning—or what she called "getting together." She narrated the following incident: Her team was set to win the state championship for the first time, but she needed the money to get her athletes there. The band director and the librarian "got together" and "went to all the teachers and they raised the money for us to go." She underscored the genuine sense of community that typified Carver, stressing, "I didn't ask a person for anything. [The teachers] brought it to me."[67]

The practice of teacher cooperation sometimes occurred through interdisciplinary networks that wove together multiple forms of knowledge and expertise to accomplish a common goal or orchestrate an important school event. Clarence Righteous relays that the second greenhouse at Carver was built "with the help of the brick-masonry class."[68] After brick-mason students put down the chain wall, he explained, "the carpentry department came in and helped frame that."[69] In this way, industrial arts teachers and students not only built community but parts of the campus together.

In the same way, Carol Righteous recalled with Lenora Condoll the cooperative effort of planning class night, a tradition highly valued by Carver's graduating seniors. Righteous made clear that "class night is a big thing."[70] Condoll, as senior advisor, called on Righteous and another teacher to plan class night; it was Righteous's first time doing so. In Carver fashion, interdisciplinary networks activated to bring this event to life. At the time, the movie *ET*, a lovable extraterrestrial that came to Earth, was popular. Righteous wrote a script for students to perform, and she "involved all extracurricular activity within that play."[71] Condoll revealed how things unfolded: "What made our senior class night so spectacular was the fact that we involved all or most . . . of the departments in the school. For example, when we needed the spaceship, carpentry did the spaceship."[72] This was not a one-time affair. Condoll noted other instances of getting together to create the best Carver possible for students. "I can recall one time . . . our drapes were not too good in the auditorium," said Condoll, "they were really raggedy."[73] With the homemaking teacher, she got some scissors and straightened things out.

Marilyn Pierre reported similar forms of engagement during her time at Carver. As a business education teacher, Pierre had her classroom designed as a model office, equipped with typewriters and computers purchased through a federal grant. However, the environment was somewhat sterile to recruit students. Thus, she divulged, "We would go to Mr. Righteous and the kids could get plants from the horticulture department and put 'em on their desk."[74] The horticulturists helped beautify the classroom for the business folks. Avis James disclosed that the childcare center functioned along the same lines. She said it was common practice for "the home ec[onomics] students [to] go over there and volunteer."[75] In fact, Pierre added, the home economics teachers taught parenting classes that coordinated with activities at the childcare center.[76] In this way, community was built across classrooms and generations.

Community-building traditions at Carver were far-reaching. If the cafeteria staff was part of the family, so were the hall monitors. Pierre and the Jameses said Ms. Gettridge, Ms. Mosley, and Ms. Wheeler were invaluable. When the hall monitors—one of whom had children at Carver—spoke, students listened.[77] Ultimately, what happened in the hallways filtered into classrooms. Ensuring a seamless educational process required a distinct way of working together—an everyday way of being that defined Carver's culture. Avis James clarified that these traditions did not necessarily permeate every school. "One of my coworkers who had come from another school was surprised at how much we worked as a family," she reflected aloud.[78] When teachers planned events like the Christmas social, the custodians were invited too. "They're part of the school as a whole," James asserted.[79] At times, she said, the custodians would talk to a child when the teacher could not—"it takes everybody" to build and sustain a school community.[80]

Teachers spent time together formally and informally. Sometimes this meant carpooling in the morning to Carver, as Lamar Smith and Enos Hicks, who also sent their children to Carver's summer camp together, did.[81] Other times, it meant sharing a kitchen table. Moore reminisced about the end of basketball season when everyone would go to the home of one coach and "have a big plate of red beans," a unique New Orleans culinary tradition. Savoring the memory and the food, he smiled, "Them red beans tasted like steaks!"[82] Pierre and the Jameses recalled casual gatherings among teachers, which contributed to the cohesiveness of the community. When Pierre started teaching at Carver, teachers were paid once per month. "It's on the first of the month," chimed Vermon James. "We got paid and we partied," Pierre declared.[83] In another tradition that marks New Orleans, she said teachers would "play cards and eat crawfish."[84] They would gather at a little family-oriented bar on Gentilly Road, bring a sack of crawfish, and play bid whist. It was the "whole gang," including Coach Hicks and fellow coaches Warren Braden and Johnny Harris. Social studies teacher Wilbert Young also joined and "would make you laugh so hard," Pierre recollected.[85] Mr. James beckoned Young aloud, stating that if he were there, "he could remind us of some of the stuff we did."[86] The sense of community and energy were palpable as the teachers—now convened to offer oral histories—re-membered the good times.

Parents were included as well. Condoll declared, "If the senior class had a prom, then we had a prom for the parents," who came "dressed in their gowns and their tuxedos."[87] Teachers also had a talent show for faculty. Clarence Righteous painted a picture: "The kids just went wild when the teachers walked out." "Remember Diana Ross?" queried Condoll as Carol Righteous echoed, "The Supremes!"[88] They laughed recalling that the musical group was played by three white teachers during one show.

Pure joy was exhibited by students as they recalled special events during their years at Carver. Teachers exhibited the same emotional register as they recounted daily acts of mutual support, interdisciplinary collaboration, and memorable traditions at Carver, not to mention get-togethers at homes and neighborhood venues. All of this generated a shared commitment to one another as members of a specific community—Carver Senior High School.[89] At a visceral level, these community-building traditions and other aspects of Carver's culture combined to generate a more panoramic reality: positive feeling and an unyielding affiliation centered around their collective identity as RAMs.

CHAPTER 8

"THEY LOVE THAT GREEN AND ORANGE!"

Positive Feeling and Affiliation Among Carver RAMs

They love that green and orange!

—DR. LINDSEY MOORE,
a 1965 graduate (and principal)
of Carver Senior High School[1]

It was a feeling. It was how you felt about
what Carver was doing for you in your life.

—MARY POLK,
a 1968 graduate of Carver Senior High School[2]

Together, the various dimensions of Carver's school culture—proactively embracing place, an intergenerational network that sustained connections over time, ethic of self-determination and achievement, commitment to not only academic content but consciousness in the context of racial inequity, and long-standing community-building traditions—produced strong, positive emotions among students and teachers. Carver was a place where people felt a sense of community and well-being. Students and teachers viewed themselves not as atomized individuals who happened to once be at Carver but as a group that shared a collective identity as RAMs. This collective identity was not temporary or fleeting. It was sustained over time, generating for teachers and alumni an abiding sense of belonging and ongoing commitment to the Carver community, not unlike a family. This love for Carver and the Carver community existed in real time on campus and endured long after graduation or retirement. The sentiments shared, the stories told, and the words invoked all spoke to the deep feelings and strong affiliations fostered through the school's culture over the course of five decades. The failure to understand the structure of feeling generated by the Carver experience is to miss something essential about the school and its legacy.

STUDENT EXPERIENCES

Althea Merricks still had her class ring, with the year 1959 etched in gold. "We had an opportunity to purchase a ring," said Merricks as she held it. "That's all my mama could afford for twenty-one dollars, but . . . it's over fifty years old."[3] She still possessed a mimeographed copy of Carver's alma mater and her diploma signed by Principal Milton Becnel. She retained a yearbook picture of Homeroom 307 headed by Thomas Hoover. She also kept programs from her twenty-five-, thirty-, and fifty-year reunions. At the thirty-year reunion in 1989, the invited speaker was Becnel. A 2016 photo taken with fellow alumni at an informal home gathering also featured among special mementos.[4] Yet they were not artifacts of the past. They were part of an ongoing life story in which ties to Carver were central. They were kept because they meant something then—and now.

Merricks explained her strong attachment to Carver, telling a story about slipping away to school against her mother's wishes. On this day, her mother and siblings needed her help due to illness, but she "didn't like to stay home from school." Thus, she left because "I loved to go to school" and said she "always recalls" that story because you "never disrespect your parents."[5] Merricks concluded: "I just wanted to go to school." At Carver there were "all of these people that you've seen day in and day out" and "everybody has school pride."[6]

It was Mary Polk who said of Carver's alma mater, "It wasn't just words. It was a feeling. It was how you felt about what Carver was doing for you in life, not just present, not past, but in your future."[7] Riley emphasized the "strong school spirit" that bonded a "network" of teachers and students, noting his lifelong relationship with Busch.[8] Kelly O'Guinn invoked a long history of Carver alumni returning to support student-athletes. It was intimidating to visiting teams because "even if you weren't the best player," said O'Guinn, "you felt very comfortable because you had that sense of community" and knew people "had your back."[9] These and other countless examples speak to the sense of personal well-being and collective belonging associated with the Carver community.

Theron Lewis, for instance, spoke of his awe in being mentored by Coach Hicks: "When Hoopy said something, that was it. It was gospel."[10] The emotional connection and admiration for his teacher ran deep. But this connection existed with other teachers, who he "respected" and whose names he remembered years later, such as Leroy Gray, a social studies teacher, and Irma

Jean Sales, a science teacher. Lewis still knew the alma mater "by heart" and recalled that the rooms of Yvonne Busch and Zenobia Stewart were "adjoining" with a shared back door. "It was a great time to be in school," pondered Lewis as he recalled the words of deceased schoolmate Earl Edwards: "He said something that really give the whole [picture]. . . . He said, 'You know, T [Theron], we were at school at a great time. It was just a wonderful time to be in school. There was a lot going on and I'm just glad I was a part of it.'" Lewis shared his sentiments fully.

For Rhea Joseph, going to Carver created affiliation among students from different locales—Desire, Lower Ninth Ward, Gentilly, Pigeon Town, and others. She explained: "[I] got to know students from other areas of the city [and then] we started bonding—there was a bond that's just unbelievable."[11] Joseph further elaborated, "I get a chill when I say that we have a saying . . . 'A RAM forever.'" A sense of belonging grew not only between students but students and their teachers. "You're in their care so many hours, six hours of the day," said Joseph. "They nurtured you." Joseph considered Carver to be a family: "There are people who are relatives and then you have people who are family. Relatives, you're just related to them, but you may not feel they're family. Carver was like family." At Carver, she contended, "the majority of us built a bond." Whether from Desire or the Lower Ninth Ward, "a lot of us had the same values. We wanted to get an education . . . and come to be productive citizens." All of this generated an abiding commitment to one another as Carver RAMs.

In terms of the solidarity between those at Carver, Ernest Charles said it was felt by the students as well as "the teachers who cared about us."[12] He continued, "We had teachers that we thought really cared about us. When you havin' a bad day, you could go to the teacher and they'll call you to the side and say, 'Hey, what's happening?'" For students, Charles said, "If you went to Carver, they had your back." He explained it this way: "If you went to Carver and you played ball, that gives us something so we had some type of knowledge [of one another]. Hey, that's Squirrel [Charles's nickname], or that's Joe. . . . Hey man, what's happening, brother? . . . We did something that we knew each other from, where we could vouch for each other."[13]

Charles was drafted into the military after high school, and then went to Grambling State University after almost three years of service. Thinking back, Charles reflected: "When I got to Grambling, I saw my 1965 class were right there. They about to leave out of Grambling. . . . Man, we saw a bunch of people, all these people from Carver. We had a little class reunion right there. . . . That was a beautiful thing."

Irvin Blackburn, class of 1968, also felt grateful for his experiences at Carver. He reported that when it came to interactions with principals, teachers, and counselors, "all the encounters . . . were positive ones."[14] Like Charles, he felt "blessed to have had the people who taught us, and put us on the right path," and said he "wouldn't change anything—I really wouldn't." Again, like Charles, reunions for Blackburn have been a time to reconnect, see people, shake their hands, and laugh about "things that happened when we were in school." He told a story that illustrated the expansive network and strong sense of identity held by Carver alumni. During the fiftieth class reunion that included a brunch on the steamboat *Natchez*, the boat's captain announced on the loudspeaker that he had "the pleasure of having members of the class of 1968 . . . on board." As those at the reunion clapped, he chimed in again, "They went to real good school. The reason I know that is because I went to that school. I graduated in 1976."

This shared sense of identity stood out for Willie Calhoun as an elemental part of the Carver experience. "The cohesiveness of the community," he said, "impacted us." To be sure, he continued, "we had a bond."[15] Even as time passed, Calhoun said mutual commitments were sustained: "Fifty years later and we still have the comradeship. We still have that partnership that we had way back then with each other. Seein' each other, tryin' to help one another, doin' what we can." Indeed, Calhoun asserted, "If you talk to anyone now, they will tell you that one of the most energetic alumni is the RAMs." Ella Shaw said the same: "One thing for sure, when a Carver RAM see each other, they acknowledge it."[16] Shaw was in the process of getting ready for her forty-fifth class reunion when she provided her oral history.

Riley, who graduated in 1974 with Shaw, demonstrated an abiding sense of respect for his teachers. "When Ms. Busch walked the halls, she got respect," he stressed. With deep regard, he underscored, "She was a beautiful woman. What can I say? She was just a great teacher."[17] In fact, for Riley, the positive emotions surrounding Carver extended beyond his beloved music teacher. He emphasized that "the general attitude of the teachers was that they cared." To this day, he said, there is "still strong school spirit," partly tied to the nurturing environment that alumni experienced in their youth. Trenesse Mosley graduated almost a decade after Riley and holds similar feelings for Carver. She is on the RAM Jam committee and has been "since day one," she explained. Mosley reflected, "My love for Carver runs deep 'cause I'm still there giving back and still working with alumni and doing the RAM Jam every year."[18] For her, the community of feeling and affiliation only grows stronger as the years proceed.

Mosley's deep commitment to Carver was fostered early on. She recollected the profound influence that Gwendolyn Tate-Smith had on her and the deep commitment she felt for her teacher. "Gwendolyn Tate would curse you if she really got mad," Mosley recalled. "You know what? We all feared her because we know she cared."[19] More specifically, "[Tate] would get up and she would close that door. She would say, 'What's your problem in here today? I'm not having it.'" Mosley said teachers knew students well enough that "they didn't have to call your parents 'cause they could reel you in." It all goes back to the idea that Carver was a family, a kinship network among not only students but students and their teachers.

One telling illustration of mutual commitment and feeling related to Mosley's pregnancy as a teenager. Harkening back to that time, Mosley remembered: "I think I was more ashamed to tell [Tate] than anybody else because I knew the disappointment that—because she had so much hope for me. . . . Because I knew they [teachers] cared about me. . . . I wasn't going to let them down. I wasn't going to turn around and do it again. I came back [after temporarily transferring to a school for pregnant girls]."[20] When Mosley returned, Tate told her, "Well, you gonna have to work your behind off 'cause you way behind and I'm not cutting you no slack." Mosley went on to receive a coveted English award from her teacher. Indeed, the connection she felt to teachers at Carver is part of what motivated her during this major life change. By the late 1980s, Carver had the on-site nursery to support teen mothers and fathers, enabling them to continue at Carver and graduate without interruption.[21]

Kelly O'Guinn captured the essence of this community of feeling when she reflected on her time at Carver in the mid-1980s. As a student-athlete, O'Guinn was "really impacted" by her coaches.[22] Under Danielle Foley, she did shot put and discus for track and played volleyball. Under Coach Earl Edwards, she played basketball. She noted that such relationships were "extremely close because I spent a lot of time [at Carver] after school or before school playing sports." She appreciated that "they pushed you beyond your limits. . . . They knew you had skills and talent." They encouraged you to "do your best" and signaled that "failure was not an option." Describing the emotional connection and care that coaches fostered through mentorship, O'Guinn underscored, "They would not allow you to just sit down and give up. They're gonna let you know [when you need to push yourself]. I think that's a part of love." Put another way: "A coach is gonna make you perform and do well. That's what type of coaches we had. That's the type of teachers we had. They wanted the best for us, and you can tell by the way they talk to you. Sometimes you don't have to tell a person you love 'em to determine that this person really cares." Teachers' investment in students was experienced and understood by O'Guinn as a form of love.

Dwan Julien spoke fondly of her teachers. She had Carol Righteous for English. She giggled: "Oh, my God. Honestly, I always looked at Ms. Righteous as a style expert. She was so fashionable when I was in school. It was her and Ms. [Lenora] Condoll. . . . I had Ms. Condoll for economics."[23] Dr. Lindsey Moore, principal during Condoll's time at Carver, was "a ball of energy," according to Julien. She said: "He was the most energetic principal I had ever seen. He was so involved with the students and always making sure that if we needed anything or if I was under the breezeway, he would say, 'Hey, Ms. Julien, whatcha doin'?' I would say, 'Nothing, just waiting for class.' 'All right,' and then, 'Let's make sure you get to class.'" She said Moore had "an open-door policy," so that students could "go to the principal and actually have a conversation with him." She recounted there was not "ever a moment that I felt like I couldn't go to the principal if I needed to [go]," even though she never had cause. All of this engendered a sense of well-being, of being cared for. In one case, Julien's biology teacher, Albert Jordan, passed away. It saddened the class, she said, because Jordan was "very engaged with us on a day-to-day basis." Jordan, who must have been terminally ill, wrote a letter to the class before his passing, saying, recalled Julien: "It was a pleasure being able to teach us, to be a part of our lives, to be able to instill in us different things or share his love of science with us [and conveyed] how much he would miss us."[24] These are the kinds of bonds that existed between administrators, teachers, and students at Carver.

Hasan Sparks had comparable experiences with Principal Moore in the early 1990s. He laughed with a kind of awe, stating: "He was active. He was always moving. It was like this guy never had any office work. He bonded with us. He had a lot of energy—I mean a lot of energy."[25] Sparks also bonded with Coach Eddie Flint, who oversaw track and football and taught math. Sparks said, "I played these activities, and I was very good in math. . . . I had to do extra better by him being my teacher as well as my coach." In short, Sparks connected with Flint in the classroom and on the field, and these interactions were mutually reinforcing. His connection with Flint also meant having a nickname; he "used to call me Watusi," Sparks recalled with delight.

This community of feeling persisted into the early 2000s when Martaz Lynch, Catherine White, and Adrienne Gladney attended Carver. Lynch considered band leader Wilbert Rawlins and brick-masonry teacher Jerry Reynolds to be "like father figures," even though he had a father, as both would "make sure I was doing what I needed to do."[26] In retrospect, as an adult, Lynch appreciated this "because there's a lot of my counterparts that are dead or in jail. I'm not in that number."[27] Reynolds also coached baseball, so Lynch connected with him on and off the diamond. White felt strongly that "Carver was the best school overall in New Orleans." She valued that "we had so many things going—it prepared you for life after graduation" through mechanics, gardening, agriculture, nursing, and more.[28] Gladney, who ultimately graduated from another high school, emphasized, "I still say [Carver is] the best." Gladney "was not doing what I'm supposed to do," but said "it was my fault." As for her teachers at Carver, she attests, "They tried to pull me back."[29] To this day, Lynch, White, and Gladney continue to attend Carver games, reunions, and the RAM Jam, sharing in a collective RAM identity that spans generations.

TEACHER EXPERIENCES

At Avis and Vermon James's house, on the day that they shared oral histories, stacks of Carver yearbooks rested on the dining room table, from 1972, '73, '74, '75, '76, '78, '80, '81, '82, '84, '85, '86, '92, '96, '99, and 2001, along with decorative glass mugs for the senior classes of 1979, 1980, and 1990. Draped nearby was an academic stole with the words *George Washington Carver*.[30] Mr. James' last year at Carver was 1988. Ms. James's last year was 2005.[31] Decades after their time at Carver, in 2018, their cherished collection of school yearbooks and other artifacts remained in pristine condition.

Even more telling was the 2001 yearbook.[32] Ms. James had been teaching at Carver for almost thirty years by then. Still, she cared enough to personally inscribe countless handwritten notes throughout the album, including small corrections. Two students, Nyasha Smith and "George" Torres, are pictured singing at the Coronation Ball; James had crossed out "George" and corrected it in pen to "Jorge." Another photo included "Kichelle" Gibson looking at the previous year's yearbook with two friends. James had scratched out the incorrect first name, writing "Kerchelle" in its place. She took the time, and had the intimate knowledge, to do this in several instances, ensuring that students' names were spelled correctly. She knew the students well. She cared. It mattered.

A yearbook photo of the Carver school-based health clinic this same year showed three staff members—two in professional dress and one wearing nurse's scrubs. By the photo labeled "Clinic Staff," Ms. James had written: "Mrs. R. Armour, Ms. Joan Thomas, Mrs. Bernard," with an arrow pointing to Mrs. Armour with the words "Rosemarie/Zulu Queen 2001" to commemorate Armour's participation as queen in New Orleans' long-standing African American Zulu parade.[33] (Most of the city's Mardi Gras organizations or krewes elect an annual king and queen who attend a celebratory ball and ride on special floats.) Ms. James knew her colleagues at a professional, social, and personal level, with a bond strong enough that she wished not to forget the details about them.

In fact, there are notations throughout the 2001 yearbook.[34] In one section, faculty are featured by academic department but are not identified; all their names have been inscribed by James. In another photo, student Marquita Pellerin offers a cute smile; next to it, James noted: "Had Top Grades 2000–01." Only genuine emotions and real relationships result in such heartfelt inscriptions. For James, Carver was a community of care and connection.

Charles Hatfield's "beautiful yearbooks," as Foley described them, were a testament to the collective identity shared by Carver RAMs.[35] Lamar Smith's "thing" about putting on a finely pressed shirt and tie each day communicated his deep regard and commitment to the Carver community. The r-e-s-p-e-c-t given to Busch as an uber-talented musician and a commanding teacher and band director grew from the same kinds of feelings. There is no doubt that Coach Enos Hicks felt similarly about Carver, where he spent every waking hour mentoring student-athletes for what he hoped would be bright futures. These early teachers dedicated most of their teaching years—counted in multiple decades—to Carver. Foley, a thirty-four-year veteran of Carver, attested, "Most everybody stayed there until they retired."[36] Carver *belonged* to them.

These positive emotions were the result of shared experiences between students and teachers. Coach Foley explained her approach after arriving at Carver:

> [I told the students:] "I'm not gonna holler at you. I'm not gonna scream at you. I'm not gonna curse you." I'd say, "That's not the way I am." I'd say, "I'm gonna respect you and you're gonna respect me. This is how we're gonna get along." That was the attitude I took with the kids. It wasn't like I'm gonna be dominant over you. No, we're gonna work together. . . . I'd say, "I'm gonna treat you like my own children. I love you all," I'd say, "but I'm gonna discipline you. I'm not gonna let you get away with anything."[37]

To treat students like your own children, to care for them, and to challenge them when they need it—these actions foster a sense of well-being and show youth they are deserving of your time and energy. This is something teachers do only if they are invested in the people around them and the community they share. "'I don't want anything to happen to you,'" Foley said she told students, "and they understood where I was coming from."[38] More than a decade after she had retired, Foley spoke with passion about her time at Carver.

Clarence Righteous talked about the good vibes among students and teachers during the learning process:

> The kids came to me and we talked theory, talked about plant propagation . . . but then when they get out and do it, then you're talking about it while you're doing it and saying, "This is what I've been talking about, [this is]

propagating right here. There are different methods of—"They'd say "Oh, okay." . . . They get all enthused about this kind of thing . . . Then they go out and tell everybody else in the community . . . how they plant the gardens. "No, Mr. Righteous said we have to do it this way." Yeah.[39]

Students were "enthused," sharing what they had learned with neighbors and other community members. Righteous had planted something in them; Carver was a source of light and they were compelled to "do it this way" because they trusted their teacher and knew he cared.

Dr. Lindsey Moore felt the same way as a student at Carver, years before he led the school: "[I] made some very good friends at Carver—felt safe— teachers very caring."[40] Thelma Crowe, his English teacher, was someone he recalled with fondness: "She really cared for the kids." Moore shared wonderful recollections of Lamar Smith in the science classroom as well. At the same time, Moore stressed that there "was a lotta Mr. Smiths" at Carver—"the teachers were caring and nurturing back in those days." He pondered, "They were young, so they really could identify with us. [They were] just old enough to be our teachers." At a visceral level, Moore said, "we knew they cared." For example, at dances, "You'd see 'em tryin' to dance out there. We just felt at home." This was during the first half of the 1960s, but the culture of care continued long after. He spoke of becoming principal in the 1980s and how he noted "a difference about people in our community." He emphasized, "They love that green and orange!" A tearful gaze occasionally accompanied Moore's recollections and stories.

Condoll recollected the strategic racial project that gave birth to Carver and other black schools on the city's outskirts. In spite of such a "bad situation," she said that she "had never seen kids so loving."[41] And "resilient," added Carol Righteous. "I think that's what kept us at Carver," Righteous concluded.[42] Giving further thought to what Carver meant to her, Condoll expounded: "When I say family, I can't even emphasize that enough."[43] She described herself as the "most blessed person" as she "did all she set out to do" in her life, much of which unfolded on Carver's campus.[44]

Carol Righteous shared a telling observation about the structure of feeling at Carver. "I'll tell you what," she announced. "The teachers who passed through Carver and left, always wanted to come back because we . . . had a camaraderie."[45] The students surely felt it. Righteous said students "bleed orange and green" because "they love Carver," an assertion supported by their own emotional reflections on their alma mater.[46] Teacher Marilyn Pierre also felt an enduring sense of belonging and commitment to Carver. She chronicled what happened during racial integration in New Orleans during the late 1960s and the 1970s, an effort that largely focused on integrating faculty: "They started grabbing teachers. [They would] send some teachers to [the white] Kennedy [High School] and some of the other schools outside of Carver. When my supervisor approached me, I said, 'No, if I have anything to offer at all [it will be at Carver].' And so I stayed at Carver. That was it."[47] Vermon James felt Carver was "one of the best schools" at the time.[48] He remained there just shy of thirty years, with chalk dust on his clothes as he taught his beloved students.

As Carver RAMs, those beloved students could be found everywhere. For teachers, seeing students after graduation was like encountering a relative. Connections remained. Carol Righteous put it this way: "Everywhere you go, you could not help but run into a Carver RAM. That's the truth. I mean, no matter where. You went out on the moon, you'd find a Carver RAM."[49] Condoll was once on a cruise with her husband in Hawaii. While she was waiting for the attendant, she said she uttered aloud, "Dang, it's so hot out here." The next thing she said she heard was a man announcing, "I'd know that voice anywhere. That's Ms. Condoll."[50] One of her former students was a chef on the cruise. The sense of kinship and shared identity transcended the campus; it was enduring.

Based on Condoll's time at Carver—from the school's first year in 1958 through 1996—she deemed Carver "a family." She proclaimed, "The parents and the students were—we were all involved. It was a community. Carver was different from, I think, any other school ever."[51] Undoubtedly, there were other black schools in New Orleans with their own nurturing traditions—and Condoll was aware of it. Her use of the word "ever" was her way of conveying emotions difficult to put into words (Figure 8.1).

Condoll chronicled efforts by the class of 1986 after Katrina struck New Orleans in 2005, destroying most of the city's schools. Back in 1986, seniors worked with the brick masonry department to build and install a RAM statue on campus. "They were able to save the RAM after Hurricane Katrina," she expounded. Ultimately, she conveyed with emotion, "We just left a legacy."[52]

FIGURE 8.1 Emotive Word Collage from Student and Teacher Oral Histories

CHAPTER 9

"THE SYSTEM SPREAD FEW RESOURCES VERY BROADLY"

Historical Perspectives on Who Failed Carver

To ignore the history of racism is to ignore
the enormous weight against which dedicated [black]
educators have pulled and strained for decades.

—AL KENNEDY,
"The History of Public Education
in New Orleans Still Matters"[1]

It is disappointing that greater achievement gains
were not made . . . but this may reflect the fact that
the system must spread few resources very broadly.

—SUPERINTENDENT GENE GEISERT
and the director of research and evaluation,
ELLEN PECHMAN,
New Orleans Public Schools Summary
of 1977–78 Test Scores[2]

The teachers at Carver Senior High School created a culture where they attempted to "mak[e] things happen that wouldn't happen otherwise."[3] They invested themselves "back in a corner someplace" and made the school their own.[4] They embraced students like they would their own children. They were determined to educate students well, guided by a desire for self-determination and achievement. Moreover, they prioritized more than high academic standards; they demonstrated concern for the context of students' lives, which required consciousness of self and community amid enduring racism. They communicated to students that the world was theirs, while recognizing that the world was biased against black people, demanding even more effort, excellence, and resistance. Their efforts should not be taken for granted. Teaching well is hard work, especially in systematically underfunded schools designed to preserve a racially subservient class. This was the reality in New Orleans.[5]

The history of white supremacy has shown itself in several ways: first, the legal denial of education to blacks; second, white resistance to establishing and funding black public schools; third, the development of an inferior, second-class school system for African American students; and fourth, white flight from public education after racial segregation was declared unconstitutional, followed by further abandonment of a public school system that became increasingly black.[6] Then there was Carver Senior High School, built on the geographic margin because whites wished to avoid desegregation.

White policymakers' neglect of black public schools in New Orleans is a long-standing problem. The perennial failure to allocate funds to build and maintain black schools, provide them with the necessary educational resources, and invest in the infrastructure to support black student achievement has been consequential. Historic data on the education budget in Orleans Parish, school resources and conditions, school performance, and Carver offer insight into the problem of chronically underfunding the public schools attended by black students.

The neglect of black education by white officials was only one dimension of a wider social and political system organized to oppress African Americans. Neglect of black schools was connected to housing discrimination and substandard public housing, limited access to healthcare, low-pay employment and exclusion from white labor unions, police brutality, the absence of African Americans in public office, and more.[7] Despite this, the black community in New Orleans forged resistance. The work of Carver teachers, documented in this book, is a powerful illustration. African Americans also built a robust infrastructure consisting of black-owned businesses, churches, and cultural and educational organizations, but this infrastructure could not compensate for grossly deficient state funding.[8] Given these conditions, the work of Carver teachers and their contributions to student well-being and excellence can be more fully appreciated. Poor standardized test scores did not reflect student or teacher deficiencies but a deeply rooted problem: racism in New Orleans. In the history that follows, it is evident that white policymakers' neglect was intended to have real and lasting effects. Withholding educational resources from black students was but one link in a chain of structural violence.

THE CHAIN OF STRUCTURAL VIOLENCE
AND NEGLECT OF BLACK PUBLIC SCHOOLS

There is a tendency to use test scores as a measure of school failure without consideration of the history that explains and, in many ways, was designed to produce "disappointing" achievement data. Blaming teachers for unfavorable student performance on standardized tests is another tendency. Gloria Ladson-Billings urges a more nuanced understanding in her explanation of the education debt: "the foregone schooling resources that we could have (should have) been investing in (primarily) low income kids." Reducing the education debt that has accumulated over time, she argues, is necessary for closing the so-called achievement gap or disparities in student performance by race.[9] In other words, schools do not exist in a vacuum. Sociologist Peter Iadicola makes the same point when he contemplates the "chain of violence" in New Orleans.[10] Iadicola argues that homicide statistics, when viewed in isolation, tell a distorted story. For example, the typical account of a neighborhood shooting in which one person assaults another focuses narrowly on proximal violence without addressing that interpersonal violence is the result, not the starting point, of a longer chain of structural violence against African Americans. "It is important to start with a definition of violence," he emphasizes, "that not only includes the violence that we criminalize . . . but also includes the violence that is part of the nature [or history] of our society."[11] He goes on: "Rarely are the acts of violence that we read about in our newspapers, that are part of police reports, isolated events."[12]

Thus, it is crucial to begin with a more encompassing definition of violence, described by Iadicola as "any action, inaction, or structural arrangement that results in physical or nonphysical harm to one or more persons" in a community.[13] "The violence of inaction can be as powerful as the violence of action," he explains; he offers child neglect as one example.[14] Iadicola examines violence that occurs in the education system, with an emphasis on institutionalized or structural violence rather than interpersonal violence alone: "Violence can take many forms; from the physical violence of assault or homicide, to the . . . symbolic violence of the denigration and exclusion of one's culture from the curriculum in schools, to the *social violence of denial of educational resources* that allow students to grow and develop their talents and abilities."[15]

Rather than focusing on fights at school or in the neighborhood, which may turn violent, Iadicola broadens the lens by linking these incidents to the state's failure to provide educational resources and the detrimental effects on marginalized youth, their schools, and their opportunities. But Iadicola does not stop there. He extends the lens to connect concerns about child welfare to the harsh reality of poverty and history of class- and race-based neglect in New Orleans and Louisiana. He writes:

> The state of Louisiana is second only to Mississippi in having the greatest concentration of poverty in the nation. The poverty rate in New Orleans is approximately twice the national average. The rate of poverty among children is also significantly higher than the rate for the United States as a whole, 34 percent versus 20 percent. The State of Louisiana ranks forty-seventh in the nation in overall child welfare. . . . This is the beginning of the chain of violence where because of one's position in terms of class, ethnicity, and/or gender you are defined as less to be invested in, whether the investment is in education, health, or protection by government.[16]

He concludes that not enough attention has been paid to structural forms of violence at the beginning of the chain.[17] Put plainly, in the context of Carver's history, poor test scores at school or incidents of physical violence in the Desire area reflected broader forms of disinvestment by white policymakers, whose decisions ultimately impact youth and their life outcomes.

From this vantage point, I argue systemic deprivation of black schools like Carver and the withholding of essential resources is a form of structural violence. This view rejects simplistic scapegoating of teachers whose work takes place within—and whose success with students occurs despite—chronic resource deprivation. It situates poor test scores as a measure of structural violence rather than of student-teacher failure. It is not scores or teaching that need to be addressed but systemic white supremacy and its educational consequences.

Early in the book, I referenced negative news depictions of the Desire area. In the 1980 article "Life Is Crime, Poverty, Fear for Housing Project Dwellers,"[18] the Desire area (and by association Carver) is considered a crime-ridden hellhole: "The symptoms are . . . familiar. Widespread crime . . . drug addiction . . . not enough police protection . . . overcrowded conditions inside the buildings . . . poor lighting . . . severe health hazards . . . outdated and poorly maintained buildings . . . exposed electrical wires . . . broken, backed-up sewers . . . holes in floors and ceilings . . . and nests of rats."[19] A sketch above the article shows a building with drug needles, trash, a large rodent in the foreground, and the face of a tearful black man. In this illustrative article, Desire, unlike Leonard Smith's more intimate portrayal, is depicted as uniformly horrible.[20] The article says little about deteriorated buildings or the racial politics of housing, only that Desire residents filed a class action suit against federal, regional, and local housing authorities, asserting that the development was "unfit for human habitation."[21] It states, "Desire, regarded as the worst project, is by no means the only one with serious problems," and goes on to list more than ten others in New Orleans.[22] Lacking is any systematic or structural analysis of why black communities have encountered these struggles. The article points out that housing authorities claim Desire residents "do not take care of [their] apartments."[23] However, it fails to examine that Desire was deliberately built cheaply for black residents.[24]

The same goes for mainstream depictions of school performance, as highlighted in a 1986 news article: "Almost half of New Orleans' public high school students are failing one or more academic subjects." Again, there is no examination of the wider causes, rooted in the racist denial of education resources. The associate superintendent of the city's high schools attributed student grades to "inadequate academic preparation," which sounds like blaming teachers. The superintendent also called out the city's "Mardi Gras mentality," suggesting that Carnival season is a distraction and that youth "play video games, loiter in shopping malls, and go to discos instead of doing their school work."[25] There is no historical or structural analysis of the consistent inaction of white policymakers in funding black schools or the lack of infrastructure in black neighborhoods.

Carver teachers and students needed no structural analysis because they directly experienced discrimination and neglect. Charles Hatfield confronted these realities firsthand when he was excluded from LSU's all-white law school. Marilyn Pierre understood the broader forces at work when Carver students were denied the hotel rooms they had reserved for a competition. Irvin Blackburn and his business teacher grasped the racism at play when he was initially not trusted with responsibility for the cash register during his A&P internship. Lenora Condoll offered a structural analysis by teaching students about exercising long-denied, hard-won voting rights. Principal Lindsey Moore saw the deeply rooted issues, which led him to establish a health clinic at Carver for those with limited access to healthcare. Denise O'Guinn "got the message" when black speakers visited Carver and encouraged students to challenge racial barriers. Coach Danielle Foley took a holistic view when she acknowledged that while resources at Carver were scarce, the teachers were nonetheless dedicated to teaching. They all knew what the above superintendent did not articulate or address: racism accounted for the neglect of black schools like Carver—and there were real consequences.

I now turn to this history of neglect, as it is the only legitimate place to begin any conversation about teaching and learning in urban school systems like New Orleans. It also elevates the contributions of black teachers, who strained against the weight of history, and locates the problem where it belongs.

WHITE NEGLECT OF BLACK SCHOOLS IN NEW ORLEANS, 1900 TO 1970

In New Orleans and throughout Louisiana, there was "active neglect" of black public schools by white officials.[26] Historian Donald DeVore explains that Warren Easton, one of the longest-serving superintendents of New Orleans public schools, "failed to mention the needs of black students in his annual reports from 1900 to 1910," indicating "the low or nonexistent priority given to African American education."[27] James Fortier, a white supremacist who was president of the city's school board from 1922 to 1926, likewise pursued a "policy of educational neglect and limitations" with the support of the all-white school board. DeVore notes this greatly "affected the quality and quantity of school facilities" available to black communities.[28] The African American struggle to obtain state-funded school facilities in New Orleans was not undermined only by the board's failure to allocate monies. White residents also protested the location of black schools in white neighborhoods, sometimes attempting to remove African Americans from schools they had populated for many years.[29]

The racial inequities of education were apparent in the number, condition, and value of public schools in New Orleans. In 1901–02, blacks had twelve schools while whites had sixty. In 1910, a decade later, there were sixteen black schools compared to sixty-eight white schools. Newly constructed schools were usually for white students while black students were relegated to poorly constructed and maintained buildings, former white schools, or annexes added to already overcrowded schools.[30] Between 1900 and 1910, for example, twenty-one new schools were built, but only three of them for black students. The land and building value of the new black schools averaged $25,000, while the value of the new white schools was nearly double; black schools were wood frame, and white ones were brick. In 1920–21, such inequities persisted.[31]

Various black advocacy groups fought for additional and better public schools, including the Colored Educational Alliance and the NAACP. The lack of schools resulted in both overcrowding and part-time attendance in shifts. This also affected access and enrollment more generally for black students.[32] During the early 1900s, black schooling in New Orleans was limited to grades first through fifth; access to middle and high school education was a separate ongoing struggle.[33]

In the late 1930s, Alonzo Grace and his Citizens' Planning Committee surveyed public school infrastructure in New Orleans and released a report revealing the consequences of historic neglect.[34] The Grace Report documented what was already well understood by African American communities in New Orleans: black schools, systematically underfunded, lacked critical infrastructure. This translated into too few schools, substandard buildings, and a perpetual lack of educational supplies and resources for learning.

In 1940, following the release of the Grace Report, the Louisiana legislature funded a statewide survey of public schools. Fisk University sociologist Charles Johnson was commissioned to oversee the "Negro side of the study."[35] His focus would be on "the impact that segregated schools had upon the lives of black students and society in general."[36] Twenty of the state's sixty-four parishes, chosen for their economic and social diversity, were investigated; Orleans Parish was excluded because of the recently released Grace Report. Classrooms were observed, and community members were interviewed about schools and other facets of parish life, such as living standards, health and recreation practices, and culture.[37] Importantly, Johnson "tried to set black students within the matrix of their schools, families, and communities."[38] For example, blacks in Louisiana were denied the right to vote; among those interviewed, researchers found only one registered voter.[39] As for black schools across the state, the majority were single rural buildings with one or two teachers. Not unlike New Orleans, however, "white parish boards and superintendents determined the number, type, and cost of each black school in the parish, and for the most part, the courses offered, length of terms, appointment of teachers, and the distribution of state and parish funds."[40]

Monies for black education were regularly diverted to white education. In 1941, parish school boards spent an average of seventeen dollars on each black student and sixty-nine dollars on each white student.[41] Thus, the inequitable, racialized patterns of resource allocation/non-allocation that characterized New Orleans existed in parishes across the state. Johnson's team found that "most black elementary schools suffered from extreme neglect and over-crowding" and were "often without lights, desks, blackboards, libraries, toilet facilities, adequate heating, bus transportation, or supervision."[42] Among the twenty parishes, there were only twenty-seven high schools and training schools for black students—and they suffered from the same problems as the elementary schools, such as overcrowding and a lack of resources.[43]

During the same period as Johnson's study, black teachers in New Orleans sought to address another disparity in educational resources: the city paid black teachers less than their white counterparts. In fact, black teachers were paid less than white teachers with the same credentials throughout Louisiana. In New Orleans specifically, the average white teacher received an annual salary of $1,880 while the black counterpart received $550.[44] In 1939, NAACP attorney Thurgood Marshall visited New Orleans and encouraged teachers to "organize a special committee, raise money, and find suitable plaintiffs" to advance a lawsuit on salary equalization—and he agreed to collaborate with A. P. Tureaud, one of the few black lawyers in Louisiana.[45] In 1941, Tureaud filed a petition with the school board asking for salary equalization. When the board did not respond, Tureaud filed suit in federal district court in New Orleans.[46] During the trial in 1942, the defense attempted to justify race-based salary inequities because of a shortage of funds. The judge ruled black teachers were entitled to equal salaries.[47] Notably, some black teachers' salaries in 1943 were as much as $1,300 more than they had been before the legal battle.[48]

During the 1940s, the struggle over equalizing separate school facilities continued. In 1948, the NAACP, along with Wilfred Aubert, a community activist from the Ninth Ward, filed suit in 1948, demanding that the school board fulfill the "equal" part of "separate but equal." But the board's efforts to change remained slow.[49] By 1951, the NAACP's calls for equalization evolved into demands for racial desegregation. Tureaud presented a petition to the school board to immediately desegregate New Orleans public schools, but the board refused.[50] The next year, in 1952, Tureaud filed a suit on behalf of Earl Benjamin Bush to force desegregation of the city's schools, but the all-white, all-male board remained unmoved.[51] Further action was delayed until the NAACP's *Brown v. Board of Education* school desegregation case progressed with the US Supreme Court. In the meantime, tensions grew in the black community over the best strategy: to focus on the equalization of black schools or the racial desegregation of all public schools.[52]

In 1954, the Supreme Court ruled on *Brown*, declaring "separate but equal" was unconstitutional. Within days, there was mass resistance from white communities. From the Louisiana legislature to White Citizens' Councils in New Orleans, the federal order to desegregate was challenged. By the end of 1954, several state laws had been enacted to preserve racial segregation. Act 555 prohibited local school boards from establishing desegregated schools, while Act 556 enshrined a pupil placement law banning cross-race assignments. The school board in New Orleans supported these legislative actions.[53] The Supreme Court's 1955 decision on implementation of *Brown*—requiring desegregation "with all deliberate speed"—emboldened resistance. The school board's refusal to develop a desegregation plan led to ongoing litigation by black leadership, including pursuing the *Bush* lawsuit.[54] Whites were determined to prevent blacks from accessing the educational resources that had long been reserved for them—and they had no intention of sharing seats in classrooms.

By May 1960, federal judge Skelly Wright had issued his own desegregation plan for New Orleans, as the board had failed to submit one. A 1961 report by the education subcommittee of the Louisiana Advisory Committee to the US Commission on Civil Rights highlighted the ongoing New Orleans crisis. In a stunning seventeen-page chronology of events from January 1960 to January 1961, the brazen resistance of white segregationists to educational equity was made clear. Louisiana governor Jimmie Davis vowed to uphold separate but equal schools in his inaugural address.[55] The Louisiana legislature once again passed myriad bills to preserve segregation, allowing the governor to close all public schools (if any should desegregate) and prohibiting the distribution of state funds to any desegregated school.[56] The Orleans Parish School Board, in a vote of four to one, asked Davis to oppose the federal mandate and preserve segregated schools.[57] Davis seized control of the New Orleans public schools while the NAACP filed suit in federal court to restrain the state from taking any action to nullify Judge Wright's desegregation order.[58] A three-judge panel ruled that "all Louisiana statutes which would directly or indirectly require segregation of the races in the public schools for the Parish of Orleans, or authorize the closure of such schools, or deny them public funds because they are desegregated, are unconstitutional."[59] Wright granted the board until November 14, 1960, to implement the plan.[60] Board member Emile Wagner, a rabid segregationist, advocated the abolition of public schools. The White Citizens' Council petitioned to remove board members who, though reluctantly, had conceded to federal pressure to preserve the public schools rather than close or abolish them.[61]

On November 14, 1960, William Frantz Elementary School and McDonogh No. 19, both in New Orleans' Ninth Ward, were desegregated. Ruby Bridges braved mobs outside Frantz; Leona Tate, Tessie Prevost, and Gail Etienne did the same at McDonogh. Many white parents withdrew their children.[62] Again relying on resource deprivation to preserve racial oppression, "the State had forbidden banks to lend money to the school board and the legislature itself had refused to pay the teachers."[63] When the legislature finally allocated funds for Orleans Parish, Frantz and McDonogh were excluded.[64]

It should be noted that when Carver opened its doors in 1958, it was during this period of mass white resistance and political unrest. Carver was born from the school board's desire to preserve racially and spatially separate schools for whites—and quell the push for desegregation—by responding to black demands for facilities. Ten years after *Bush*, eight years after *Brown*, and four years after Carver's founding, only twelve black students were attending desegregated schools in New Orleans.[65] Black enrollment in New Orleans public schools continued to rise, alongside rapidly decreasing white enrollment.[66]

It was not until 1968—a whole decade after Carver opened—that Dr. Mack Spears, a longtime teacher and former principal of McDonogh No. 35, became the first African American elected to the Orleans Parish School Board.[67]

ONGOING WHITE FLIGHT AND NEGLECT IN THE 1970S

Gene Geisert, the white superintendent of New Orleans public schools, was appointed in 1971. He later recollected how the city's media highlighted his selection as superintendent with two cartoons.[68] One depicted him as the "skipper of a storm-buffeted dinghy named 'Orleans Schools.'" The other was "a desk marked with [his] name on which sat an oversized apple tagged 'old problems' [with a] worm . . . poking its head out of the apple."[69] Public education leadership in Orleans Parish and Louisiana had been white before and after Reconstruction. In other words, whites had long controlled the allocation (and non-allocation) of educational resources to white and black public schools. At the time of Geisert's appointment, there were 108,000 students in New Orleans public schools, 70 percent of whom were black.[70] Geisert's superintendency occurred amid ongoing resistance to school desegregation and white flight.[71] While the public schools of New Orleans became increasingly black, another 42,000 white elementary and secondary students "among whom were numbered the children of most of the city's leadership, attended parochial and private schools."[72] One long-standing issue—racism—not only persisted but deepened.

By the 1970s—the same period during which Leonard Smith, Ella Shaw, and Herlin Riley attended Carver—the number of white students in Orleans Parish had declined precipitously. Only ten years earlier, Ruby Bridges had desegregated Frantz under the watch of federal marshals; Tate, Prevost, and Etienne had done the same at McDonogh No. 19.[73] Whites resisted desegregation by removing their children from New Orleans public schools and sending them to the city's Catholic or private schools. Many more moved out of Orleans Parish altogether to newly developing suburbs.[74]

The Orleans Parish School Board's *Facts and Finances* report indicated that the percentage of white students in public schools from 1963–64 to 1977–78 decreased from 46 percent to 38 percent.[75] Moreover, the total number of whites in the city's public, Catholic, and private schools during this period dropped from 84,000 to 44,000—halved over a span of fifteen years. Public school enrollment for black students remained steady at 85 percent of all black students.[76] Meanwhile, the trend of white flight continued in the following decades: from 1950 to 2000, two-thirds of the white population left Orleans Parish.[77] In the 1977–78 school year, Carver Senior High School had the second highest enrollment among all black public high schools in New Orleans, with a student body of over two thousand; on the same campus, Edwards Elementary and Carver Junior each enrolled one thousand students.[78]

In 1978, Superintendent Geisert and the director of research and evaluation, Ellen Pechman, issued a report on district test scores.[79] It was twenty years after Carver's founding. From 1976–77 to 1977–78, test scores had remained consistent, with "no statistically significant gains or losses." More specifically, "Except in twelfth grade math and reading and in tenth grade math, all achievement falls within the average range of scores (the fourth and fifth stanine) by comparison to other schools in large cities."[80] The summary stated it was "disappointing" that no further gains were made and underscored "this may reflect the fact that the system must spread few resources very broadly."[81] It emphasized that the absence of performance gains "can be expected in educational settings where there are not enough resources available to meet the complex needs of the diverse student population."[82] A few years earlier, a 1974 report on demographic data and test scores revealed that 80 percent of students in New Orleans public schools qualified for free lunch. The report also highlighted that "the inadequate level of financial support for public schools has handicapped the ability to compensate for children with weak fundamental skills."[83]

As in the past, adequately financing a school district serving low-income black students was not a priority for white leadership. But test scores failed to capture the full story or reflect the daily reality of students and teachers in New Orleans public schools, where most teachers labored with skill and determination to develop the talents of their students. Pechman, responsible for the test score summary, directed the district's testing program during the 1970s and early '80s. She recalled "a lot of pressure to publish the test scores from the white community to prove how bad the schools were." She further emphasized, "As the testing director, I tried very hard to resist those kinds of smear tactics."[84]

Stagnant or declining test scores could not be attributed to a lack of teacher care or expertise. From 1962 to 1978, the percentage of black teachers with a master's degree increased by 6 percent, while the number of white teachers with a master's remained virtually unchanged. In fact, more black teachers had master's degrees than white teachers—860 compared to

552—impressive considering the racial and economic barriers of the time.[85] Total elementary and secondary instructional staff in November 1977 was 1,500 whites versus 3,000 blacks, with black individuals constituting 71 percent of all district employees.[86] In short, black teachers stepped up and pushed forward despite more than a century of neglect and "smear tactics."

In 1978, John Finney, the district's director of maintenance services, provided data from the most recent 1972 school plant survey to Superintendent Geisert, who had requested the information.[87] Finney's memorandum offered some insight on the results of neglect in a majority-black school district. The cost of rehabilitating the entire system in 1978 was estimated at $130 million, but it would likely be closer to $208 million in light of "the continuing inflationary spiral . . . on construction costs" and "the fact that this would be . . . a ten-year project."[88] Total building repairs contracted for 1978–79, however, totaled only $6 million, with a meager $9,000 allocated for Carver to replace the folding partition in the gym and $14,000 set aside for electrical work in the auditorium; a new roof was planned for Carver Junior at a cost of $16,000.[89]

The results of neglect were alarming. Finney communicated that in New Orleans public schools:

- 50 percent of fire alarm systems are wholly or partially inoperative, with exit doors inoperative in the majority of our schools
- 11 buildings are under continual structural observation[90]

He clarified that "various state and city regulatory agencies have demonstrated an understanding of our [financial resources] problem and thus have not enforced their regulations to the letter of the law," such as those set by the state fire marshal.

In the 136 school plants inspected, Finney reported the following deficiencies:

- Site and Play Area—30 need drainage repair, 15 require clearance of hazards, and 4 require fencing from traffic
- Buildings—107 need repair and paint for appearance, 5 need heat and ventilation, and 16 need natural and electric light

- Toilet Facilities—15 have unclean floors and walls, 17 need light and ventilation, 38 need toilets due to problems with type, number, or condition, 58 need soap and towels, and 37 require a supply of toilet paper
- Water Supply—24 have drinking fountain problems

His report continued: among the 130 cafeterias inspected, 59 floors, 76 walls and ceilings, 23 doors and windows, and 52 lavatory facilities were unsatisfactory; 29 required utensils and equipment; and 9 needed rat-proofing. The "greatest problem," he stressed, "still lies in the elimination of peeling paint and repairs to floors, walls, and ceilings." An additional 44 schools needed student handwashing facilities.

When his superintendency ended in 1980, Geisert reflected on the link between declining test scores and inadequate school funding. He wrote that, during his tenure of almost a decade, "analysis of progressive pupil performance showed that test scores began around the twenty-fifth percentile in kindergarten and deteriorated one or two percentage points with each succeeding grade. Thus twelfth graders were functioning somewhere around the tenth or twelfth percentile."[91] He went on to clarify:

> At meetings of the school district's top management, talk about potential strategies to reverse the downward spiral of student achievement kept returning to the problem of funding. Neither the city of New Orleans nor the State of Louisiana has historically given high priority to the support of public education. During the 1978–79 school year, the New Orleans Public Schools ranked third-to-last in per-pupil expenditure among the 50 largest school systems in the country. The funding situation in 1971 was similar.[92]

To repeat: public education had historically never been a high priority in New Orleans, which ranked third-to-last in per pupil expenditures among urban districts nationally. Graduating seniors scored at the tenth percentile. Significantly, discussion of strategies to reverse the downward spiral of student achievement kept returning to the *problem of funding*.

Geisert never explicitly linked deteriorating conditions and achievement with a history of racism and white flight, though he separately noted it was a majority-black school system.[93] Additionally, Geisert had navigated struggles over racial desegregation and participated in ongoing dialogue at the district level about financial constraints and the lack of adequate educational infrastructure, issues that were clearly interconnected.

The challenge of building infrastructure—the physical and academic resources required by New Orleans public schools—was evident throughout Geisert's tenure. Initially, he focused on improving elementary education, which meant "raid[ing] accordingly from the administrative, maintenance, and custodial services budgets."[94] Only by implementing further austerity in these areas was he able, in 1973, to expand kindergarten from a half-day to a full-day program.[95] This zero-sum game operated in tandem with the earlier school plant survey. In short, black students could either have full-day kindergarten or toilet paper, but they could not have both.[96] Well-maintained buildings were a distant possibility, regardless.

The problem was equally evident when Geisert pursued his high school improvement plan, an initiative called the Secondary Curriculum Improvement Program (SCIP).[97] Regarding SCIP, Geisert opined: "It was not clear what form such a program should take or how much it would cost. It was clear, however, that a great deal of preparation would be required to get the program established . . . and that it would almost certainly make a tremendous demand on an already strained budget."[98] The development and implementation of SCIP put into sharp relief the depth of the school system's funding problems and the implications for black students; SCIP was not remotely up to the task of remedying more than a century of racially targeted neglect. SCIP began in the summer of 1977 with a reading and language arts resource and training center at John F. Kennedy Senior High School, a formerly all-white high school.[99] Each high school was expected to undertake a needs assessment to develop its own instructional model with a corresponding action plan focused on reading, language arts, and math. When students returned to school in 1977, high schools initiated the needs assessment.[100]

Next came a funding debacle, which mirrored the challenge of improvements at the elementary level. First, to support the new high school initiative, Geisert "made a plea to Title I to use some of its funds to develop some SCIP models in Title I schools." This would be "appropriate," argued Geisert, since "the majority of these students were from disadvantaged backgrounds."[101] The Title I Citywide Advisory Committee agreed and negotiations with the Louisiana Department of Education enabled funds to be used in eight Title I secondary schools.[102] Second, as a result of "the collection of some additional unanticipated tax revenues," the school board had a budget surplus. Geisert advocated for the board to provide him with funds to give all high schools "a grant" allowing them to work on their five-year SCIP proposals the next summer. The board's windfall provided grants ranging from $500 for small schools and up to $20,000 for the largest senior high schools.[103] But this was made possible by unexpected funding and was intended for planning purposes only.

In drafting the 1978–79 budget, Geisert and his administrative team "realized that funds had to be set aside to begin implementation of the SCIP proposals."[104] The school board approved $1.4 million for SCIP, which would mostly be "prorated among the 13 senior high schools and the 21 middle and junior high schools." A portion would be used for "support services from the Office of Curriculum and for other expenses to be incurred for the program systemwide."[105] A rough distribution, which assumes even allocation of *all* the $1.4 million to the thirty-four senior and junior high schools, would translate into only $45,000 per school. To supplement its allocation, the school board earmarked an additional $2.5 million in Title I funds to twenty-two of the eligible senior and junior high schools. However, Geisert lamented, a teachers strike in Orleans Parish during this same period resulted in a "settlement with the teachers' union [that] necessitated the Board's slashing $1.95 million from its $108 million budget." By Geisert's report, twenty-two budget items were affected and SCIP's funding was cut by $400,000. Once again, limited funds for vast needs, though distributed creatively, never eliminated the historic deficit.

Although Geisert and several school board members blamed striking teachers for undermining students' education at the start of the 1978 school year—and warned of consequences if they did not return to classrooms— teachers, for the most part, had the support of students and the community.[106] The 1940s lawsuit that sought to equalize teacher salaries by race, along with two previous strikes—in 1966 and in 1969—had challenged the low teacher salaries in the public schools of New Orleans.[107] Still, as DeVore and coauthor Joseph Logsdon point out, in the late 1960s, the salaries of New Orleans teachers "lagged behind those of most other Southern cities," including Shreveport, Louisiana, where teachers were paid a minimum of

$3,900 annually.[108] The final agreement between Geisert, the school board, and the teacher union included a 7 percent raise for teachers and a larger contribution to employee health insurance.[109] As before, monies for one necessity would come at the expense of another necessity in the budget. New Orleans teachers deserved to be well paid; New Orleans students deserved, at the very least, full-day kindergarten and SCIP. In the end, the budgetary constraints imposed by state policymakers undermined black education, creating a terrain on which limited resources were constantly in flux as they were moved to avert one problem, then another, then another.

As one example, during the 1978 teachers strike, Geisert and the school board asked the state legislature to allow citizens to vote on a proposed half-cent sales tax increase to support salary increases, but the "legislators adjourned without passing the tax bill," leaving the school board to consider a property tax increase, an idea that "fizzled, largely because of the historical aversion of New Orleanians to property taxes."[110] Of course, those with the highest property taxes were white and enrolled their children in private and parochial schools. From their perspective, there was little motivation to approve higher property taxes to subsidize public schools attended by black students—the same students with whom whites refused to integrate.

In sum, two decades after *Brown*, whites had fled, creating a nearly all-black public school system in New Orleans. White flight, compounded by historic state neglect of black education, further worsened the financial infrastructure for black students and teachers still in the system. Conditions in the schools deteriorated, as facilities aged and went without repair due to the lack of resources. School programs suffered as well, and any attempt to plug one hole translated into the creation of new ones elsewhere.

THE WAR ON DRUGS, THE WELFARE STATE, AND STUDENTS, 1980–2000

The forces of racism did not disappear after *Brown* and mass resistance. Jim Crow as de jure segregation (mandated by law) was replaced by de facto segregation (maintained by whites through choice and custom). Additionally, civil rights activists were considered lawless and responsible for widespread social discontent. A "new Jim Crow" system emerged in this reactionary atmosphere.[111] The 1980s was an era in which white supremacy was reinvented, with a new set of racially targeted policies. These policies developed on two fronts: the War on Drugs and the political assault on the welfare state, both of which shaped the wider climate navigated by Carver students and teachers.

The War on Drugs, introduced in 1982 by President Ronald Reagan, was advanced on the ground by local police in urban centers, such as New Orleans. Officially, the War on Drugs was touted as an initiative to reestablish "law and order" and curb the spread of drugs, violence, and crime on city streets. In reality, however, illegal drug use was on the decline when the War on Drugs began. It was "crack"—the kind of cocaine found in poor communities of color as opposed to the powder form used by wealthier whites—that was most heavily criminalized.[112]

The federal government invested significant resources in the War on Drugs. Between 1981 and 1991, FBI antidrug allocations increased from $38 million to $181 million.[113] Large cash grants were given to state and local law enforcement agencies such as Special Weapons and Tactics (SWAT) teams that conducted raids in public housing development, schools, and elsewhere.[114] Meanwhile, funding for drug treatment, prevention, and education plummeted. The budget of the National Institute on Drug Abuse fell from $274 million to $57 million between 1981 and 1984, and the antidrug funding for the Department of Education was reduced from $14 million to $3 million.[115] The number of incarcerated people, mostly of color, soared from 300,000 in 1980 to two million in 2000. Most were charged with nonviolent minor offenses.[116]

The War on Drugs ultimately amounted to a war on youth of color in poor urban neighborhoods like the Desire housing development, where many Carver students lived. New Orleans' first black school superintendent had to navigate this difficult terrain. DeVore and Logsdon write:

> By the time Everett J. Williams, a veteran teacher and administrator became the system's first black school superintendent in 1985, the main issue of the preceding three decades—desegregation—had been replaced by the problem of operating an urban school system amid the many societal ills that plagued New Orleans. . . . [Dr. Williams] realized . . . that urban schools, if they were to succeed or even survive, had to find ways of solving many non-educational problems. Violence, drugs, and teenage pregnancy constituted some of the new challenges.[117]

It was a bitter irony that while the War on Drugs accelerated, significant cuts were made to drug treatment, prevention, and education programs.[118]

In 1987, Carver hosted an antidrug retreat facilitated by the National All-Star Program to prevent substance abuse, the first of its kind in Louisiana and the first at an all-black school nationwide.[119] During this same period, however, the state defunded a program that Coach Danielle Foley ran at Carver to combat alcoholism.[120] In addition, between 1984 and 1990, the black citizens of New Orleans, according to the US Department of Justice, filed more complaints about police brutality than any other city in the nation.[121] Louisiana's incarceration rate grew to be the highest in the United States, and the New Orleans Police Department was ultimately put under a federal consent decree to remedy corruption and abuse.[122]

The War on Drugs was partly intertwined with an attack on the welfare state, and associated public benefits, in the 1980s. The welfare state is best understood as a system of policies through which the government provides citizens with social supports, benefits, and entitlements. It first emerged in the 1930s with Depression-era government programs and expanded in the 1960s.[123] With the passage of the Civil Rights Act of 1962, which prohibited discrimination in public accommodations, and President Lyndon Johnson's War on Poverty, which established an array of social programs to assist the poor and other marginalized communities, a backlash coalesced. Political leaders asserted that government interventions for the poor only served to bolster a so-called culture of poverty.[124] Laziness, or the lack of a work ethic and educational aspirations, was often cited as the result of the welfare state's anti-poverty programs, in addition to civil rights legislation that many whites felt unfairly advantaged people of color. This narrative suggested that lawlessness worsened, driven by a lack of incentive and discipline in low-income communities of color. It followed that social welfare programs focused on food, health, and housing were gutted.[125]

During this period, then, black communities subjected to historic neglect and racial marginalization faced even deeper neglect. Long overdue monies for school and community infrastructure were spent instead on criminalizing and incarcerating youth. The few existing social supports were cut. That the school community was left to shoulder the burden with fewer and fewer state resources partly explains why Moore established the Carver childcare center and health clinic. These services provided nutrition, dental care, mental health, drug and alcohol abuse, and testing for pregnancy and sexually transmitted diseases, funded not by the city or state but a private foundation.[126]

Amid the War on Drugs and an attack on the welfare state, chronic underfunding and disinvestment took a devastating toll. A 1983–84 Carver school profile from the district's Division of Planning, Testing, and Evaluation shows a 12 percent dropout rate. The Blight Index, published by City Hall, designated Carver's Desire Area as "endangered," twenty-sixth out of seventy neighborhoods in terms of condition. Meanwhile, Carver Senior had 1,100 students, with one principal, two assistant principals, forty-five regular teachers, fifteen special education teachers, one part-time nurse, two librarians, two teacher aides, ten custodians, and one security guard, supported by a budget of only $1.7 million, with a meager $1,600 for repair and maintenance, $8,500 for instructional materials, and $4,500 for custodial supplies. The average teacher's salary was $18,500.[127]

Results from the 1983 Comprehensive Test of Basic Skills were informative. Of the approximately 650 Carver students in grades nine through twelve who took the reading and math tests, 65 percent scored in the bottom percentile for reading and 49 percent for math. Only 1 percent were in the top percentile for reading and 2 percent for math. More specifically, 12 percent were at or above grade level in reading and 18 percent at or above grade level in math.[128] *In sum, while experienced teachers taught with all their might, they could not fully compensate for the structural violence of neglect and disinvestment, measured by poor test scores.*

Decades of resource deprivation had real, documented effects. A 1987 report on Carver by the Southern Association of Colleges and Schools (SACS), which accredits educational institutions, reveals the effects of neglect and the gross lack of educational resources.[129] It also underscores the herculean efforts of veteran teachers to support student achievement, despite inadequate infrastructure. Reviewers made clear that they were "deeply impressed by the high morale of the faculty" and saw "much evidence of realization of many of the educational objectives," with Carver demonstrating "a significant influence on the lives of students."[130] However, the report is replete with statements about the lack of school resources and crumbling infrastructure (Figure 9.1).[131]

AREA ASSESSSED	RECOMMENDATIONS
School Facilities	• Maintenance of grounds . . . should be given serious attention • Bleachers and furniture in the gym should be replaced • The Industrial Arts and Music Building needs to go through extensive repair • Student lockers in hallways need to be repaired or replaced • More drinking fountains are needed on campus • Complete accessibility should be considered for handicapped persons • Plumbing for water in the science labs needs to be installed or repaired
Art	• Sufficient materials, supplies, and equipment, including art desks and tables, should be acquired
Business Education	• A need exists for additional computer equipment, with appropriate software
English	• The department requires more reading materials and supplies
Foreign Language	• Audiovisual materials should be obtained
Health Education	• Fire extinguishers are needed in food lab as well as bookshelves • Textbooks should be updated
Industrial Arts	• Lighting should be improved in the drafting room • Models, drafting equipment, and other teaching aids need updating
Math	• Computers should be increased to improve ratio of students to computers
Music	• There is a need for procurement, replacement, and repair of school-owned instruments, electronic and audiovisual equipment, repair [of] facilities • Acoustics and soundproofing of band and choral rooms should be improved • Music library should be expanded
Science	• Urgent attention is needed to repair and maintain plumbing in labs to provide water • Immediate attention should be given to the installation of safety equipment • Additional supplies are needed
Social Studies	• Consider purchasing a video recorder
Trades	• Hot water should be made available in all shops

FIGURE 9.1 Excerpts from SACS Report on Carver, March 25–27, 1987

Despite these challenges, the faculty are lauded as "well qualified, dedicated, with a positive professional approach to education" and doing "an excellent job with limited resources" and maintaining "very low" teacher turnover.[132] Science teachers ensure that lab experiments are done "with the available resources."[133] The committee concluded that "the entire educative program of [Carver] is appropriate for the total growth and development of students."[134] In the previous twelve months, the school experienced a 16 percent dropout rate, a reality explained by structural violence rather than teacher-student deficits.[135]

Carver students reflected on the cumulative impact of neglect during their time at school. Trenesse Mosley reported that, by the 1980s, the school was "starting to fray" with things "break[ing] down." She said there were "leaks in the ceiling so they had to close off part of the gym" and the "bleachers didn't come out all the way like they used to." There was a limited supply of sports equipment, so it was reserved for sports teams rather than physical education classes. Library books were not replaced; teachers had to borrow and share the library's projector, making it sometimes unavailable.[136] Kelly O'Guinn, a Carver student in the 1980s, said her first real chemistry experiment occurred in college, a testimony to the condition of the science lab.[137] Her sister Denise O'Guinn, at Carver until 1990, provided a thoughtful analysis of these challenges, saying she left high school feeling "unprepared" and "knew something was lacking."[138] Dwan Julien said during her time there in the late 1980s and early 1990s, "they hadn't updated anything." She reflected, "Our school was in a lower-income area. They didn't give us as much money or financing toward our education." "I didn't feel like my teachers didn't care," she said, but "the resources weren't there."[139] She further recalled: "The books were old. They were falling apart. They were outdated. They could only teach us from the curriculum that they [created]. . . . Bathrooms needed to be fixed; lockers weren't operable. . . . You carried all your books with you if you had your books. . . . Lights didn't always work for night games. . . . A lot of things around the school needed to be fixed."[140] Adrienne Gladney, Catherine White, and Martaz Lynch said the auditorium was closed by the 2000s. Gladney said students "never were able to use it." Despite this, she continued, "The teachers were definitely there to teach. They were there early every day. If you asked for help after school, they would stay and help you."[141]

Lynch followed, "We may not have had a set of books to bring home. . . . We may not have had no lockers, [but] teachers taught."[142]

A 1991 school improvement and accountability plan by Carver students, parents, teachers, and administrators underscored the commitment to a "climate where students can achieve high expectations." To sustain this climate, they focused on instructional leadership, invited parents into classrooms, practiced peer teaching, focused on reading and writing, and drew on community services and resources. The school even hosted a "Parents as Partners in Education" seminar during which Mrs. Sholes-Ross introduced the Carver health clinic, Mr. Larkins spoke about the drug-free school program, and Coach Foley covered AIDS and safe sex interventions. Parents were reminded that the school counselors, nurse, librarian, and social worker were available for support.[143]

The plan addressed the wider racial and political context of the time and the challenges for Carver. For example, teachers sought to develop an atmosphere "free from the threat of physical harm and . . . conducive to teaching and learning." Evidence of success would be measured by "fewer recorded instances of: intruders, class cutting, suspensions involving fighting and weapons."[144] Finally, the plan concluded with a pledge signed by the principal as well as parents, teachers, counselors, custodians, and others.[145] The school community was striving to succeed with the resources available. As shown throughout this book, most of those resources were cultural and human rather than economic.

A few years before Carver issued its unfunded school improvement plan, a *Times-Picayune* headline announced: "Remedial Programs Ended at Orleans High Schools."[146] The article explained: "A federal program providing extra help for students weak in reading and math will be discontinued in New Orleans public high schools so that it can be restored at three elementary schools." The school board had "$2 million less to operate the program for 1987–88," resulting in the layoff or reassignment of 149 teachers and tutors. A principal at Nicholls High School lamented, "At a time when test scores are improving they are taking away some of our methods of remediation." Carver's principal at the time, Dr. Moore, called the district and was reported as "not happy at all" with the programmatic cuts.[147] The zero-sum game once again impacted Carver and other public schools in the city's all-black district.

The punches kept coming. In 1992, a *Times-Picayune* article warned that "students may find classrooms packed" in the fall. One hundred high school teachers, among others, would be terminated to offset a $19 million deficit. Dr. Moore registered dismay again: "As it stands now, every teacher is going to be responsible for thirty extra children a day. We've already got hot [unair-conditioned] classrooms. Now you'll be putting more bodies into those classrooms."[148]

In 2003, Anthony Amato, the newly elected superintendent of New Orleans public schools, toured school facilities and surveyed teachers and students about their needs.[149] He visited Helen S. Edwards Elementary School, part of the Carver complex. When asked about "one thing" that should be changed, an Edwards third grader asked Amato for "a million dollars in school supplies."[150] A Carver Middle School teacher informed Amato, "I've got a list forever long," then showed the superintendent "laptops that are wearing out and supplies that are running thin." Next, Amato toured the gym, sports fields, and auditorium shared by Carver middle and high schoolers. He "grew frustrated at what he found," declaring conditions to be "a disgrace." The *Times-Picayune* article concludes: "In what was once a state-of-the-art auditorium, seats are falling apart; the orchestra pit is littered with trash and leaves, and the stage is stripped of its wood floor. . . . [The] gym, which has had considerable repairs, is still in no shape to host basketball games, and the football field and track have been overrun by weeds."[151] A few months later, another *Times-Picayune* article appeared, reporting that state test scores were getting worse in New Orleans public schools.[152]

LOOKING BACK, LOOKING FORWARD

The first version of the state's testing program, Louisiana Educational Assessment Program (LEAP), was implemented in 1986. Under Governor Mike Foster, LEAP was redesigned as Leap for the 21st Century (LEAP 21). LEAP 21 introduced test scores as a factor in student promotion and graduation. It is worth mentioning that Foster, the son of a wealthy sugar planter, was backed by Ku Klux Klan member David Duke in 1995 and later pleaded guilty to buying a mailing list of Duke's supporters for $150,000. When the revised LEAP tests were introduced in 1999, a source within

Foster's administration revealed that the eighth-grade tests were more difficult than the existing high school exit exam.[153]

A New Orleans–based group, Parents for Educational Justice, formed in 2000. Its legal representative sent letters to the state education superintendent, citing public records law and requesting information about the development of the test and the contractors responsible as well as old and new versions of the LEAP tests. In response, the House Education Committee introduced legislation protecting LEAP from public records law, and a resolution passed exempting LEAP from inspection. While education officials and lawmakers claimed that LEAP would most benefit black students, members of the African American community had grave doubts. "The secrecy . . . and [graduation] penalties associated with the LEAP," writes education historian Erica DeCuir, "fueled Blacks' skepticism of high stakes testing as a school excellence reform model."[154]

The history of black education in New Orleans is a story of black determination in the face of state antipathy to racial equity. Black student achievement was consistently underfunded by the state and white school district leadership. By the late 1990s, New Orleans public schools confronted a financial crisis: per-pupil spending in New Orleans as of 1997 was 26 percent below the national average and 16 percent lower than the average of badly underfunded urban school systems nationally. "Public school students regularly had to bring their own supplies to school, from writing paper to toilet paper. The school system was on the brink of financial collapse and struggled to even meet its payroll."[155]

A facilities assessment of New Orleans public schools three years after Hurricane Katrina struck in 2005 highlighted the seriousness of the issue. With 330 buildings in the system, only 72 had been constructed between 1970 and 2005; 247 were built before 1970 and 55 of those before 1930.[156] The assessment revealed that 77 percent of buildings were categorized as "poor" in condition or in need of *at least* a major renovation. The condition of half the buildings was rated as "very poor," meaning replacement might be more cost-effective than a complete renovation.[157] New Orleans public schools were estimated to be "in the worst physical condition of any public school system in the United States"[158] and require an estimated $2 billion to address.[159]

In a report, Williams, the first black superintendent of New Orleans, reflects on the school system's history:

> Public education has grown despite a history of neglect. The schools have not lost financial support so much as they have never been able to rally the city around its schools. . . . There are no nostalgic days of abundant and generous financial support. . . .
>
> Education has always been viewed as the pathway to success and the good life. For many of our children, that pathway seems closed. . . .
>
> Born into poverty in an environment that is chillingly brutal, the youngsters would face lives of hunger and hopelessness were it not for the schools. . . . Yet, people point fingers at these children in alarm and ask, "Why aren't their test scores higher?"
>
> How much time in a classroom will compensate those children whose families are torn asunder by the problems of poverty . . . ? This is not a rhetorical question. It sums up the difficulties the schools—and particularly the teachers—face as they try to fulfill the responsibilities of their profession. The public schools will never give up on those children, but the city must not give up on its schools.[160]

The inspiration and success that many Carver students experienced is a tribute to the teachers' unwavering commitment and the supportive culture they created. They never gave up on their students, even when those in positions of power did.

CHAPTER 10

"THEY DON'T WANT US"

The Mass Termination of Black Teachers and the Fate of Carver

They don't want us [New Orleans educators].
They want people [from] outside the community.

—CAROL RIGHTEOUS,
Carver Senior High School English teacher[1]

I arrived at the home of Avis and Vermon James and knocked on the door. The day before, I had visited with them and fellow teacher Marilyn Pierre to hear about their experiences as veteran educators at Carver Senior High School. I had returned to go through the stacks of Carver yearbooks on the kitchen table, which had taken me by surprise the previous day. After thumbing through some of the yearbooks, I paused to chat with Ms. James. The house was quiet. "I didn't ask it yesterday," I said, but "could you recollect what it was like just before Hurricane Katrina when everyone was evacuating?" I asked, "What was it like being in the halls of Carver? And what happened when you realized it wasn't gonna be so easy to come back?" I knew it was a difficult question, and a sad one, because of teachers' termination after the storm.

Katrina, a monstrous Category 5 hurricane, struck New Orleans at the end of August 2005. As it strengthened in the Gulf of Mexico, city officials waited and watched. The evacuation order came just one day before landfall. James recalled:

I didn't even know that Hurricane Katrina was headed right for New Orleans. On Friday night I left [Carver] at 6 [and] missed the 6 o'clock news. It was 10 [pm] before I knew that it was even coming [here]. . . . When I left Carver [that evening], I didn't even know. . . . So, there was no [emotional] closure to anything. Then afterwards, we were like, "Oh, we're not going back." So, there was no closure. It took me a year and a half to realize [this].[2]

James was tearful, thirteen years later.

"People need to know the lifework that teachers put into that school," I consoled her. "They really did" work tirelessly, James affirmed. She had served as a math teacher and counselor at Carver for thirty-two years while her husband taught math at the school for twenty-seven years.

James continued with great emotion:

> I don't know if you know this, but there was talk—one of my coworkers was at a meeting in Baton Rouge [after Katrina] and she said she heard someone say, "Too bad New Orleans can't just go off the face of the earth and into the ocean." I'm not talking just the school system; I'm talking about the city. Okay? Because a lot of Louisiana thinks that we're all the bad part of [the state] right here in this area.

She continued, explaining, "When [Louisiana's state-run] Recovery School District came in and started taking over the [New Orleans public] schools [after] Katrina, that was their reason." As James spoke, I acknowledged her tears and offered reassurance that what transpired post-Katrina "could not have been easy." She added: "We were all scattered everywhere. There's some teachers that I know where they are, and there's some teachers I've never heard from again. It was difficult. It was very difficult."

TEACHER TERMINATION, PUBLIC SCHOOL CLOSURES, AND CHARTER SCHOOL EXPANSION IN NEW ORLEANS

Avis James referred to the city's veteran teachers not having the option of returning to post-Katrina schools. Hurricane Katrina radically altered the city's public education landscape. Historic all-black public schools like Carver were either closed or converted to charter schools—public schools privately operated by entrepreneurs under charter, or contract, with the state education board and Recovery School District. Before most African American residents had the chance to return to see if their homes were still standing, critical decisions had been made about the public schools in their neighborhoods. Perhaps most troubling, as mentioned, the city's teachers—most of them black—were informed they would be let go in early 2006.[3]

Many of those educators—including those at Carver—had taught for decades in schools systematically deprived of resources by white policymakers. However, this history was ignored by those who wished to "reform" the city's struggling schools.[4] The mass termination of black educators and principals in post-Katrina New Orleans was a bold move for a city that needed to rebuild its school system. Why did this happen?

James referred to the desire that New Orleans slip into the ocean from those in power, such as Baton Rouge legislators. She pointed out that after Katrina, the city's public schools were taken over by the Recovery School District (RSD), a state entity authorized to assume control of and reform "failing" public schools across Louisiana. Regarding the actions of the state-run RSD in Orleans Parish, James explained that the state regarded New Orleans schools as "bad," which provided a justification for the takeover. Her claims were not without basis.[5] Once again, racism and power would be central.

Hurricane Katrina made landfall in New Orleans on August 29, 2005. Approximately one week later, James Reiss, a real estate investor, chair of the New Orleans Business Council, and a member of the Bring New Orleans Back Commission, declared: "Those who want to see this city rebuilt want to see it done in a completely different way: demographically, politically, and economically."[6] It was a racially coded call for whites to take back what he conceived as *their* city, as New Orleans was majority black when Katrina struck.[7] During a landmark special legislative session in November 2005, lawmakers in Baton Rouge donned "Rebuild It Right" pins as they passed legislation to maximize the number of "failing" public schools in Orleans Parish that could be taken over by the RSD. White flight since the mid-1950s had slowly shifted the racial makeup of the city, which along with its public schools, had become increasingly black.[8] Local government had likewise become increasingly black and Democratic over the two decades preceding Katrina. Outside of New Orleans, Louisiana's white Republican lawmakers hoped to alter this political terrain.[9]

Additionally, as Reiss's commentary demonstrates, local power brokers, particularly white elites, sought to bolster control over the city's assets and future. Katrina provided an opportunity to enhance direct power and institute new reforms quickly and at a scale previously unimagined, particularly as communities—especially black ones—were displaced and destroyed.

Perhaps most crucially, beyond local and state authorities, federal officials in the George W. Bush administration and powerful national stakeholders saw post-Katrina New Orleans as an "opportunity zone."[10] With the city on its knees, the time seemed ripe for unfettered experimentation in public education. New Orleans was poised to become the model for overhauling public schools through mass charter school expansion.[11] But the slate first needed to be wiped clean.

FATE OF THE HISTORIC CARVER SENIOR HIGH SCHOOL: TAKEOVER, PHASEOUT, AND CLOSURE

After Katrina, Carver was among the hundred-plus public schools in New Orleans taken over by the RSD. The Carver school building was damaged by the storm. Avis James left Carver on August 26, 2005, three days before the storm. It would take two years for the high school to reopen. Although the RSD could have temporarily relocated Carver to a viable building, it chose to wait. In August 2007, the historic Carver Senior High School reopened as a public school run by the RSD (hereafter referred to as Carver-RSD), rather than the local board.[12] Its veteran teachers had been terminated. At first, the school was housed in portable units located elsewhere in the city, rather than on the original campus, but about two months later, the portables were moved to the historic site.

From the outset, alumni and community members sought to reclaim and rebuild the historic Carver. This determined effort grew from the school's legacy, the community's sense of ownership, intergenerational connections, and strong affiliations among Carver RAMs. The school-based traditions had helped sustain a place that many considered a lifelong home. In April 2009, the George Washington Carver Charter School Association (CCSA) was incorporated as a nonprofit in Louisiana.[13] In the new education landscape, CCSA securing a charter to operate the school was the only viable way of restoring some community control over the institution. In 2008–09, the RSD received a grant from the pro-charter school Walton Family Foundation to engage in a high school redesign process in New Orleans. Part of this process involved the development of steering committees for specific high schools, including Carver.[14] Steering committee members were invited to form nonprofit 501(c)(3) corporations that could apply for the school's charter.[15] In a letter from RSD superintendent Paul Vallas to CCSA, Vallas supported "CCSA seeking charter status for Carver High School." He also approved "CCSA holding majority interest on the Carver High School Steering Committee," a group encouraged to "build the capacity needed to become an autonomous governing school board, if and when charter status is awarded."[16]

Meanwhile, in a related but separate process, a broader group of students, teachers, alumni, and community members affiliated with Carver initiated a visioning process for reclaiming and rebuilding the school.[17] Many aspects of the culture built by Carver teachers over the previous fifty years were evident in the community's vision:

- Student success, including a curriculum that affords college preparation as well as trade preparation, so that students have an "economic safety net" and do not spend their lives "surviving rather than thriving"
- A "safe, nurturing, just environment" because students "deserve love" and should be surrounded by "caring adults who strive to provide students with everything they need"
- A nursery on campus, like Carver had "before Katrina" to enable "students who are parents to focus on school"
- "Democratic principles" that ensure teacher, parent, and "student voices . . . [are] heard on all important decisions" because "without ownership, there can be no cooperation"
- A school "legacy that deserves to be honored and continued," with "the history of the school and community . . . intentionally woven into the school's curriculum," through the assistance of "alumni mentors" who can "provide this important consciousness"[18]

This planning occurred while Carver-RSD operated in portable units from 2007 to 2012.

When Carver-RSD first opened in 2007, the principal was a black veteran educator. However, the RSD assigned an almost all-white, first-year Teach For America (TFA) teaching staff to the newly reopened school, with only one or two black teachers among them.[19] Carol Righteous, a twenty-six year veteran English teacher from the historic Carver, was hired to serve as a "master teacher" alongside one other black master teacher. Righteous recalled working with novice teachers at Carver-RSD:

> [They had] very poor, limited classroom management. I would go into classrooms. . . . I would sit in the back. I'd observe and take notes. Well, one day I was in a class. The students were just screaming and hollering across the room. . . . [The teacher] was up there just trying to teach. . . . I couldn't take it anymore, so I asked, "Please, can I say something?" Then I settled them down and told them what they're supposed to do and all of that. . . . That's the kind of stuff that I saw all the time.[20]

Despite their inexperience in the classroom, Righteous recalled overhearing conversations around the table among new teachers, with one querying another, "Did you get your stipend yet?" She reflected on the deep irony of the circumstances: "You're coming in here. You can't even handle your class and you're getting a stipend for this and housing. This is not right."[21]

The high attrition of TFA teachers at Carver-RSD opened the way for black veteran teachers to be (re)hired. By 2011–12, the school's teachers were nearly all black experienced educators.[22] Then, on November 1, 2011, during the fifth year of operation as a public school in the RSD, teachers were informed that they would be terminated at the end of the academic year; for many, it was the second time since Katrina. Carver-RSD would be phased out and closed. Nine other public schools in the RSD received the same news that day.[23]

The news about Carver-RSD's closing was met with frustration by CCSA. In late January 2012—a few months after the announcement—the group convened.[24] By this time, several applications to secure a charter for CCSA to operate the school had been rejected. A January meeting agenda outlined various strategies to challenge the phase out and closure and secure a community charter. Strategies included letter-writing campaigns directed at politicians, state officials, and RSD education leaders; mobilizing alumni, ministers, community groups, students, and teachers; and utilizing social media, radio, television, and local and national newspapers. Petitions and protests were also discussed, including an action on February 7.[25] Anticipating the termination of veteran teachers at the end of the year and their replacement during the school's phaseout, the protest would feature signs that read, "Carver Needs Highly Qualified Teachers" and "No Teach For America."[26]

The following month, on March 7, CCSA released a *Student Visioning Committee Report*.[27] Again, anticipating transition to another staff entirely, students called for a principal who "knows" and "respects" students. They also demanded a school leader who "take[s] the time to understand what is going on in students['] lives" as well as "Black History Programs."[28] This vision reflected the culture of historic Carver, where teachers had a dual commitment to academics and the consideration of students' life circumstances as part of a race-conscious curriculum. A related statement by students expressed a desire for both "college and career guidance," "leaders and teachers, who genuinely care about the students and the community," and "a large loyal network of Carver Alumni who have great affection for their school."[29] In a signed letter issued by an alumni vision committee, the links between "past, present, and future" are emphasized, with a demand made for the "restoration of all of the artifacts of . . . Carver Senior High School . . . in a position of prominence in the school." It was essential that "this great institution" be "restored" through "culturally sensitive" teachers, counselors, and nurses; options for trade education, such as nursing, industrial arts, technology, and distributive education; mentorship programs, career days, and apprenticeships; and a continually growing "Alumni Association to keep in touch with the needs of the school." In the spirit of Carver RAMs, the letter concludes: "We envision victory."[30]

CHARTER SCHOOLS PHASE IN

A week later, on March 16, the RSD released a letter to the staff of Carver-RSD, revealing more about the planned phaseout: "Next fall, the Carver campus will house three high school programs that will be part of the Carver community."[31] One would be Carver-RSD as it phased out; the other two would be new charter schools. The very same day that the RSD issued its letter, the Save Carver Committee met. They planned meetings with the RSD and the Louisiana Board of Elementary and Secondary Education (BESE). They discussed strategies to advance the campaign to stop Carver's impending closure—from door-to-door outreach, parent letters, and a Carver Unity Day to a press conference and possible complaint to the Justice Department.[32] Another vision statement from the period makes clear: "We want to receive a charter in the name of CCSA."[33]

As community organizing continued, another turn of events further galvanized the historic Carver community. On April 18, Carver-RSD teachers were summoned to a meeting after school, where RSD officials introduced the young white TFA teacher who would be principal during the school's phaseout.[34] Isaac Pollack was a founding teacher at Sci Academy, a charter school that opened in New Orleans in 2008.[35]

Sci Academy owes its existence to New Schools for New Orleans, which provided a paid fellowship for its founder to develop and open the school, and it was the first school in a new charter school network called Collegiate Academies.[36] The plan was to open two new charter schools on Carver's campus in the 2012–13 academic year, beginning with a ninth-grade cohort and adding a grade each year until there were four grades. Alternatively, Carver-RSD would not admit a new ninth grade and served only grades ten, eleven, and twelve, phasing out the youngest grade at the end of each year. In short, while the two Collegiate Academies charter schools pushed in with each new grade, Carver-RSD would be pushed out (Figure 10.1).[37]

At the meeting, Pollack shared background on his work with Sci Academy and his rationale for assuming control of the phaseout and closure of Carver-RSD. Standing before a room full of black veteran educators, he declared:

> You've poured your heart and soul into these kids. And so it's a hard thing to see someone else [like me] come in here and say, I want to do this [new model of education as we phase out]. And I want to make clear I'm only doing it for two reasons. Reason number one is that I cannot sleep at night thinking about the fact that Collegiate Academies, which will make an amazing ninth grade next year, will not make an amazing tenth through twelfth. And when I think about those students [at Carver-RSD] not having as good of an education as I've been able to provide for my students [at Sci Academy] . . . it makes me scared and nervous and not be able to sleep at night. So, point number one: I just want to do right by those kids [as the school phases out].[38]

In short, Pollack implied that the black veteran educators in the room were not "doing right" by their students—and surely not as well as the "amazing"

SCHOOL	TEACHERS	GOVERNANCE	OPERATION
Historic Carver Senior High School ("Historic Carver")	Veteran black teachers	Orleans Parish School Board	1958–2005
	Teachers terminated and operation of the school is suspended	Hurricane Katrina and RSD Takeover	2005
Carver-RSD	TFA white, then veteran black (after attrition)	Recovery School District	2007–2014
		Pollack as phase-out principal	2012–2014 (closed)
Historic Carver, Post-Katrina	Envisioned: Veteran black teachers	Carver Charter School Association (CCSA), incorporated by alumni and community members	2009
		Submission of charter school applications to operate the school	2009–2013
Sci Academy	TFA white	Charter school under contract with BESE/RSD	2008–
		Became part of newly incorporated Collegiate Academies network under contract with BESE/RSD	2012
Carver Collegiate	TFA white	Collegiate Academies network under contract with BESE/RSD	2012–2016 (merged 2016)
Carver Prep	TFA white	Collegiate Academies network under contract with BESE/RSD	2012–2016 (merged 2016)
Carver High School	TFA white	Collegiate Academies network under contract with BESE/RSD	2016–
		Merger of Collegiate and Prep in new building on historic site at beginning of 2016–17 academic year	

FIGURE 10.1 Chronology of Carver: Founding, Takeover, Closing, and Chartering

Collegiate Academies charter schools. He could not rest knowing that students were receiving a substandard education from their black teachers. One teacher at the meeting with Pollack later reflected: "Immediately, [Pollack's] frame of reference is that we're dysfunctional, and we don't know what we're doing."[39] Existing teachers were then informed they could reapply and potentially be hired as part of the Carver-RSD phase-out staff; Pollack would visit their current classrooms and observe them.

Pollack's remarks did not only lack cultural and historical knowledge regarding black teachers' contributions to New Orleans public schools over the past century; they were insulting, even arrogant. Word quickly spread to alumni of the historic Carver, the one with a fifty-year legacy in the community. When Pollack returned to do his classroom observations, he was unable to enter the school. Alumni holding signs, reading "Hands Off Carver," formed a human chain barricading him from entry. He left and did not return.[40] A "Hands Off Carver" petition supporting CCSA was also circulated during this period, declaring that Carver:

> has been a pillar of education in New Orleans for over fifty years. It has served as a pathway to success for generations of residents from many parts of the city. The school has been instrumental in preserving the cultural heritage of New Orleans' Black community. Thousands of students have been nurtured under its wings. Above all, Carver Rams learned that we are a family.[41]

Regarding Carver's planned closure and the charter schools pushing in, the petition did not waiver: "We need to inform RSD that we are not accepting this as the final decision. We must insist that our school be run by the community. . . . These are our children. This is our school. This is our community. Hands off Carver!"[42]

In the meantime, another CCSA application was submitted to operate Carver as a charter school in the RSD.[43] The proposed board consisted of highly qualified individuals and alumni with a deep commitment to carrying on the culture of achievement that they had experienced at the historic pre-Katrina Carver. Among the board members was a clinical psychologist, certified public accountant, Circuit Court of Appeals judge, licensed attorney, and retired educators.[44] The application was nevertheless denied, even as corporate charter operators were approved to run schools throughout the city, including the schools that Collegiate Academies was permitted to operate on Carver's campus.[45]

THE "NO EXCUSES" MODEL COMES TO CAMPUS

By mid-summer 2012, Pollack had hired an entirely new staff to teach during the phaseout of Carver-RSD. The staff consisted almost completely of white TFA teachers with three years or less of experience; only a handful of black staff members from the 2011–12 school year remained, including a secretary and a security guard.[46] During four weeks of professional development prior to the start of the school year, new and rehired teachers learned about the "amazing" educational model that Pollack had referred to at the April meeting: "No Excuses." The "No Excuses" model revolves around a highly structured, harsh set of disciplinary rules and consequences; it has been implicated in what is known as the school-to-prison pipeline, a component of the "New Jim Crow."[47]

Teachers prepared for the arrival of students with heavily scripted lesson plans, repetitive chants, taped lines on hallway floors to control student movement, a host of classroom management techniques, and SPARK, an acronym for strict rules of comportment for students in the classroom: Sit up, Pay attention, Ask and answer questions, React to show I'm following directions, and Keep tracking the speaker. Further, they were asked to role-play misbehaving students and teachers enforcing discipline techniques.[48] "This is not really what teaching is," explained a teacher at Carver during its phaseout.[49]

This same "No Excuses" model, practiced at Sci Academy, where Pollack first taught, would be in use at the two new charter schools in the Collegiate Academies network: Carver Collegiate Academy and Carver Preparatory Academy. Carver Collegiate and Carver Prep would be the charter schools pushing in as Carver-RSD was phasing out. A teacher queried Pollack about this new educational model, reminding him of Carver's historic past. Pollack, however, appeared to believe that the school's past had nothing to offer current students, who presumably had been failed by black teachers since the school's founding in 1958.[50] Another teacher, reflecting on Pollack's utterances during staff recruitment, characterized his view of Carver's past: "The way he messaged was the school has been failing. This charter organization is taking over the ninth grade. Somebody has to make sure that these [remaining Carver-RSD] kids in tenth, eleventh, and twelfth grade are provided with a good education."[51] Another new recruit recollected Pollack explaining that teaching at Carver-RSD was "going to be a really challenging thing [because] this is a school that is known for violence and failures." The teacher's distinct impression was that "people had been fired because they weren't able to do their job," so the school "needed us to come do it." Further, Pollack proclaimed that Collegiate Academies had "figured out the way to fix failing urban schools," thus he and they were obligated to "bring [the "No Excuses" model] to as many kids as we can."[52]

Many students saw things differently. Rather than embracing the new and improved "No Excuses" education model instituted at Carver-RSD, they organized themselves in protest. Within weeks of Pollack's principalship in fall 2012, students were wearing shirts with "Free Carver" handwritten on them and demanding the taped lines be removed from floors, among other things.[53] The tape disappeared, but the disciplinary approach remained in place and grew even stricter as Pollack "doubled down."[54]

The next fall, in 2013, students from the chartered Carver Collegiate and Carver Prep walked out, along with students at another charter high school, in protest of "No Excuses" discipline policies.[55] In a letter to the Collegiate Academies board and administration, the Carver Collegiate and Carver Prep students wrote:

> We get disciplined for anything and everything. We get detentions and suspensions for not walking on the taped lines in the hallway, for slouching, for not raising our hands in a straight line. . . .
>
> We get suspended for trying to ask why we must do certain things—teachers consider this to be "disrespect." . . .
>
> Students don't have a voice at the [chartered] Carver schools [operated by Collegiate Academies]. . . . We don't have any say in school policies. . . . We also get talked to like we are little kids, or sometimes like animals.[56]

In addition to worries about the zero-tolerance school culture, students voiced concerns about their teachers, writing: "The teachers don't connect with us or where we come from. There are no black teachers. . . . Some of the teachers are racially insensitive. None of the teachers are from New Orleans. They can't relate to us, our neighborhoods, or our community. They have no respect for our customs and culture, and simply want to make us more like them without understanding us and our background."[57] There was a clear link between many of the white teachers' limited and racialized understandings, cultural disrespect toward students and their communities, the lack of place-based knowledge, and the adoption of rigid policies to "control" students that they failed to engage in more meaningful, culturally relevant ways.

Several weeks later, the Southern Poverty Law Center wrote a letter in support of students at the Collegiate Academies charter schools.[58] They pointed out "constitutionally suspect and punitive disciplinary measures" and a "poor school climate."[59]

On the same day the letter was issued—December 18, 2013—students, parents, Carver alumni, and other community members gathered for a press conference and rally at Joe Brown Park, followed by a march to the Collegiate Academies board meeting.[60] Two days later, Collegiate Academies founder and CEO wrote an open letter, asserting that "a small group of activists has been making inaccurate claims." Further, the letter reads, "Our approach to discipline is a key component in the success of our academic program" in which "we use positive reinforcement frequently and effusively."[61] The charter network's suspension rates told a different story: 60 to 70 percent of students at Sci Academy, Carver Collegiate, and Carver Prep were suspended at least once a year, based on state data.[62] By comparison, Louisiana's suspension rate was 9.2 percent.[63]

In early 2014, Collegiate Academies hosted meetings with concerned community members, but no concerns were answered.[64] While *U.S. News & World Report* ranked Sci Academy as the "number two" high school in Louisiana, a community group called the Better Education Support Team, led by Carver alumnus and minster Willie Calhoun, filed a civil rights complaint with the assistance of Loyola University's School of Law attorneys against the Collegiate Academies charter school network for its harsh discipline policies.[65] At a rally and press conference held on Poydras Street outside the Recovery School District office, the group called for state and federal investigations of discipline policies and school culture at Collegiate Academies.[66]

According to the complaint, existing "policies and practices endanger the safety and welfare of students, violate students' rights under state and federal laws, push students out for minor infractions and ultimately deprive students of a right to education guaranteed by the Louisiana constitution."[67] It further alleges that students were:

- Isolated without academic work for minor infractions
- Suspended and sent home without parental notification
- Detained until after dark for detention
- Bullied and harassed due to special needs
- Locked out of bathrooms, with permission to go refused and door handles removed from stalls
- Denied food if they refused to serve lunch detention
- Penalized for out-of-school protests despite First Amendment rights[68]

Meanwhile, the white business community in New Orleans embraced the entrepreneurial spirit of charter school operators, with *New Orleans City Business* magazine naming Collegiate Academies as the city's "number one" place to work.[69]

The investigation of the civil rights complaint was held up by requests, perhaps unsurprisingly, for more documentation from the Louisiana Department of Education (LDOE)—documentation that the attorneys reported they offered to provide, with no further response from the state.[70] At the time, LDOE, RSD, and BESE were all headed by charter school proponents.[71] At the federal level, the US Department of Education closed the complaint, asserting that the state was investigating parts of it, though that was not true. The attorneys were told that they had failed to provide requested documentation to the Office of Civil Rights, a request that attorneys specify they never received.[72] Once again, it is worth noting that the US secretary of education at the time was a staunch advocate of charter schools.[73]

Although public revelation of exceptionally high out-of-school suspension rates appeared to shake Collegiate Academies leadership, it did not, by students' reports, address the underlying problem. The network deemed school discipline "an area of [needed] growth" and boasted in 2014–15 that it had implemented the Collegiate Academies Restorative Initiative (CARe), which "focused on non-traditional discipline methods." According to Collegiate Academies, all three of its charter schools had decreased suspensions to "about 12% network wide compared to 56% in the 2013–2014 school year."[74] Students, however, reported that the Restorative Center (RC) on campus was a dreaded in-school-suspension room that helped the network bring down its out-of-school suspension rate. In the RC, covered windows blocked natural sunlight as students were warehoused, often all day, in complete silence, seated in partitioned cubicles, and given work packets on how to amend countless violations.[75] One student described the RC this way:

> It's just small and got [a] couple holes [cubicles]. Then, you got to complete a paper talkin' about why you here, what you could do better about your mistakes. . . . You don't finish [the packet], you gonna stay there all day. . . . [Students were] in here [RC] for some petty stuff: Wrong color socks. Wrong color shoes. Not follow directions. . . . They just sit [with nothing educational to do]. Just you gotta finish that packet. Ain't got nothin' to do with learnin'. . . . The whole day, cooped up in that one space all day lookin' at four walls.[76]

This was the future that lay ahead for students who could have otherwise been at a school operated by CCSA. CCSA's school, by contrast, would have been guided by historic Carver's time-tested culture of student care and what Principal Milton Becnel called "intelligent self-direction." Instead, alienating forms of punishment, with little educational value, were enforced in Carver's name.

Back at Carver-RSD, Pollack oversaw the phaseout for only two years, 2012–14. The senior class of 2015, the only grade remaining before closure, was scattered across the city at other schools, with Carver-RSD phased out one year earlier than planned. A new school for senior year was more than some students could bear, and some never completed high school.[77] Moreover, at the end of each year, the newly hired teachers for the grade level that was phased out were laid off or moved elsewhere.[78] What had once been a proud Carver legacy for black teachers and students during the previous fifty years was dismissed by reformers with other plans. Collegiate and Prep, the new "Carvers," would enter the vacuum, but in name only. They did not resemble the historic Carver, where black educators with community roots had built an intergenerational pipeline founded on self-determination, achievement, and pro-black racial consciousness.[79]

CARVER IS BACK? THE BETRAYAL OF CARVER'S LEGACY

Ultimately, the chartered "Carvers" would reside in a new building on the historic site. It was highly controversial, given the community's long-standing investment in Carver both before and after Katrina. When the city's post-Katrina School Facilities Master Plan was being developed to decide which schools would be rebuilt, Carver was not included on the list for rebuilding.[80] Carver alumni fought hard for the allocation of funds to construct a new building where the historic Carver once stood—and successfully secured Carver's inclusion in the final plan.[81] The building would not be home to a charter school operated by community members, however. Collegiate Academies would be given the new building for its operation of "Carver." In 2016–17—the year after Carver-RSD closed—Collegiate Academies merged Carver Collegiate with Carver Prep into a single charter school named G. W. Carver High School, which occupied the newly constructed building on the historic site. At historic Carver, veteran teachers had taught in a building that, by the 1980s, was deteriorating from decades of neglect. Meanwhile, Collegiate Academies was given a new $55 million dollar building (Figure 10.2).[82]

No matter the name or location, the Collegiate Academies' "No Excuses" school was not continuous with the Carver tradition, dedicated to educating students well rather than alienating, punishing, and pushing them out. As a student who attended one of the chartered "Carvers" reported:

> I really went to [the charter] Carver because my grandmother went to [the historic]Carver, so I just wanted to relive the tradition 'cause they said how good it was . .
>
> [But in the "No Excuses" charter classroom] . . . they'll tell you one time and if you don't listen the first time, they'll send you in the hall and talk to you. You do it again, you're going straight home. . . .
>
> It took me about a week to get really fed up. . . . I feel like the school was really mostly disciplining rather than really teaching—period. They'll wait to see you do something wrong. I feel like they'll criticize you more than uplift you.[83]

In other words, the historic Carver was not "back." Something very different and destructive had literally taken its place.

When Carver Collegiate and Carver Prep merged, Collegiate had a state-issued school performance score of C; Prep had a D; and Sci had a B.[84] This, combined with extraordinarily high suspension rates and civil rights complaints, made Collegiate Academies charter schools less than "amazing." Yet, the newly hired white teachers and administrators in the charter school network were never criticized as failing. Instead, they were given accolades and contracts by the RSD to operate more charter schools.[85]

FIGURE 10.2 Sign for George Washington Carver High School, operated by Collegiate Academies, announcing that the school is "back," with new building in the background. (Photo by Kristen Buras, 2017)

Considering the rich legacy of the historic Carver—despite the challenges from state neglect—the failure of the well-financed charter school network that replaced it deeply troubled many.

CARVER TEACHERS AND STUDENTS ON THE MASS TERMINATION OF BLACK EDUCATORS AND CLOSING OF THE HISTORIC CARVER

"We tried to open a charter school" to continue Carver's legacy after Katrina, explained Carol Righteous as I sat with her, Clarence Righteous, and Lenora Condoll. She went on:

> I was on the board with some people with master's [degrees] and PhDs, all with more than thirty years of service [in the city's public schools]. We had every kind of resource. We had everything we needed to open a school . . . [They] didn't approve anybody from Orleans. . . . We tried it three times and it never worked. . . . They don't want us. They want people [from] outside the community. That's what they want because that's the ones who get approved [to operate charter schools].[86]

Regarding newly recruited teachers and charter school operators, she explained: "They come with the attitude that they came here to save the children."[87]

Clarence Righteous reflected on the important role of intergenerational connections at the historic Carver, when veteran teachers knew students and their families. "That's what's lacking now with Teach For America," chimed Ms. Righteous. "Three years," she continued, as Condoll echoed, "Then they're gone." Emphasized Ms. Righteous: "They don't have an educational background. They don't know how to manage the classes. They don't know the culture. They don't understand the children."[88]

Regarding intergenerational connections, it should be noted that Carver's early teachers had children who grew up to be teachers in New Orleans public schools; they were terminated post-Katrina. This included Coach Enos Hicks's son, a longtime coach, and three of Lamar Smith's daughters.[89] These dramatic changes in the schools were disturbing to Condoll and her fellow teachers, who also lamented that children were getting put out of the city's zero tolerance charter schools "for anything."[90]

Avis James shared, "I don't really feel much connection to [the Collegiate Academies] Carver because it's not the Carver that I knew." She further explained, "I don't know any teachers there. I don't know any students there. . . . I feel very detached from the whole school system because it's so different."[91] Seeing inexperienced teachers with so little knowledge of how to work with students "hurt" Marilyn Pierre. "It's a travesty to do that to the kids," she asserted.[92] Dr. Lindsey Moore similarly reflected: "Looking over the high rise bridge [near Carver], it's not the same neighborhood, not the same community. . . . This is a different era. That was then. This is now."[93]

Students who graduated from the historic Carver demonstrated similar concerns about the displacement of teachers and the newly chartered system. Herlin Riley, for example, had the following to say:

> Carver was closed as a public school. It was taken over by the charter school system. . . . There are very few black teachers in the schools now. [The new teachers] don't necessarily have the dedication to students that we experienced in my years at school. Ms. Yvonne Busch—and many other teachers—were in the community. Coach Hicks was living around the corner from us. There was so many teachers who lived in the community and in the neighborhood who had a real—they took ownership of each

student. This is *my* child. This is *my* child. . . . The village was responsible for all the children.[94]

"Now," he said by comparison, "everything is individualized. You don't have that kind of communal thing."[95]

Kenneth Royal, whose wife and two sons attended New Orleans public schools, paused to think about the mass termination of veteran teachers and the fate of Carver, his alma mater. "I think that the teachers got a very raw deal in this whole thing," he pondered, "because they literally threw the baby out with the bath water so that they could get what they wanted." Royal contended that, since Katrina, "New Orleans has become corporate America's cash cow." He clarified further: "It was just a money grab. . . . [State officials] didn't plan on Katrina happening, but once it happened, disaster capitalism kicked in. . . . [After Katrina] I'm [displaced] in Texas in a hotel trying to figure out what's gonna happen to the rest of my life, and they're busy doing this [takeover]."[96] Fewer kids are graduating now than "back in the day," said Royal, who believes "the problem with the murder rate in our city has more to do with what they did to the schools than anything." He pointed out that Louisiana incarcerates more people "than anybody does," with the majority from New Orleans. "Why would [charter schools] want to contribute to this problem?" he questioned aloud. Regarding the "new George Washington Carver," Royal did not "even consider that my high school." He elaborated: "These new [charter] high schools with the same name as the ones that were there [before Katrina], they're not the same, especially when I don't even know what your agenda is. I don't feel welcome in this place you call by the same name . . . and it's kind of sad."[97] Royal said he would prefer to bring back "community schools . . . and make sure that the schools had the resources they need." Looking back historically, he concluded, "[Policymakers] never did put the resources in [the public schools] that needed to be in."[98]

CLOSING THOUGHTS ON CARVER AND SCHOOL CLOSINGS

This book is an effort to restore and re-member the knowledge, experiences, and cultural traditions that characterized a historic, all-black high school in New Orleans.[99] This kind of "re-membering," says Joyce King, constitutes a form of heritage knowledge critical to groups whose histories have been ig-nored.[100] Carver's fifty-year history challenges the decontextualized narrative that public schools like Carver were "failing" and highlights the long-standing existence and value of black educational traditions—and the teachers who created and sustained them. The vacuous narrative of "failure," unmoored from a history of white policymakers' neglect of black schools, fostered creation of the nation's first all-charter school district in New Orleans, now touted as a national model. As a part of this, historic schools like Carver have closed while zero-tolerance charter schools multiply.

The termination of veteran teachers and closing of neighborhood schools in urban black and brown communities is more than unjust—it represents a national crisis. In 2014, a civil rights complaint was filed with the US Department of Justice and the US Department of Education by Journey for Justice Alliance, a coalition of grassroots organizations that includes groups in New Orleans, Chicago, and Newark.[101] They invoked history: "As we commemorate the landmark civil rights victory that struck down the 'separate but equal' doctrine and the system that codified racism in our public schools, we respectfully request that you open an investigation of the racially discriminatory school closings that are the subject of these complaints."[102] Despite the fact that charter school operators have "cloaked themselves in the language of the Civil Rights Movement," they went on to describe racial dynamics that are just the opposite: "[T]oo many of the charter and privately managed schools that have multiplied as replacements for our beloved neighborhood schools are test prep mills that promote prison-like environments, and seem to be geared at keeping young people of color controlled, undereducated, and dehumanized."[103]

Tragically, this story repeats itself in cities across the US, from New Orle-ans to Chicago, from Houston to Detroit, from Little Rock, Memphis, and Nashville to New York City, Milwaukee, and beyond.[104] The story of historic Carver—and similar schools around the nation—reveals what we stand to lose when policymakers dismiss teachers with deep community roots and close historic schools at the center of black and brown communities. We cannot be whole without both, and prison-like school environments will not get us there.

In her book on school closings in Chicago, Eve Ewing opens with the words, "Failing schools. Underprivileged schools. Just plain *bad schools.*"[105]

Yet, as Ewing explains, rather than relying on the numeric data as evidence of school failure, community members often possess a "different understanding of what should count in determining the value of a school and a different understanding of what racism is and the huge scale on which it functions."[106] She cites the testimony of former principal Carla Watts, who compares the effects of teacher termination and school closings to the slave auction that served the economic interests of white slaveholders: "So now we put [teachers] out to pasture when they have built all these skills for these children and now they're going to be put out there with other teachers trying to grapple for jobs. I feel like I'm at a slave auction. I'm very full right now. Because I'm, like, begging you [begins to cry] to keep my family together. Don't take them and separate them."[107] As Watts conveys, through tears and experience, teachers from the community and their neighborhood schools are like home.

To put someone out of their home is an act of cruelty. It is even more devastating when they are told that they are being evicted because they were not keeping up the house, especially when the authority evicting them is responsible for the neglect. In the schoolhouse where history matters, there is abundant evidence of community care and an education worthy of its name. In New Orleans, the history of the public schools "shows that when times were at their toughest, teachers stepped up to guide children, comfort them, deal with their personal and family issues, provide desperately needed nutrition during school hours, and offer alternatives to suspension and failure."[108] The historic Carver Senior High School is a powerful example.

ONE, TWO, READY, BEGIN . . . AGAIN

When the Federal Emergency Management Agency (FEMA) came to New Orleans to assess post-Katrina damages to Carver's school campus, the final report noted:

> While the archival record contains extensive information on the planning, design, and opening of the Carver Complex, documentation is scarce regarding the academic, extracurricular, and social history of the school from 1958–2005. Carver alumni, the people who lived this history, are best suited to provide information about the people and events that made George Washington Carver a special place to attend school during its forty-seven

years before Hurricane Katrina. They also can offer a unique perspective regarding some of the more sensitive . . . aspects of Carver's history, including African Americans' fight for civil rights.[109]

Carver alumni and teachers have indeed brought clear light to the school's invaluable culture and contributions. It is imperative to set straight the historical record, especially if we are to develop a full understanding of the problems in urban schools and how to fix them. In the final analysis, we need to confront white supremacy, not scapegoat "bad" teachers and "failing" public schools by closing them.

During her forty years of teaching, Condoll consistently encouraged her students: "Have your voice heard."[110] The 1959 *Carver Times* included "famous quotes" from teachers who taught with Condoll when the school first opened, and for many years to come. Their words ring true to their legacy and no doubt echo in the hearts and minds of students, like they once did in Carver's hallways:

MR. HATFIELD: "And keep that seat until June 3rd!"

MR. SMITH: "Matter is . . ."

COACH HICKS: "Take ten."

MS. BUSCH: "One, two, ready, begin!"[111]

Charters schools are not permanent. They are failing and eventually their operators will move on to other lucrative ventures, leaving behind the children that they betrayed and a public school system in need of rebuilding. Inevitably, a new generation of black teachers will step into the void left by charter schools and one-two-ready-begin *again* the critical work of educating black youth. When they do, the history of Carver Senior High School may serve as a reminder of how to create a culture that supports, challenges, prepares, values, and educates black students. When the time comes—and that should be now—it is imperative that the education debt be remedied and that the teachers, students, and public schools in New Orleans be given the resources they were wrongly denied.[112] It is high time that we stop blaming teachers and the institutions they teach in and start addressing the problem of racism.

It seems apt to conclude with the words of students, teachers, alumni, and community members of the historic Carver. Together, they created a vision statement describing the Carver they wanted to rebuild post-Katrina, which opens:

> Our students are black in a racist country. Our students are New Orleanians. Our students live in poverty. Our students are too young to have lost so many friends and relatives to violence. Our students are being raised by their mothers, aunts, grandmothers, and each other. . . . Our students experienced one of the worst disasters in American history. They have not been provided support for the inevitable trauma caused by the destruction of their city, neighborhoods, and schools. Our students face challenges every day before they even set foot on the campus of George Washington Carver Senior High School. We ignore the realities of their lives at their peril and ours. It is our solemn responsibility to provide nothing less than our students deserve: love, understanding, guidance, education, and preparation. Without us, they are lost. Without them, we are lost.[113]

"A REALITY OF LIFE FOR BLACK PEOPLE IN CITIES ALL OVER"

Public School Closures and the Assault on Civil Rights

S ince the early 2000s, thousands of public schools have closed in urban communities of color nationwide. Sociologist Ebony Duncan-Shippy calculates that "education officials shuttered approximately 24,000 K–12 public schools between 1999 and 2013, displacing on average a quarter of a million students each year."[1] From Atlanta to Detroit, from Little Rock to Washington, DC, Duncan-Shippy and other researchers document the racialized process of urban school closures and the devastating effects. More to the point, communities never benefited; they were harmed, and historic inequities deepened.[2] Terrance Green cites the National Center for Education Statistics, which tallied 1,959 school closings during 2010–11. Between 2000–01 and 2010–11, school closings increased by 62 percent nationally.[3] Ewing and Green reveal that in the past decade, at least six hundred public schools have closed in eight urban school districts: Chicago, Detroit, Philadelphia, Washington, DC, St. Louis, Cleveland, Tucson, and Boston.[4] Additional closures occurred in Austin, Oakland, Salt Lake City, and Indianapolis.[5]

In each of these cities, historic neighborhood schools mattered; they had a past and offered something valuable to the life of the community. Like Carver Senior High School, they were nevertheless closed. The losses were real. Also real was the failure of policymakers, who first neglected these educational institutions, then shifted blame to teachers and schools, all the while ignoring chronic disinvestment in children of color.

This explains why, in 2014, the Journey for Justice Alliance (J4J) issued a report aptly titled *Death by a Thousand Cuts*. J4J fights public school closures and charter school expansion in cities across the country. The report chronicled racially discriminatory public school closings and the harms inflicted on black and brown communities in numerous cities, including Boston, Chicago, Detroit, Jersey City, New Orleans, New York, Newark, Paterson (NJ), Philadelphia, Pittsburgh, St. Paul, and Washington, DC. "America's predominantly Black and Latino communities are experiencing an epidemic of public school closures," declared J4J.[6] On the report's first page, a state-by-state map showed recent closings. Detroit, New York, and Chicago shut down more than one hundred public schools each, while Columbus, Pittsburgh, St. Louis, Houston, Philadelphia, Washington, DC, Kansas City, Milwaukee, and Baltimore each closed more than twenty-five public schools. In just seven years, Camden, San Antonio, Los Angeles, Indianapolis, and Cleveland lost between one-fifth and one-third of their student populations as a result of closures.[7]

One of the leading reasons offered was school "failure," but J4J warned that such explanations are "largely superficial."[8] The "real, underlying cause" for school closures, the alliance explained, is that "right-wing conservatives have long sought to eliminate public goods such as public education, and dismantle organized labor, especially teachers' unions." J4J explained further:

> There emerged a well-organized and extraordinarily well-funded group of individuals and organizations that has exploited any political opening they could find to destabilize neighborhood public schools—almost exclusively within communities of color—and instead promote the expansion of charter schools. . . . In many cases, "reformers" . . . simply capitalized on the disillusionment with public schools caused by the longstanding lack of commitment, by both policymakers and the broader public, to the education of students of color.[9]

Between 2005 and 2013, New York City, as one example, had a 428 percent increase in charter school enrollment.[10]

Firsthand testimony from affected groups revealed that "closing a school is one of the most traumatic things than can happen to a community." Not only does it "strike at the very core of community culture, history, and identity," but it simultaneously has "far-reaching repercussions that negatively affect every aspect of community life."[11] Among the reported harms of school closure and charter expansion are weakened connections between schools and communities (a "gaping hole" in neighborhoods once anchored by local public schools[12]); diminished teacher effectiveness (experienced educators are "being made to leave the field" and replaced by "less experienced, and often brand-new and uncertified teachers"[13]); limited educational access and lower quality schooling (charters selectively enroll and exclude students and "are no better than the [public schools] that were closed"[14]). In New Orleans, for example, 79 percent of charter schools were rated as D or F by the Louisiana Department of Education in 2013.[15]

J4J's findings resonate with the findings of other researchers, who affirm that school closings are "a high-risk/low-gain strategy that fails to hold promise for improving student achievement and non-cognitive well-being." In fact, school closings have "the tendency to cause political conflict and incur hidden costs for both districts and local communities, especially low-income communities of color that are differentially affected." These communities may be better served by state policymakers "investing in persistently low-performing schools" rather than "closing them."[16]

Modeled after Louisiana's Recovery School District (RSD) and its take-over of public schools in New Orleans, other states have taken over entire schools districts in black and brown communities by creating "achievement" or "opportunity districts."[17] In 2010, the Tennessee Achievement School District began taking over schools in Nashville and Memphis. In 2013, the Michigan Education Achievement Authority took over schools in Detroit. In 2015, Georgia legislators enacted Opportunity School District legislation to take over schools in Atlanta, but the required constitutional amendment did not pass.[18] From 2010 to 2015, under the "One Newark" plan instituted by the New Jersey governor and the city mayor, many public schools were closed in Newark, while charter school operators were "handed the keys." There were eight charter schools in Newark in 2000; by 2015, there were twenty-two. Yet, as Roberto Cabañas, a Newark community organizer, explained, "State-control of Newark Public Schools has stripped the community of our voice and our self-determination. [Community members] have been told that we do not know what's best for our own children. This type of colonialism is not 'reform'—it's anti-democratic."[19] According to New York University researcher Domingo Morel, over one hundred school districts have been taken over by their state.[20]

The vigor with which communities of color fight against school closings speaks to the legacy of neighborhood public schools. In New Orleans, the Lower Ninth Ward community successfully fought to rebuild Martin Luther King Elementary School after Hurricane Katrina.[21] King first opened in 1995, after a decade of community work to pressure the school board for a new neighborhood elementary school. After Katrina, King's principal traveled to the state capital in Baton Rouge to communicate plainly: "Hey, we know what's going on. We know what you all are trying to do. But, if there is any indication . . . that you are going to print that King was taken over because it's a failing school, you better watch and see our attorneys because we're going to sue."[22]

The RSD had no intention of rebuilding schools in the Lower Ninth Ward. Teachers and community members had to submit a charter application, seek approval, fight for access to the building to begin repairs, march and sit-in at RSD headquarters to obtain a habitable building to educate students while the damaged school was rebuilt, and more.[23] Through these efforts, the school was successfully chartered and reopened by the community. As one veteran teacher explained: "I guess a lot of people thought if you keep [black residents] down so long, they'll surrender. It don't work like that here. This is all we have. This is home. We're not going nowhere."[24]

In a similar vein, Green documented the successful efforts of a Midwestern community (likely in Detroit) to organize against a school closure.[25] He revealed that Lawrence High School, opened in 1927, was "the hub of the community" and drew from three surrounding neighborhoods, each with century-old centers offering essential social services to residents.[26] In 1973, under a school desegregation mandate, one-way busing was ordered for African American students from the urban district to other township schools. Enrollment declined and, in 1995, the district closed Lawrence High School; moreover, between 1967 and 2007, the district closed approximately one hundred schools. Closing Lawrence and its feeder schools left the area with "zero public schools."[27]

Over the course of five years, community center leaders mobilized with advocates from a local university, forming a coalition that pushed to reopen the school. The coalition gathered data on the impacts of the Lawrence closure and presented it to the superintendent and school board, including "how badly the school was wanted by the neighborhood."[28] Initially, they were unsuccessful. This led the group to examine successful community schools nationally, develop a concrete plan for Lawrence's reopening based on community support, and present a new plan to the board. "This time, instead of just presenting data about *why* the school should be reopened, they explained *how* the community would support [it] as a community school."[29] The board finally agreed to reopen Lawrence in 2000.

A similar effort to contest the proposed closure of the mostly black Dubois High School in a Southwest city was documented in 2010, with more than nine hundred parents and community members participating in a protest.[30] While district and school administrators focused on test scores and economics, community members emphasized the link between school and community, where the school was considered a central institution in uplifting the community. A parent advocate expressed concern that Dubois was slated to be closed on several different district plans, stating, "*And what would that do to our community?* You know, if you kill the school you know you're killing the community."[31] Whereas district administrators referred to the school's problems, and only vaguely in historical context, community members highlighted an ongoing history of racism, including "continual neglect" by policymakers that shaped the school's performance.[32] Community members adopted a broad, contextualized view of the school's history, importance, challenges, and successes; those in power assessed the school narrowly, focusing on immediate problems and quantitative metrics, without considering its role in community survival and uplift, despite its shortcomings.

Struggles over school closures have been documented in Chicago as well, where Renaissance 2010 (Ren2010), a corporate-driven plan, resulted in mass school closings and charter school expansion in black and brown communities across the city. As scholar Pauline Lipman explains, Ren 2010 "began with an educational rationale for closing 'failing schools.'" The proposal to close at least sixty Chicago public schools and open one-hundred new schools, one-third of them charter, one-third contract (which operate like charters), and one-third public performance schools under five-year contracts, mandating adherence to Ren2010 policies.[33] After community protest, Chicago Public Schools (CPS) added a "turnaround" strategy: instead of closing schools, students remained in schools, all the teachers were fired, and outside entities hired new staff, introduced new programs, and managed the schools.[34] Once again, as in New Orleans, Chicago developed and implemented the plan without community participation.[35]

The effects were devastating, according to Lipman, with "increased student mobility and greater neighborhood instability." Additionally, "most displaced students from public housing units were reassigned to schools academically and demographically similar to those they left."[36] More than two thousand black teachers and one hundred principals and administrators lost their jobs.[37] Every year, reports Lipman, parents and children—mostly black and Latinx—and teachers "fill buses, compile elaborate binders documenting their school's actual enrollment and achievement, and pack the Board of Education chambers to argue that their school should not be closed."[38] Marches, pickets, community meetings, press conferences, and other forms of resistance demonstrate community opposition to Ren2010.[39] This raises a critical question: Why do communities defend "failing" neighborhood schools?

Eve Ewing and other activists explore this question in relation to Chicago's Walter Dyett High School, which was closed under Ren2010. In her chapter, "What a School Means," Ewing provides historical perspective on the school, named after Walter Dyett, a widely respected music teacher who began at Wendell Phillips High School in Chicago's Bronzeville neighborhood in 1931. Phillips, relocated in 1936, was renamed Du Sable High School, after Chicago's founder, Jean Baptiste Point du Sable. Walter Dyett taught at Du Sable.[40] His pedagogy melded the joy of music with the teaching of discipline, which he believed would be "carried over into whatever field of endeavor they may choose for a vocation."[41] In 1975, a Chicago middle school was named after Dyett as a tribute to his teaching twenty thousand students and inspiring another half million through band activities, programs, and concerts.[42] Ewing writes:

> The decision to name a school after Dyett—a local titan who dedicated his life to young people . . . someone who in sharing his passion and his care with generations of students did what all teachers set out to do—appears to be a tacit way of celebrating the community itself. It is a way of saying that a life lived in the service of Bronzeville is a notable life, and that the legacy of someone so dedicated to the community is worth memorializing with something important.[43]

In 2000, Dyett Middle School was converted into a high school, with the goal of serving students not admitted into nearby selective enrollment high schools.[44] This move foreshadowed the expansion of school choice in the coming decade. In November 2011, the CEO of Chicago Public Schools sent Dyett families a letter stating: "Nothing is more important to me than making sure your child is getting access to a high quality education. . . . For too long, Dyett High School has been one of the schools not meeting the needs of its students. . . . This is why we are proposing today . . . to phase out Dyett."[45]

"There are just some schools that are so far gone that you cannot save them," the CEO told local news.[46] Ewing thoughtfully ponders in response: "*So far gone.* With these matter-of-fact words, [the superintendent] painted Dyett as a failing school. . . . We see this language . . . frequently in our society. The notion that the school is a failure creates a supposedly urgent space for the public to support policymakers in whatever drastic methods may be needed to address the failure."[47]

Yet, as Ewing shares, a group of community members not satisfied [with] "characterizing Dyett as an unsalvageable failure" organized to reverse the school board's decision. Aside from filing a civil rights complaint, citing the proposed closure as a form of racial discrimination, they established the Coalition to Revitalize Dyett in 2013. The group developed a plan to keep the school open and held rallies and sit-ins—some of which led to arrests—to protest the planned phaseout.[48]

A few months later, school officials reversed their decision and announced they would reopen Dyett as a neighborhood high school.[49] However, after issuing a call for proposals, the board delayed the process for review, ignoring the fact that the coalition's vision and organizing had driven the change in plans. Coalition members addressed the board, calling Dyett a "historic institution" that should remain a public school honoring "our history and Bronzeville and the legacy of Walter Dyett."[50] Ewing points out, "The 'failing' school label itself failed by not encompassing a crucial detail: that [Dyett's] very existence was a testimony to the history of black education in Bronzeville, to a hero and the geniuses under his care, to an institution that successfully educated black children to be great in an era when the expectations for their lives were meager."[51] As the weeks dragged on, it became increasingly evident that the board's decision-making process was opaque and inexplicably slow.

Members of the coalition, with community allies, planned a hunger strike, vowing not to eat until the mayor agreed to support their vision for Dyett.[52] Ultimately, CPS leadership decided it would reopen Dyett as an open-enrollment arts high school, but it would not adopt the coalition's plan.[53] The thirty-four-day hunger strike ended, more than a week later, on September 10, 2015. Ewing again poses an important question: "Why do people fight for schools like Dyett?"[54] She replies: "It was about honoring the everyday moments that make a school a place of care, a home, a site of history. It was about saying *this is not a failed school, and we are not a failed people. We know our history. We will prevail. You will not kill us.*"[55]

J4J leader Jitu Brown was intimately involved as a hunger striker trying to save Dyett. He writes, reflecting on the experience: "There was no acknowledgement of the failure of the system to educate our children. Instead, the blame for so-called failing schools was placed on the children, the teachers, the parents, and community residents. We said, 'No, our schools are not failing; *we've* been failed.' Then we mobilized . . . to oppose the city's plan."[56] Brown served on Dyett's local school council in 2004, when the school library had just seven books. By 2006, the school was faced with an influx of students from another closed school. Yet teachers "transformed an explosive school climate into a great school climate" by using student-led restorative justice and other innovative partnerships; the school doubled its graduation rate and decreased discipline violations by 85 percent.[57] Nevertheless, in 2012, the board voted to close Dyett. In turn, the hunger strike "raised a simple question for thousands of black people in this city: Why can't our community have a say in what kind of school we want for our children?"[58] Brown sums up the naked truth: "The basic quality-of-life institutions that white Americans take for granted, such as schools and health clinics, are intentionally denied in black communities. You build a community by investing in those institutions; you destroy a community by denying those institutions. That is a reality of life for black people in cities all over this country."[59]

The termination of teachers and shuttering of neighborhood public schools constitutes the civil rights crisis of our time. Black teachers and the institutions they built and sustained have always been at the center of the freedom struggle.[60] From King Elementary School to Carver Senior High

School, from Lawrence High School to Dubois, Dyett, and beyond, communities have raised their voices to honor neighborhood schools and their invaluable contributions as bedrock institutions.

The struggle against school closings must continue. We have too much to lose.

ACKNOWLEDGMENTS

For two decades, I have worked with dear friends, fellow activists, and community groups as a part of Urban South Grassroots Research Collective (USGRC). I cofounded USGRC with long-standing educational and cultural groups in New Orleans to ensure my research reflected community concerns and experiences. This bottom-up approach means that I am indebted to countless allies for their insight and guidance.

I want to recognize, in particular, the following USGRC members: Reverend Willie Calhoun for his resolute efforts to sustain communities (and for pointing the way to early Carver graduates); Dave Cash for his genuine commitment to teaching, careful eyes on early drafts, and an ear to the ground always; Phoebe Ferguson for conversations on honoring black history and a vast video archive of struggles to defend New Orleans public schools; Karran Harper Royal for the good fight; Cherice Harrison Nelson for her contributions as a veteran teacher and cultural guardian; the late DJ Markey for his deep laugh and wisdom that continues to inform; the late Amelie Prescott, my sister friend, for teaching and healing in the ways of the ancestors; and Dr. Raynard Sanders for his unwavering commitment, vision, and camaraderie. I am forever grateful.

In addition, I offer my gratitude to Jim Randels and Kalamu Ya Salaam as well as Derek Roguski, Mia Rotondo, and Hannah Sadtler. Barbara Cook and Ernest Charles have also been partners in this work. Ms. Cook, I will never let go of the blue binder full of invaluable information; Mr. Ernest, thank you for taking a ride with me through the Desire area and sharing history. For providing space to gather around this work, I am thankful to Vera Warren Williams and Mama Jenn of Community Book Center. I also appreciate the support of Beverly McKenna and Anitra Brown of the *New Orleans Tribune*.

Al Kennedy has provided many resources through his research and writing, and his ongoing effort to curate an archive on public schools in New Orleans, where I discovered materials on Carver. Thanks for your generosity of spirit. Along these lines, I also appreciate the assistance of Connie Phelps, Louisiana and Special Collections, University of New Orleans, and Lisa Moore, Amistad Research Center, Tulane University. Importantly, the study of Carver Senior High School would not have been possible without the well-networked RAMs or past students and teachers who willingly shared their stories and personal documents with me; a special word of thanks goes to Leonard Smith, a Carver graduate and brilliant documentarian. I am also indebted to teachers Avis and Vermon James for access to their extensive Carver yearbook collection. I extend my appreciation as well to Lamar Smith Jr. and the late Reverend Douglas Haywood for their recollections on Lamar Smith Sr.; to Enos Hicks Jr. and Sarahlilly Hicks for stories about their father, and to Charles Hatfield Jr. for access to a recorded interview with his father.

Many scholars have been encouraging over the years, including historians Derrick Alridge, Jon Hale, and Tondra Loder-Jackson, who published the first piece on Carver teachers as part of an edited book on black educators as historic civil rights activists. The work of historian Walter Stern on schooling and housing in New Orleans was informative. Additionally, I am indebted to Bill Ayers for connecting me with Beacon Press; editor Rachael Marks and editorial assistant Rebecca Johnson have been highly supportive. I likewise appreciate the friendship of colleagues—Michael Apple, Wayne Au, Keffrelyn Brown, Chris Buttimer, Melia Cerrato, Katherine Dunn, Luís Armando Gandin, Dave Gillborn, Sandy Grande, Cheryl Harris, Darryl Kilbert, Joyce King, Zeus Leonardo, Bekisizwe Ndimande, Larry Parker, Tom Pedroni, Bill Quigley, Kenneth Saltman, Beth Sondel, Dave Stovall, David Terrie, Julian Vasquez Heilig, Cirecie West-Olatunji, Terrenda White, and many others—throughout this project and my work in New Orleans more generally. I am always inspired by Eve Ewing's words and scholarship. Thanks to Kevin Welner and colleagues at the National Education Policy Center for publishing my reports. Carol Burris and Diane Ravitch at the Network for Public Education have been allies as well. I also appreciate the truth-telling efforts of teacher, author, and blogger Mercedes Schneider.

Finally, I am ever grateful to my husband, Joe; my son, Ian; my parents, Christine and Michael Buras; and my other parents, Minnie and Joe Aguilar, for their lifetime of support in doing this difficult but meaningful work.

I hope that I have in some small way marked the historical record by documenting the valuable educational and cultural contributions of New Orleans' black veteran teachers. It is my hope that when the community rebuilds its schools—the *community*—this book may serve as a reminder of what is worth preserving. I extend great respect to the Carver community and the beautiful people who taught and learned there. Let us remember.

LIST OF FIGURES

CREDITS

"Principal Moore, Lower 9th Ward, New Orleans" is printed with permission of Amelie Prescott and the Mos Chukma Arts-as-Healing Institute, Azura Prescott, Merlin Ramsey, and Uma Arrhenius-Till.

Material from the documentary film *A Place Called Desire* is used with permission of Leonard Smith III, LS3 Studios. Additional information on the film may be found at www.aplacecalleddesire.com.

A version of chapter 3 appeared in Derrick Alridge, Jon Hale, and Tondra Loder-Jackson's *Schooling the Movement: The Activism of Black Educators from Reconstruction Through the Civil Rights Era* and is reprinted with the permission of University of South Carolina Press.

The signature pages of *Charles Hatfield vs. Board of Supervisors, Louisiana State University, W. B. Hatcher, President, Paul M. Herbert, Dean of the Law School*, October 10, 1946, Charles Hatfield Collection are reprinted with permission of the Amistad Research Center, New Orleans, LA.

The school emblem and photos from the 1962 G. W. Carver Senior High School yearbook are reprinted with permission of the Earl Long Library, Louisiana and Special Collections, Orleans Parish School Board Collection, G. W. Carver Junior-Senior High School, University of New Orleans.

Oral history testimony and associated photos and documents from personal archives are used with the written informed consent of interviewees.

G. W. Carver Senior High School yearbook materials are printed without copyright restriction, as reported by the United States Copyright Office.

NOTES

CHAPTER 1: "THEY DON'T KNOW THE HISTORY"

1. Al Kennedy, "The History of Public Education in New Orleans Still Matters," History Faculty Publications, Paper 5 (Feb. 2016): 1–4, https://scholarworks .uno.edu/hist_facpubs/5/.

2. Trenesse Mosley, interviewed by Kristen Buras, June 10, 2017, New Orleans, Louisiana.

3. Mary Landrieu, "School Turnaround 2.0: How Federal Policy Can Support School Turnaround," video, Center for American Progress, June 30, 2011, https://www.americanprogressaction.org/events/2011/06/30/17119/school -turnaround-2-0-how-federal-policy-can-support-school-turnaround/.

4. Kristen Buras, *Charter Schools, Race, and Urban Space: Where the Market Meets Grassroots Resistance* (New York: Routledge, 2015), 125–59.

5. Steve Ritea, "Nagin's Schools Panel Issues Reforms," *Times-Picayune*, Jan. 18, 2006, www.nola.com. In author's possession.

6. Buras, *Charter Schools, Race, and Urban Space*; Kristen Buras et al., *Pedagogy, Policy, and the Privatized City: Stories of Dispossession and Defiance from New Orleans* (New York: Teachers College Press, 2010); Raynard Sanders, *The Coup d'État of the New Orleans Public Schools: Money, Power, and the Illegal Takeover of a Public School System* (New York: Peter Lang, 2018).

7. Landrieu, "School Turnaround 2.0"; for other illustrations, see Kristen Buras, "The Mass Termination of Black Veteran Teachers in New Orleans: Cultural Politics, the Education Market, and Its Consequences," *Education Forum* 80, no. 2 (2016): 154–70.

8. Sanders, *The Coup d'État*, "Appendix E: Reasons for Judgement, *Eddy Oliver Versus Orleans Parish School Board*."

9. Dana Brinson et al., *New Orleans–Style Education Reform: A Guide for Cities—Lessons Learned 2004–2010* (Chapel Hill, NC: Public Impact and New Schools for New Orleans, 2012), https://publicimpact.com/new-orleans -guide/.

10. Buras, "The Mass Termination of Black Veteran Teachers in New Orleans"; Buras, *Charter Schools, Race, and Urban Space*.

11. Buras et al., *Pedagogy, Policy, and the Privatized City*; Sanders, *The Coup d'État*.
12. Sanders, *The Coup d'État*, "Appendix E."
13. Kennedy, "History of Public Education in New Orleans Still Matters."
14. Wayne Au and Joseph Ferrare, eds., *Mapping Corporate School Reform: Power and Policy Networks in the Neoliberal State* (New York: Routledge, 2015); Raynard Sanders, David Stovall, and Terrenda White, *Twenty-First-Century Jim Crow Schools: The Impact of Charters on Public Education* (Boston: Beacon Press, 2018).
15. Ebony Duncan-Shippy, ed., *Shuttered Schools: Race, Community, and School Closures in American Cities* (Charlotte, NC: Information Age Publishers, 2019); Sonya Douglass Horsford, Janelle Scott, and Gary Anderson, *The Politics of Education Policy in an Era of Inequality: Possibilities for Democratic Schooling* (New York: Routledge, 2019); Eve Ewing, *Ghosts in the Schoolyard: Racism and School Closings on Chicago's South Side* (Chicago: University of Chicago Press, 2018); Domingo Morel, *Takeover: Race, Education, and American Democracy* (New York: Oxford University Press, 2018); Keith Benson, *Education Reform and Gentrification in the Age of #CamdenRising* (New York: Peter Lang, 2018); Kevin Henry and Adrienne Dixson, "'Locking the Door Before We Got the Keys': Racial Realities of the Charter School Authorization Process in Post-Katrina New Orleans," *Educational Policy*, 30, no. 1 (2016): 218–40; Alliance to Reclaim Our Schools, *Out of Control: The Systemic Disenfranchisement of African American and Latino Communities Through School Takeovers*, Aug. 2015, http://www.reclaimourschools.org/sites/default/files/out-of-control-takeover-report.pdf; Journey for Justice Alliance, *Death by a Thousand Cuts: Racism, School Closures, and Public School Sabotage*, Voices from America's Affected Communities of Color, May 2014, https://dignityinschools.org/resources/death-by-a-thousand-cuts-racism-school-closures-and-public-school-sabotage/; Kenneth Saltman, *The Failure of Corporate School Reform* (Boulder, CO: Paradigm Publishers, 2012); Pauline Lipman, *The New Political Economy of Urban Education: Neoliberalism, Race, and the Right to the City* (New York: Routledge, 2011); Michael Apple, *Educating the "Right" Way: Markets, Standards, God, and Inequality* (New York: Routledge, 2006).
16. Eve Ewing and Terrance Green, "Beyond the Headlines: Trends and Future Directions in the School Closure Literature," *Educational Researcher* 51, no. 1 (Jan./Feb. 2022): 1.
17. Ewing and Green, "Beyond the Headlines," 5.
18. Derrick Alridge, Jon Hale, and Tondra Loder-Jackson, eds., *Schooling the Movement: The Activism of Southern Black Educators from Reconstruction Through the Civil Rights Era* (Columbia: University of South Carolina Press, 2023); see Kristen Buras, "'They Were Very Low Key, but They Spoke from Wisdom and Experience': How Black Teachers Taught Self-Determination at Carver Senior High School in New Orleans," in Alridge, Hale, and Loder-Jackson, *Schooling the Movement*, 126–47.

19. Ewing and Green, "Beyond the Headlines"; Duncan-Shippy, *Shuttered Schools*; Journey for Justice, *Death by a Thousand Cuts*.

20. Buras et al., *Pedagogy, Policy, and the Privatized City*; Daniel Solórzano and Tara Yosso, "Critical Race Methodology: Counter-Storytelling as an Analytical Framework for Educational Research," in *Foundations of Critical Race Theory in Education*, 2nd ed., eds. Edward Taylor, David Gillborn, and Gloria Ladson-Billings (New York: Routledge, 2016), 127–42.

21. Ewing, *Ghosts in the Schoolyard*; see also Mark Warren with David Goodman, *Lift Us Up, Don't Push Us Out: Voices from the Frontlines of the Educational Justice Movement* (Boston: Beacon Press, 2018).

22. E. Meese, S. Butler, and K. Holmes, *From Tragedy to Triumph: Principled Solutions for Rebuilding Lives and Communities* (Washington, DC: Heritage Foundation, 2005), 1.

23. George W. Bush speech, Sept. 15, 2005, www.cbsnews.com. In author's possession.

24. S. M. Butler, J. J. Carafano, A. A. Fraser, D. Lips, R. M. Moffit, and R. D. Utt, *How to Turn the President's Gulf Coast Pledge into Reality* (Washington, DC: Heritage Foundation, Sept. 16, 2005), www.heritage.org/research/reports /2005/09/how-to-turn-the-presidents-gulf-coast-pledge-into-reality.

25. Margaret Spellings, letter from the US secretary of education to states affected by Hurricane Katrina, Sept. 14, 2005, in author's possession.

26. Meese, Butler, and Holmes, *From Tragedy to Triumph*; Paul Hill et al., *Portfolio School Districts for Big Cities: An Interim Report* (Seattle: Center on Reinventing Public Education, Oct. 2009); Paul Hill and Jane Hannaway, "The Future of Public Education in New Orleans," in M. A. Turner and S. R. Zedlewski, eds., *After Katrina: Rebuilding Opportunity and Equity into the New New Orleans* (Washington, DC: Urban Institute, 2006), 27–35; Mind Trust, *Creating Opportunity Schools: A Bold Plan to Transform Indianapolis Public Schools* (Indianapolis: Mind Trust, 2011), www.themindtrust.org/files/file/opp-schools -full-report.pdf; Nelson Smith, *The Louisiana Recovery School District: Lessons for the Buckeye State* (Washington, DC: Thomas B. Fordham Institute, Jan. 2012), www.edexcellence.net/publications/the-louisiana-recovery-school -district.html; David Osborne, *Born on the Bayou: A New Model for American Education* (Washington, DC: Third Way, 2012).

27. United Teachers of New Orleans, Louisiana Federation of Teachers, and American Federation of Teachers, *National Model or Flawed Approach? The Post-Katrina New Orleans Public Schools* (New Orleans: Author, Nov. 2006).

28. Sanders, *The Coup d'État*, "Appendix B: Act 35."

29. Louisiana Federation of Teachers and American Federation of Teachers, *The Chronology: Scenario of a Nightmare* (Baton Rouge, LA: Author, Jan. 2007); Louisiana Federation of Teachers, letter to Kathleen Blanco regarding Executive Orders 58 and 79, Nov. 2, 2005.

30. Julian Vasquez Heilig and Su Jin Jez, *Teach for America: A Review of the Evidence* (Boulder, CO: Education and the Public Interest Center and Education Policy Research Unit, 2010), https://nepc.colorado.edu/publication/teach-for-america; T. Jameson Brewer and Kathleen deMarrais, eds., *Teach for America Counter-Narratives: Alumni Speak Up and Speak Out* (New York: Peter Lang, 2015).

31. Bring New Orleans Back Commission (BNOBC), *Rebuilding and Transforming: A Plan for World-Class Public Education in New Orleans* (New Orleans: BNOBC, Jan. 17, 2006).

32. New Schools for New Orleans (NSNO), *Lead, Serve, and Start*, 2008, http://newschoolsforneworleans.org/.

33. Sarah Usdin, "Meet Sarah," 2012, www.sarahusdin.com/meetsarah/.

34. Lesli Maxwell, "Foundations Donate Millions to Help New Orleans' Recovery," *Education Week*, Dec. 13, 2007, https://www.edweek.org/policy-politics/foundations-donate-millions-to-help-new-orleans-schools-recovery/2007/12.

35. Michael Tisserand, "The Charter School Flood," *The Nation*, Aug. 23, 2007.

36. Tisserand, "The Charter School Flood."

37. Z. Conway, "Education 'Revolution' in New Orleans," BBC, Apr. 8, 2010, http://news.bbc.co.uk/2/hi/americas/8608960.stm.

38. Will Sentell, "Charter Schools Praised: BESE Member Chas Roemer Calls Them Wave of Future," *The Advocate*, Sept. 12, 2009, http://theadvocate.com.

39. In 1975, Orleans Parish School Board member Harwood Koppel wanted to "link salary increases for teachers to performance evaluations," according to Donald DeVore and Joseph Logsdon; see *Crescent City Schools: Public Education in New Orleans, 1841–1991* (Lafayette: Center for Louisiana Studies, University of Southwestern Louisiana, 1991), 281. This approach is the predecessor to more recent policies centered on merit pay for teachers. In general, policies such as these adopt an atomized view of the teacher that is disconnected from the larger social, economic, and historical context of the school and the ways in which this context affects teaching and learning in schools systematically neglected by the state. Most often, these schools are where there are teachers of color and their students.

40. Buras, "The Mass Termination of Black Veteran Teachers in New Orleans."

41. Sarah Carr, "Many Orleans Schools Have Lack of Veteran Teachers," *Times-Picayune*, Feb. 14, 2009, www.nola.com; Howard Nelson, *Teacher Quality and Distribution in Post-Katrina New Orleans* (Washington, DC: AFT, 2010), 19–20.

42. Nelson, *Teacher Quality and Distribution in Post-Katrina New Orleans*, 11.

43. J. Zubrzycki, "TFA Alumni Aid New Teachers in New Orleans," *Education Week*, Apr. 19, 2013, http://www.edweek.org/ew/articles/2013/04/19/29neworleans_ep.h32.htm.

44. For *Oliver* ruling by New Orleans Civil District Court judge Ethel Julian, see Sanders, *The Coup d'État*, "Appendix E: Reasons for Judgement, *Eddy Oliver Versus Orleans Parish School Board.*"

45. Sanders, *Coup d'État*, 8.

46. Sanders, *Coup d'État*, 20.

47. Sanders, *Coup d'État*, 22.

48. Sanders, *Coup d'État*, 23.

49. Sanders, *Coup d'État*, 23; Phoebe Ferguson, "A Perfect Storm: The Takeover of New Orleans Public Schools," https://www.aperfectstormthemovie.com/.

50. Danielle Dreilinger, "Recovery School District Will Be Country's First All-Charter District in Sept. 2014," *Times-Picayune*, Dec. 20, 2013, www.nola.com.

51. Lovell Beaulieu, "Life Is Crime, Poverty, Fear for Housing Project Dwellers," *Times-Picayune*, Jan. 7, 1980.

52. Beaulieu, "Life Is Crime, Poverty, Fear for Housing Project Dwellers."

53. Molly Moore, "School Secretaries, Clerks Given OK to Hold Union Vote," *Times-Picayune*, Mar. 10, 1981.

54. Kelly O'Guinn, interviewed by Kristen Buras, Apr. 3, 2018, by telephone; of the nineteen interviews with Carver alumni, only four—for those living outside of Louisiana—were conducted by phone; the rest were conducted in person in New Orleans.

55. O'Guinn, interview.

56. Dwan Julien, interviewed by Kristen Buras, June 4, 2018, by telephone.

57. Hasan Sparks, interviewed by Kristen Buras, June 3, 2018, by telephone.

58. Lolis Eric Elie, "Focusing on a Different Firestorm," *Times-Picayune*, Jan. 11, 2002.

59. Elie, "Focusing on a Different Firestorm."

60. Kristen Buras, "Education Research and Critical Race Praxis: Fieldnotes on 'Making It Matter' in New Orleans," *International Journal of Qualitative Studies in Education* 36, no. 1 (2023): 42–56.

61. Emblem of Carver Ram, 1962 Carver yearbook, University of New Orleans, Earl K. Long Library, Louisiana and Special Collections, Orleans Parish School Board Collection–147, G. W. Carver Junior-Senior High School, Box 5.

62. Alliance to Reclaim Our Schools, *Out of Control*; Ewing, *Ghosts in the Schoolyard*.

63. Kennedy, "History of Public Education in New Orleans Still Matters."

64. Joyce King, Ellen Swartz, et al., *"Re-membering" History in Student and Teacher Learning: An Afrocentric Culturally Informed Praxis* (New York: Routledge, 2014).

65. King, Swartz, et al., *"Re-membering" History in Student and Teacher Learning*, xiv.

66. King, Swartz, et al., *"Re-membering" History in Student and Teacher Learning*, xiii.

67. Frederick Douglass, *Narrative of the Life of Frederick Douglass, an American Slave* (1845) (New York: Penguin Books, 1968); DeVore and Logsdon,

Crescent City Schools; John Blassingame, *Black New Orleans, 1860–1880* (Chicago: University of Chicago Press, 1973); Rodolphe Lucien Desdunes, trans. and ed., Sister Dorothea Olga McCants, *Our People and Our History: Fifty Creole Portraits* (1911) (Baton Rouge: Louisiana State University Press, 1973).

68. Keith Medley, *We as Freemen:* Plessy v. Ferguson, *the Fight Against Legal Segregation* (Gretna, LA: Pelican Publishing, 2003).

69. DeVore and James, *Crescent City Schools*; James Anderson, *The Education of Blacks in the South, 1860–1935* (Chapel Hill: University of North Carolina Press, 1988).

70. Vanessa Siddle Walker, *Their Highest Potential: An African American School Community in the Segregated South* (Chapel Hill: University of North Carolina Press, 1996).

71. Walker, *Their Highest Potential*, 5–6.

72. Walker, *Their Highest Potential*, 15.

73. Walker, *Their Highest Potential*, 16.

74. Walker, *Their Highest Potential*, 20.

75. Walker, *Their Highest Potential*, 26.

76. Walker, *Their Highest Potential*, 27.

77. Walker, *Their Highest Potential*, 31–32.

78. Walker, *Their Highest Potential*, 35.

79. Walker, *Their Highest Potential*, 44.

80. Walker, *Their Highest Potential*, 50.

81. Walker, *Their Highest Potential*, 54.

82. Walker, *Their Highest Potential*, 63.

83. Walker, *Their Highest Potential*, 96.

84. Walker, *Their Highest Potential*, 98

85. Walker, *Their Highest Potential*, 98.

86. Walker, *Their Highest Potential*, 100–102.

87. Walker, *Their Highest Potential*, 104.

88. Walker, *Their Highest Potential*, 110.

89. Walker, *Their Highest Potential*, 123.

90. Walker, *Their Highest Potential*, 123.

91. Walker, *Their Highest Potential*, 127.

92. Walker, *Their Highest Potential*, 128.

93. Walker, *Their Highest Potential*, 130.

94. Walker, *Their Highest Potential*, 197.

95. Walker, *Their Highest Potential*, 200.

96. Vanessa Siddle Walker, "Valued Segregated Schools for African American Children in the South, 1935–1969: A Review of Common Themes and Characteristics," *Review of Educational Research* 70, no. 3 (2000): 253–85; for the testimony of teachers who taught pre- and post-*Brown*, see Michele Foster, *Black Teachers on Teaching* (New York: New Press, 1998).

97. Walker, "Valued Segregated Schools for African American Children in the South."
98. Alridge, Hale, and Loder-Jackson, *Schooling the Movement*, 2.
99. Jarvis Givens, "Teaching to 'Undo Their Narratively Condemned Status': Black Educators and the Problem of Curricular Violence," in Alridge, Hale, and Loder-Jackson, *Schooling the Movement*, 26.
100. Givens, "Teaching to 'Undo Their Narratively Condemned Status,'" 26–27.
101. Sonya Douglass Horsford, *Learning in a Burning House: Educational Inequality, Ideology, and (Dis)Integration* (New York: Teachers College Press, 2011).
102. Horsford, *Learning in a Burning House*, 43–44.
103. Horsford, *Learning in a Burning House*, 44.
104. Horsford, *Learning in a Burning House*, 44.
105. Walker, "Valued Segregated Schools for African American Children in the South," 276.
106. Walker, "Valued Segregated Schools for African American Children in the South," 253.
107. Monica White, "Paradise Lost? Teachers' Perspectives on the Use of Cultural Capital in the Segregated Schools of New Orleans, Louisiana," *Journal of African American History* 87 (2002): 269–81.
108. White, "Paradise Lost?" 270.
109. White, "Paradise Lost?" 275–76.
110. White, "Paradise Lost?" 276.
111. Al Kennedy, *Chord Changes on the Chalkboard: How Public School Teachers Shaped Jazz and the Music of New Orleans* (Lanham, MD: Scarecrow Press, 2005).
112. Kennedy, *Chord Changes on the Chalkboard*, 11.
113. Kennedy, *Chord Changes on the Chalkboard*, 9.
114. Kennedy, *Chord Changes on the Chalkboard*, 15.
115. Kennedy, *Chord Changes on the Chalkboard*, 15.
116. Kennedy, *Chord Changes on the Chalkboard*, 17.
117. Kennedy, *Chord Changes on the Chalkboard*, 18.
118. Raphael Cassimere Jr., "'Our School Is Our Glory': Reflections on the Early Years of Joseph. F. Clark High School, 1949–1970," *Journal of African American History* 103, no. 4 (2018): 560–80.
119. Cassimere, "'Our School Is Our Glory,'" 564.
120. Cassimere, "'Our School Is Our Glory,'" 566.
121. Cassimere, "'Our School Is Our Glory,'" 567.
122. Cassimere, "'Our School Is Our Glory,'" 570.
123. Cassimere, "'Our School Is Our Glory,'" 571.
124. Cassimere, "'Our School Is Our Glory,'" 573–75; Principal Herbert J. McCullum's letter to the Class of 1978, 1978 Carver yearbook, Personal Collection of Avis and Vermon James, New Orleans, LA.

125. Cassimere, "'Our School Is Our Glory,'" 577.
126. Cassimere, "'Our School Is Our Glory,'" 577.
127. Kennedy, "History of Public Education in New Orleans Still Matters," 19.
128. Kennedy, "History of Public Education in New Orleans Still Matters," 19–20.
129. Kennedy, "History of Public Education in New Orleans Still Matters," 20.
130. King, Swartz, et al., *"Re-membering" History History in Student and Teacher Learning*.
131. Buras, "Education Research and Critical Race Praxis."
132. Buras, *Charter Schools, Race, and Urban Space*.
133. Solórzano and Yosso, "Critical Race Methodology."
134. Charles Lawrence, "The Word and the River: Pedagogy as Scholarship as Struggle," in *Critical Race Theory: Key Writings That Formed the Movement*, ed. Kimberlé Crenshaw et al. (New York: New Press, 1995), 336–51.
135. Matthew Miles, Michael Huberman, and Johnny Saldaña, *Qualitative Data Analysis: A Methods Sourcebook*, 3rd ed. (Thousand Oaks, CA: SAGE, 2014).
136. Ian Hodder, "The Interpretation of Documents and Material Culture," in *Handbook of Qualitative Research*, ed. Norman Denzin and Yvonna Lincoln (Thousand Oaks, CA: SAGE, 1994), 393–402.
137. Althea Merricks Haywood attended Carver Senior High School her senior year, the school's first year. From 1958–59 to 1967–68, Carver Senior High School included only grades ten, eleven, and twelve; grade nine was at Carver Junior High and thereafter at Carver Senior. Those who graduated before 1968–69, therefore, attended Carver Senior for three years.
138. This book is intended to chronicle the culture of a post-*Brown* historic black high school in New Orleans over a fifty-year period (that closed due to charter school expansion). An in-depth comparison of the historic culture with the climate of current charter schools in New Orleans is not possible here. For such a comparison, see Kristen Buras, "A Legacy That Can't Be Chartered: Carver Senior High School and the Threat of School Closures" (forthcoming).
139. King, Swartz, et al., *"Re-membering" History in Student and Teacher Learning*; Joyce King, ed., *Black Education: A Transformative Research and Action Agenda for the New Century* (New York: Routledge, 2005).

CHAPTER 2: "BACK IN A CORNER SOMEPLACE"
1. Lenora Condoll Gray, Carol Righteous, and Clarence Righteous, interviewed by Kristen Buras, June 11, 2017, New Orleans.
2. Donald DeVore and Joseph Logsdon, *Crescent City Schools: Public Education in New Orleans, 1841–1991* (Lafayette: Center for Louisiana Studies, University of Southwestern Louisiana, 1991).
3. Walter Stern, *Race and Education in New Orleans: Creating the Segregated City, 1764–1960* (Baton Rouge: Louisiana State University Press, 2018).

4. Gwendolyn Mildo Hall, "The Formation of Afro-Creole Culture," in *Creole New Orleans: Race and Americanization*, ed. Arnold R. Hirsch and Joseph Logsdon (Baton Rouge: Louisiana State University Press, 1992), 58–87.

5. Orissa Arend, *Showdown in Desire: The Black Panthers Take a Stand in New Orleans* (Fayetteville: University of Arkansas Press, 2009).

6. James Anderson, *The Education of Blacks in the South, 1860–1935* (Chapel Hill: University of North Carolina Press, 1988); John Blassingame, *Black New Orleans, 1860–1880* (Chicago: University of Chicago Press, 1973); Kristen Buras, "Benign Neglect? Drowning Yellow Buses, Racism, and Disinvestment in the City That Bush Forgot," in *Schooling and the Politics of Disaster*, ed. Kenneth Saltman (New York: Routledge, 2007), 103–22; Kristen Buras, *Charter Schools, Race, and Urban Space: Where the Market Meets Grassroots Resistance* (New York: Routledge, 2015); DeVore and Logsdon, *Crescent City Schools*; W. E. B. Du Bois, *Black Reconstruction in America, 1860–1880* (New York: The Free Press, 1992/1935); Keith Medley, *We as Freemen:* Plessy v. Ferguson, *the Fight Against Legal Segregation* (Gretna, LA: Pelican Publishing, 2003); Vanessa Siddle Walker, *Their Highest Potential: An African American School Community in the Segregated South* (Chapel Hill: University of North Carolina Press, 1996); Derrick Alridge, Jon Hale, and Tondra Loder-Jackson, eds., *Schooling the Movement: The Activism of Southern Black Educators from Reconstruction through the Civil Rights Era* (Columbia: University of South Carolina Press, 2023).

7. DeVore and Logsdon, *Crescent City Schools*, 23.

8. Blassingame, *Black New Orleans*, 117.

9. Eric Foner, *A Short History of Reconstruction, 1863–1877* (New York: Harper and Row, 1990); Medley, *We as Freemen*.

10. DeVore and Logsdon, *Crescent City Schools*, 179.

11. Ken Chujo, "The Negro Division: Public Education Policy for Black Louisiana, 1916–1941," in *The Louisiana Purchase Bicentennial Series in Louisiana History: Education in Louisiana, Volume XVIII*, ed. Michael Wade (Lafayette: Center for Louisiana Studies, University of Southwestern Louisiana, 1999), 300–325.

12. Blassingame, *Black New Orleans*, 130.

13. Chujo, "The Negro Division," 320.

14. DeVore and Logsdon, *Crescent City Schools*, 179–215.

15. Alonzo Grace and the Citizens' Planning Committee for Public Education in New Orleans, *Tomorrow's Citizens: A Study and Program for the Improvement of the New Orleans Public Schools* (New Orleans: Orleans Parish School Board, 1940).

16. Grace et al., *Tomorrow's Citizens*, 114.

17. Grace et al., *Tomorrow's Citizens*, 114–15.

18. Grace et al., *Tomorrow's Citizens*, 120–21.

19. Grace et al., *Tomorrow's Citizens*, 35.

20. Grace et al., *Tomorrow's Citizens*, 35.

21. Grace et al., *Tomorrow's Citizens*, 142.

22. Louisiana State Advisory Committee, *The New Orleans Crisis: Report of the Louisiana State Advisory Committee to the United States Commission on Civil Rights* (Baton Rouge: Author, 1961).

23. See generally Liva Baker, *The Second Battle of New Orleans: The Hundred-Year Struggle to Integrate the Schools* (New York: HarperCollins, 1996).

24. Elizabeth Heavrin, *Recordation of Certain Buildings at the George Washington Carver School Campus, New Orleans, Louisiana* (Washington, DC: FEMA, June 28, 2010), 7; University of New Orleans, Earl K. Long Library, Louisiana and Special Collections, FEMA G. W. Carver School Collection, Box 1, Folder 1.

25. Stern, *Race and Education in New Orleans*.

26. Stern, *Race and Education in New Orleans*, 199.

27. In the late 1940s and early 1950s, the NAACP pursued equalization lawsuits, a strategy to equalize funding and facilities for black and white students. Hoping to avoid desegregation, white officials attempted to remediate past neglect of black schools by increasing levels of investment. On this account, see Raphael Cassimere Jr., "'Our School Is Our Glory': Reflections on the Early Years of Joseph Clark High School, 1949–1970," *Journal of African American History* 103, no. 4 (Fall 2018): 572; Vanessa Siddle Walker, "Valued Segregated Schools for African American Children in the South, 1935–1969: A Review of Common Themes and Characteristics," *Review of Educational Research* 70, no. 3 (2000): 274.

28. Stern, *Race and Education in New Orleans*, 212–13.

29. Stern, *Race and Education in New Orleans*, 213–14.

30. Stern, *Race and Education in New Orleans*, 221.

31. Stern, *Race and Education in New Orleans*, 223.

32. Stern, *Race and Education in New Orleans*, 223.

33. Stern, *Race and Education in New Orleans*, 225.

34. Stern, *Race and Education in New Orleans*, 224.

35. Stern, *Race and Education in New Orleans*, 226–27.

36. Stern, *Race and Education in New Orleans*, 227.

37. Stern, *Race and Education in New Orleans*, 228.

38. Nathaniel Curtis and Arthur Davis, *George Washington Carver Junior-Senior High School Plan Book* (New Orleans: Curtis and Davis Architects-Engineers, circa 1955); UNO, OPSB–147, Carver, Box 5.

39. Curtis and Davis, *George Washington Carver Junior-Senior High School Plan Book*.

40. Curtis and Davis, *George Washington Carver Junior-Senior High School Plan Book*.

41. Heavrin, *Recordation of Certain Buildings at the George Washington Carver School Campus*; for more on George Washington Carver's biography, see Christina Vella, *George Washington Carver: A Life* (Baton Rouge: Louisiana State University Press, 2015).

42. Aerial photo, 1962 Carver yearbook, UNO, OPSB–147, Carver, Box 5.

43. Curtis and Davis, *George Washington Carver Junior-Senior High School Plan Book*.

44. Curtis and Davis, *George Washington Carver Junior-Senior High School Plan Book*.

45. Curtis and Davis Architects-Engineers, Carver Schematic (circa 1950s), UNO, OPSB–147, Samuel Scarnato Papers, Carver, Box 14.

46. Arthur Davis in Heavrin, *Recordation of Certain Buildings at the George Washington Carver School Campus*, 3.

47. Rosa Mae Millsap, "Impressive Dedication Program Held," *Carver Times* 1, no. 2 (May 1959): 1. UNO, OPSB–147, Carver, Box 1, Folder 2.

48. Millsap, "Impressive Dedication Program Held," 1.

49. Dedication Program, Dec. 7, 1958, UNO, OPSB–147, Scarnato Papers, Carver, Box 14.

50. Dedication Program.

51. Millsap, "Impressive Dedication Program Held," 2.

52. Alice Wilkerson, "Carverites Are on the March," *Carver Times* 1, no. 2 (May 1959): 3. UNO, OPSB–147, Carver, Box 1, Folder 2.

53. Wilkerson, "Carverites Are on the March."

54. Wilkerson, "Carverites Are on the March."

55. Mr. Provost and Rodney A. Davis, "Woodworking Class," *Carver Times* 1, no. 2 (May 1959): 4. UNO, OPSB–147, Carver, Box 1, Folder 2.

56. Carver Times Staff, *Carver Times* 1, no. 2 (May 1959): 2. UNO, OPSB–147, Carver, Box 1, Folder 2; Althalia Chauvin, "Itemettes," *Carver Times* 1, no. 2 (May 1959): 2.

57. Chauvin, "Itemettes," 2.

58. Althea Merricks Haywood, interviewed by Kristen Buras, Apr. 11, 2017, New Orleans.

59. Theron Lewis, interviewed by Kristen Buras, Apr. 10, 2017, New Orleans.

60. Lewis interview.

61. Rhea Joseph, interviewed by Kristen Buras, Apr. 10, 2017, New Orleans.

62. Ernest Charles, interviewed by Kristen Buras, Apr. 11, 2017, New Orleans.

63. Reverend Willie Calhoun, interviewed by Kristen Buras, Apr. 12, 2017, New Orleans.

64. Calhoun interview.

65. Leonard Smith, interviewed by Kristen Buras, Apr. 12, 2017, New Orleans; Curtis and Davis built Louisiana State Penitentiary at Angola in 1956, two years prior to Carver's opening. Angola is regarded as an all-black prison-plantation and is part of a prison complex in Louisiana ranked first in the world for its incarceration rate. Pondering the racial politics behind Carver's establishment by white school officials, school alumni have noted that Carver's cafeteria resembles Angola's dining hall. On the resemblance noted by alumni, see Heavrin, *Recordation of Certain Buildings at the George Washington Carver School Campus*, 1–2.

66. On Curtis and Davis's reputation for building prisons, see Karen Kingsley, "Curtis and Davis Architects," *64 Parishes* (Mar. 11, 2011), https://64parishes.org/entry/curtis-and-davis-architects.

67. Leonard Smith, interviewed by Buras.
68. Gwendolyn Mildo Hall, "The Formation of Afro-Creole Culture," in *Creole New Orleans: Race and Americanization*, ed. Arnold R. Hirsch and Joseph Logsdon (Baton Rouge: Louisiana State University Press, 1992), 78.
69. Hall, "The Formation of Afro-Creole Culture," 68.
70. Hall, "The Formation of Afro-Creole Culture," 78.
71. Hall, "The Formation of Afro-Creole Culture," 73–75.
72. Hall, "The Formation of Afro-Creole Culture," 59, 79.
73. Hall, "The Formation of Afro-Creole Culture," 80–81.
74. Hall, "The Formation of Afro-Creole Culture," 80.
75. Hall, "The Formation of Afro-Creole Culture," 83.
76. Hall, "The Formation of Afro-Creole Culture," 81.
77. John Blassingame, *Black New Orleans: 1860–1880* (Chicago: University of Chicago Press, 1973); Rodolphe Lucien Desdunes, trans. and ed. Sister Dorothea Olga McCants, *Our People and Our History: Fifty Creole Portraits* (Baton Rouge: Louisiana State University Press, 1911/1973); Keith Weldon Medley, *We as Freemen:* Plessy v. Ferguson, *the Fight Against Legal Segregation* (Gretna, LA: Pelican Publishing, 2012).
78. Keiana Belton, "My Thoughts About Blacks and Our Nation," in *The Writing Project, 1992–1993*, ed. Debra Perkins Adams and John Thompson (New Orleans: G. W. Carver Junior-Senior High School, 1993); Personal Collection of Avis and Vermon James, New Orleans.
79. Maxine Gives, "A Short, Short Story," in Adams and Thompson, *The Writing Project*.
80. Percie Ann Rodney, "My Legacy to Students Everywhere," in Adams and Thompson, *The Writing Project*.
81. Smith interview.
82. Leonard Smith, *A Place Called Desire*, LS3 Studios, 2021. For more information on this award-winning film, see https://www.aplacecalleddesire.com/.
83. *A Place Called Desire*, LS3 Studios, Leonard Smith, producer, 2:46–3:07, https://www.aplacecalleddesire.com/.
84. Malvin Cavalier interview, *A Place Called Desire*, 4:33–4:48.
85. *A Place Called Desire*.
86. *A Place Called Desire*; see also Arend, *Showdown in Desire*.
87. Tod Smith interview, *A Place Called Desire*, 1:04:30–1:04:56.
88. Smith interview, *A Place Called Desire*, 1:06:40–1:06:43; see also Michelle Alexander, *The New Jim Crow: Mass Incarceration in the Age of Colorblindness* (New York: New Press, 2012).
89. Smith interview, *A Place Called Desire*.
90. See also Rachel Breunlin and Helen Regis, "Putting the Ninth Ward on the Map: Race, Place, and Transformation in Desire, New Orleans," *American Anthropologist* 108, no. 4 (2006): 744–64.
91. Smith interview, *A Place Called Desire*, 1:13:15–1:15:00.

92. Kirk Stevens interview, *A Place Called Desire*, 1:04:10–1:04:18; for a narrative history of public housing in Alabama, see Jerome Morris, *Central City's Joy and Pain: Solidarity, Survival, and Soul in a Birmingham Housing Project* (Athens: University of Georgia Press, 2024).

93. Trenesse Mosley, interviewed by Kristen Buras, June 10, 2017, New Orleans.

94. Hasan Sparks, interviewed by Kristen Buras, June 3, 2018, by phone.

95. Debra Perkins Adams and John Thompson, eds., *The Writing Project, 1992–1993* (New Orleans: G. W. Carver Junior-Senior High School, 1993), Personal Collection of Avis and Vermon James, New Orleans; Lydia Voigt, Dee Wood Harper, and William Thornton, eds., *Preventing Lethal Violence in New Orleans: A Great American City* (Lafayette: University of Louisiana at Lafayette Press, 2015); Michelle Alexander, *The New Jim Crow: Mass Incarceration in the Age of Colorblindness* (New York: New Press, 2012).

96. Adrienne Gladney, Martaz Lynch, and Catherine White, interviewed by Kristen Buras, Apr. 12, 2017, New Orleans.

97. Condoll Gray, Righteous, and Righteous, interviewed by Buras, June 11, 2017, New Orleans.

98. Condoll Gray, Righteous, and Righteous interview.

99. Condoll Gray, Righteous, and Righteous interview.

100. Condoll Gray, Righteous, and Righteous interview.

101. Avis James, Vermon James, and Marilyn Pierre Degrasse, interviewed by Kristen Buras, Feb. 5, 2018, New Orleans.

102. James, James, and Pierre Degrasse interview.

103. James, James, and Pierre Degrasse interview.

104. Condoll Gray, Righteous, and Righteous interview.

105. Condoll Gray, Righteous, and Righteous interview.

106. James, James, and Pierre Degrasse interview; Arend, *Showdown in Desire*.

107. Danielle Foley, interviewed by Kristen Buras, May 21, 2017, by phone.

108. "A Female in a Male Dominated Department," 1982 Carver yearbook, Personal Collection of Avis and Vermon James, New Orleans.

109. Lindsey Moore, interviewed by Kristen Buras, Feb. 6, 2018, New Orleans.

110. 1986 Carver yearbook, Personal Collection of Avis and Vermon James, New Orleans.

CHAPTER 3: "MAKING THINGS HAPPEN THAT WOULDN'T HAPPEN OTHERWISE"

1. Charles Hatfield, interviewed by Al Kennedy, Mar. 12, 1993, Charles Hatfield Papers, Amistad Research Center, Tulane University, New Orleans, Louisiana, Box 4, Item 1. Videocassette obtained from Charles Hatfield Jr. by Kristen Buras.

2. Leonard Smith interviewed by Kristen Buras, Apr. 12, 2017, New Orleans.

3. Walter Stern, *Race and Education in New Orleans: Creating the Segregated City, 1764–1960* (Baton Rouge: Louisiana State University Press, 2018).

4. Elizabeth Heavrin, *Recordation of Certain Buildings at the George Washington Carver School Campus, New Orleans, Louisiana* (Washington, DC: FEMA, June 28, 2010), 5–6. University of New Orleans, Earl K. Long Library, Louisiana and Special Collections, FEMA G. W. Carver School Collection, Box 1, Folder 1.

5. Derrick Bell, "Serving Two Masters: Integration Ideals and Client Interests in School Desegregation Litigation," in *Critical Race Theory: Key Writings That Formed the Movement*, ed. Kimberlé Crenshaw et al. (New York: New Press, 1995), 5–19.

6. Gwendolyn Mildo Hall, *Africans in Colonial Louisiana: The Development of Afro-Creole Culture in the Eighteenth Century* (Baton Rouge: Louisiana State University Press, 1992); Ned Sublette, *The World That Made New Orleans: From Spanish Silver to Congo Square* (Chicago: Lawrence Hill Books, 2008); Donald DeVore and Joseph Logsdon, *Crescent City Schools: Public Education in New Orleans, 1841–1991* (Lafayette: Center for Louisiana Studies, University of Southwestern Louisiana, 1991).

7. Hatfield interview.

8. Evelyn Wilson, *Laws, Customs, and Rights: Charles Hatfield and His Family—a Louisiana History* (Westminster, MD: Heritage Books, 2008).

9. Wilson, *Laws, Customs, and Rights*, 77.

10. Hatfield interview, 17:30–18:00.

11. Wilson, *Laws, Customs, and Rights*, 78, 83.

12. Wilson, *Laws, Customs, and Rights*, 99.

13. Charles Hatfield, "The Passing Age," news clipping, Dec. 16, 1944, Amistad, Hatfield Papers, Box 1, Folder 16.

14. Wilson, *Laws, Customs, and Rights*, chapter 8; Hatfield's Draft Second Letter to the Registrar at Louisiana State University (Jan. 25, 1945), Amistad, Hatfield Papers, Box 1, Folder 16.

15. Wilson, *Laws, Customs, and Rights*, chapter 9; Hatfield interview.

16. Wilson, *Laws, Customs, and Rights*, chapter 11; Hatfield interview.

17. Legal Records, Amistad, Hatfield Papers, Box 1, Folder 15.

18. Hatfield interview, 31:00–32:15.

19. Wilson, *Laws, Customs, and Rights*, 190.

20. Wilson, *Laws, Customs, and Rights*; Hatfield's Alpha Kappa Delta Certificate (Dec. 12, 1947), Amistad, Hatfield Papers, Box 1, Folder 14.

21. Wilson, *Laws, Customs, and Rights*, 192–93.

22. Wilson, *Laws, Customs, and Rights*, 193

23. Wilson, *Laws, Customs, and Rights*, 194; Hatfield interview; Hatfield's Teaching Certificate, State Department of Education of Louisiana (Mar. 7, 1952), Amistad, Hatfield Papers, Box 1, Folder 11.

24. Building Curriculum Council photo, 1962 Carver yearbook, UNO, OPSB-147, Carver, Box 5.

25. Photo of Charles Hatfield in language lab, 1972 Carver yearbook, Personal Collection of Avis and Vermon James, New Orleans, LA; Programs, Practices, and Progress: A Ten-Year Progress Report, *Louisiana Weekly* (1968), UNO, OPSB–147, Samuel Scarnato Papers, Box 14.
26. Ella Shaw, interviewed by Kristen Buras, June 11, 2017, New Orleans.
27. Charles Hatfield, "The Passing Age," news clipping (undated version), Amistad, Hatfield Papers, Box 1, Folder 16.
28. Hatfield interview, 1:00:45–1:01:17.
29. Wilson, *Laws, Customs, and Rights*, 201–2.
30. Hatfield interview, 1:26:45–1:27–10.
31. Hatfield interview, 1:08:15–1:08:50
32. Avis James, Vermon James, and Marilyn Pierre Degrasse, interviewed by Kristen Buras, Feb. 5, 2018, New Orleans.
33. Wilson, *Laws, Customs, and Rights*, 202; Hatfield Certificate of Appreciation for Board Membership, Orleans Public School Federal Credit Union (1993, Sept. 30). Amistad, Hatfield Papers, Box 2, Item 2.
34. Hatfield Farewell to Seniors as Yearbook Advisor, 1962 Carver yearbook, UNO, OPSB–147, Carver Junior-Senior High School, Box 5.
35. Tribute to Hatfield, 1973 Carver yearbook, Personal Collection of Avis and Vermon James.
36. Wilson, *Laws, Customs, and Rights*, 202.
37. Hatfield Pioneer Award, Apr. 30, 1983, Amistad, Hatfield Papers, Box 2, Item 1.
38. Wilson, *Laws, Customs, and Rights*, 203–4.
39. Hatfield interview, 46:35–46:45.
40. "Lamar Smith: Back Bone of Community School," 1981 Carver yearbook, Personal Collection of Avis and Vermon James; Louisiana Senate Resolution No. 41 (Baton Rouge, LA, 2003).
41. 1962 Carver yearbook, UNO, OPSB–147, Carver, Box 5.
42. Theron Lewis, interviewed by Kristen Buras, Apr. 10, 2017, New Orleans.
43. "The Community School," 1972 Carver yearbook, 12, Personal Collection of Avis and Vermon James.
44. "Smith: Back Bone," 1981 Carver yearbook.
45. Lamar Smith, "The Plight of the Black Teacher in New Orleans," prepublished version for *Afro-American*, circa 1970, 2, UNO, Long Library, Louisiana and Special Collections, United Teachers of New Orleans, Local 527 Collection, Container 135–15.
46. Smith, "The Plight of the Black Teacher in New Orleans," 1.
47. Smith, "The Plight of the Black Teacher in New Orleans," 4.
48. "Smith: Back Bone," 1981 Carver yearbook.
49. "Smith: Back Bone," 1981 Carver yearbook.
50. Lamar Smith Jr. and Reverend Douglas Haywood, interviewed by Kristen Buras, June 8, 2017, New Orleans.

51. Smith and Haywood interview.
52. Louisiana Senate Resolution No. 41.
53. Louisiana Senate Resolution No. 41.
54. Smith and Haywood interview.
55. "Smith: Back Bone," 1981 Carver yearbook.
56. Smith and Haywood interview.
57. Smith and Haywood interview.
58. Enos Hicks Jr., interviewed by Kristen Buras, June 8, 2017, New Orleans.
59. "Memories of Daddy by Enos S. Hicks IV," unpublished essay, Personal Papers of Sarahlilly Hicks; "Ralph Metcalfe, Former Marquette Ace, Has Also Fashioned Enos Hicks into One of the Nation's Best Sprinters" in "J. Herbert Breaks World Record in N.Y.C.," *Indianapolis Recorder*, Mar. 5, 1938, https://newspapers.library.in.gov/cgi-bin/indiana?a=d&d=INR19380305-01 .1.3&e=-------en-20--1--txt-txIN-------.
60. "Memories of Daddy by Enos S. Hicks IV"; Dedication Program; Building Curriculum Council photo.
61. Hicks interview.
62. Lewis interview.
63. Lewis interview; Teacher of the Year 1961, 1962 Carver yearbook.
64. Lewis interview.
65. Lewis interview.
66. Lewis interview; Hicks interview.
67. Lewis interviewed by Buras; Letter from Carver Principal Milton Becnel to Assistant Superintendent John Monie, Feb. 16, 1967, on Lewis's quarter mile world record and upcoming Olympics in Mexico City, with newspaper clipping, "Theron Lewis VFW Honoree," *Times-Picayune*, Feb. 16, 1967, OPSB–147, Scarnato Papers, Box 14; "Southern U.'s Best to Run Here," *New York Times*, Jan. 13, 1966, Personal Papers of Theron Lewis.
68. Hicks interview.
69. Hicks interview.
70. Enos Hicks photo, 1973 Carver yearbook, Personal Collection of Avis and Vermon James.
71. "Coach Hicks by Lloyd Wills," unpublished essay, July 26, 2011, Personal Papers of Sarahlilly Hicks.
72. "Coach Herman Gray on Hoopy," unpublished essay, Personal Papers of Hicks.
73. Hicks interview.
74. Hicks interview.
75. Ernest Charles, interviewed by Kristen Buras, Apr. 11, 2017, New Orleans.
76. Hicks interview.
77. Al Kennedy, *Yvonne Busch: One Teacher's Role in Shaping New Orleans Music* (New Orleans: Author, 2000), 2–5.
78. Kennedy, *Yvonne Busch*, 5–7.
79. Kennedy, *Yvonne Busch*, 7.

80. Kennedy, *Yvonne Busch*, 8.
81. Kennedy, *Yvonne Busch*, 8.
82. Kennedy, *Yvonne Busch*, 10.
83. Kennedy, *Yvonne Busch*, 11.
84. Kennedy, *Yvonne Busch*, 10.
85. Kennedy, *Yvonne Busch*, 16.
86. Kennedy, *Yvonne Busch*, 24–26.
87. Dedication Program, 1958.
88. Kennedy, *Yvonne Busch*, 28–29.
89. Kennedy, *Yvonne Busch*, 30.
90. Kennedy, *Yvonne Busch*, 33.
91. Kennedy, *Yvonne Busch*; Al Kennedy, *Chord Changes on the Chalkboard: How Public School Teachers Shaped the Jazz and the Music of New Orleans* (Lanham, MD: Scarecrow Press, 2005).
92. Herlin Riley, interviewed by Kristen Buras, Apr. 12, 2017, New Orleans.
93. Smith interviewed by Buras.
94. Kennedy, *Yvonne Busch*, 34.
95. Personal Collection of Avis and Vermon James.
96. Kennedy, *Yvonne Busch*, 15.
97. LS3 Studios, 2015.
98. LS3 Studios, 2015, 43:00.
99. LS3 Studios, 2015, 49:00.
100. LS3 Studios, 2015, 33:00.
101. Rhea Joseph, interviewed by Kristen Buras, Apr. 10, 2017, New Orleans; Busch Funeral Program (Mar. 8, 2014), Personal Papers of Herlin Riley, New Orleans.
102. Lenora Condoll Gray, Carol Righteous, and Clarence Righteous, interviewed by Kristen Buras, June 11, 2017, New Orleans; Lenora Condoll Gray, interviewed by Kristen Buras, Apr. 10, 2021, by phone.
103. Condoll Gray interview.
104. Condoll Gray, Righteous, and Righteous interview.
105. Condoll Gray, Righteous, and Righteous interview.
106. Dwan Julien, interviewed by Kristen Buras, June 4, 2018, by phone.
107. Hasan Sparks, interviewed by Kristen Buras, June 3, 2018, by phone.
108. Condoll Gray, Righteous, and Righteous interview.
109. Photo, "Close Up Participants in DC, Outside Smithsonian Institute," 1972 Carver yearbook; photos, "Students Tour Nation's Capital and New York City," 1973 Carver yearbook; photos, "Close Up at Lincoln Monument, US Supreme Court," and Williamsburg, VA, 1992 Carver yearbook; Personal Collection of Avis and Vermon James.
110. Condoll Gray, Righteous, and Righteous interview.
111. Faculty Friday, Clarence Nero, from Baton Rouge Community College at https://www.mybrcc.edu/news/clarence.php.
112. Condoll Gray, Righteous, and Righteous interview.

113. "Introduction '81," 1982 Carver yearbook, Personal Collection of Avis and Vermon James.
114. "TP/SI Cites Condoll," 1984 Carver yearbook, Personal Collection of Avis and Vermon James.
115. "Teacher Superlatives," 1985 Carver yearbook, Personal Collection of Avis and Vermon James.
116. "My Favorite Teacher," 1986 Carver yearbook, Personal Collection of Avis and Vermon James.
117. Condoll Gray, Righteous, and Righteous interview.
118. Condoll Gray, Righteous, and Righteous interview.
119. Condoll Gray interview.
120. Personal Collection of Avis and Vermon James.
121. Condoll Gray, Righteous, and Righteous interview.
122. Condoll Gray, Righteous, and Righteous interview.
123. Riley interview.
124. 1959 Carver graduate Althea Merricks Haywood interviewed by Kristen Buras, Apr. 11, 2017, New Orleans; Personal Papers of Althea Merricks Haywood, "Alma Mater" mimeograph.

CHAPTER 4: "THEN I HAD MY GRANDCHILDREN"
1. Lenora Condoll Gray, Carol Righteous, and Clarence Righteous, interviewed by Kristen Buras, Feb. 5, 2018, New Orleans.
2. Althea Merricks Haywood, interviewed by Kristen Buras, Apr. 11, 2017, New Orleans.
3. Irvin Blackburn, interviewed by Kristen Buras, June 2, 2018, by phone.
4. Leonard Smith, interviewed by Kristen Buras, Apr. 12, 2017, New Orleans.
5. Trenesse Mosley, interviewed by Kristen Buras, June 10, 2017, New Orleans.
6. Kenneth Royal interviewed by Kristen Buras, Apr. 13, 2017, New Orleans.
7. The Report of the Reviewing Committee for G. W. Carver High School, SACS (Mar. 25–27, 1987), 9, University of New Orleans, Earl K. Long Library, Louisiana and Special Collections, OPSB–147, G. W. Carver Junior-Senior High School, Box 1, Folder 1.
8. Kelly O'Guinn, interviewed by Kristen Buras, Apr. 3, 2018, by phone.
9. O'Guinn, interviewed by Buras; Danielle Foley, interviewed by Kristen Buras, May 21, 2017, by phone.
10. Adrienne Gladney, Martaz Lynch, and Catherine White, interviewed by Kristen Buras, Apr. 12, 2017, New Orleans.
11. Carver 1962 yearbook, UNO, OPSB–147, Carver, Box 5.
12. Theron Lewis, interviewed by Kristen Buras, Apr. 10, 2017, New Orleans.
13. Mary Polk, interviewed by Kristen Buras, Apr. 10, 2017, New Orleans.
14. Polk interview.
15. Herlin Riley, interviewed by Kristen Buras, Apr. 12, 2017, New Orleans.
16. Riley interview.

17. Yvonne Verily Busch Funeral Program, Mar. 8, 2014, New Orleans, Personal Papers of Herlin Riley.

18. Leonard Smith, *The Power of One: The Musical Legacy of Yvonne Busch*, LS3 Studios, forthcoming. For more information on this film, see www.yvonne busch.com; see also Al Kennedy, *Chord Changes on the Chalkboard: How Public School Teachers Shaped Jazz and the Music of New Orleans* (Lanham, MD: Scarecrow Press, 2005).

19. Personal Papers of Riley.

20. Ella Shaw, interviewed by Kristen Buras, June 11, 2017, New Orleans.

21. Blackburn interviewed by Buras.

22. Smith interviewed by Buras.

23. Mosley interview.

24. Discover the Road to Careers: G. W. Carver Middle School Career Day, Mar. 17, 1989, UNO, OPSB–147, Carver, Box 1, Folder 3.

25. Shaw interview.

26. Mosley interview.

27. Kelly O'Guinn interview.

28. Dwan Julien, interviewed by Kristen Buras, June 4, 2018, by phone.

29. Gladney, Lynch, and White interview.

30. Smith interview.

31. Mosley interview.

32. Mosley interview.

33. Condoll Gray, Righteous, and Righteous interview.

34. Condoll Gray, Righteous, and Righteous interview.

35. Condoll Gray, Righteous, and Righteous interview.

36. Avis James, Vermon James, and Marilyn Pierre Degrasse, interviewed by Kristen Buras, Feb. 5, 2018, New Orleans.

37. James, James, and Degrasse interview.

38. James, James, and Degrasse interview.

39. Lindsey Moore, interviewed by Kristen Buras, Feb. 6, 2018, New Orleans.

40. Moore interview.

41. James, James, and Pierre Degrasse interview.

42. Letter from Robert E. Wall, Director of School-Community Relations, to Principal Willie C. LeBeau, Sept. 14, 1971, UNO, OPSB–147, Samuel Scarnato Papers, Carver, Box 14.

43. Letter with "Principals Workshop: Possible Topics for Discussion" Memo from Robert E. Wall, Director of School-Community Relations, to Members of the School-Community Relations Advisory Committee, Sept. 20, 1971, UNO, OPSB–147, Scarnato Papers, Carver, Box 14.

44. "Parent Social a Smashing Success," Carver 1982 yearbook, Personal Collection of Avis and Vermon James.

45. School Improvement and Accountability Plan for G. W. Carver Junior-Senior High School, Dec. 5, 1991, UNO, OPSB–147, Carver, Box 5.

46. "Parents as Partners in Education" seminar.
47. "An Action Plan for Parents."
48. "Parents as Partners in Education" seminar.
49. "Pledge."
50. Condoll Gray, Righteous, and Righteous interview.
51. James, James, and Pierre Degrasse interview.
52. Condoll Gray, Righteous, and Righteous interview.
53. Condoll Gray, Righteous, and Righteous interview; Class of 1989 twenty-five-year reunion photo, including students alongside Lenora Condoll Gray, Avis and Vermon James, Carol and Clarence Righteous, and other teachers, Personal Collection of Avis and Vermon James.
54. Moore interview.
55. Foley interview.
56. For more on Smith's work and CETA, see chapter 3.
57. Foley interview.

CHAPTER 5: "DETERMINED TO EDUCATE OUR KIDS"
1. Danielle Foley, interviewed by Kristen Buras, May 21, 2017, by phone.
2. Milton Becnel's Foreword, Carver 1962 yearbook, University of New Orleans, Earl K. Long Library, Louisiana and Special Collections, OPSB–147, G. W. Carver Junior-Senior High School, Box 5.
3. Becnel's Foreword.
4. "Programs, Practices, and Progress: A Ten Year Progress Report" (*Louisiana Weekly*, Nov. 9, 1968); UNO, OPSB–147, Samuel Scarnato Papers, Carver, Box 14.
5. "Programs, Practices, and Progress."
6. "George Washington Carver Senior High School Philosophy and Objectives, 4, UNO, OPSB–147, Carver, 1955–1994, Box 1, Folder 1.
7. Althea Merricks Haywood, interviewed by Kristen Buras, Apr. 11, 2017, New Orleans.
8. Merricks interview.
9. Merricks interview.
10. Merricks interview.
11. Theron Lewis, interviewed by Kristen Buras, Apr. 10, 2017, New Orleans.
12. Lewis interview.
13. Lewis interview.
14. Carver 1962 yearbook, 140, UNO, OPSB–147, Carver, 1955–1994, Box 5.
15. Lewis interview.
16. Personal Papers of Theron Lewis, New Orleans; "SU's Theron Lewis, SWAC Super Star," photo caption, Official Program of 28th Annual SWAC (Southwestern Athletic Conference) Track and Field Meet (May 6 and 7, 1966); "Southern U.'s Best to Run Here," *New York Times*, Jan. 13, 1966; "One of the Greatest World Records of All-Time Was Set by This Team in the

1600-Meter Relay at the LA International: Tommie Smith, Theron Lewis, Lee Evans, and Bob Frey," photo caption, *Los Angeles Times*, July 25, 1966; "Negro Sets Sugar Bowl Track Record—Theron Lewis, Southern University, Baton Rouge, La., Wins the 400-Meter Dash Event in New Orleans Today for a New Sugar Bowl Record," photo caption, AP, Dec. 29, 1964.

17. Milton Becnel letter to John Monie regarding Theron Lewis, Feb. 16, 1967, UNO, OPSB–147, Scarnato Papers, Box 14: Carver.
18. "Theron Lewis VFW Honoree."
19. Milton Becnel letter to John Monie regarding Hannah Brown (Apr. 5, 1967), UNO, OPSB–147, Scarnato Papers, Box 14: Carver.
20. "Teen Mailwoman Supplies New Postal Service Look."
21. John Monie letter to Milton Becnel (Apr. 6, 1967), UNO, OPSB–147, Scarnato Papers, Box 14: Carver.
22. Referral Slip from Milton Becnel to Carl Dolce regarding Thomas Bennett (May 22, 1969) with "Who Says Things Are Changing?" broadside by Shell Oil Co., UNO, OPSB–147, Scarnato Papers, Box 14: Carver.
23. Rhea Joseph, interviewed by Kristen Buras, Apr. 10, 2017, New Orleans.
24. Joseph interview.
25. Irvin Blackburn, interviewed by Kristen Buras, June 2, 2018, by phone.
26. Blackburn interview.
27. Blackburn interview.
28. Mary Polk, interviewed by Kristen Buras, Apr. 10, 2017, New Orleans.
29. Polk interview.
30. Polk interview.
31. Senior Class Officers, "Vice President–Leonard Smith," photo, 1973 Carver yearbook, Personal Collection of Avis and Vermon James.
32. Leonard Smith, interviewed by Kristen Buras, Apr. 12, 2017, New Orleans.
33. Smith interview.
34. Smith interview.
35. Smith interview.
36. Ella Shaw, interviewed by Kristen Buras, June 11, 2017, New Orleans; "COE" photos, 1972 Carver yearbook, Personal Collection of Avis and Vermon James.
37. Smith interview; "Automotive Professional Training," photo, 1973 Carver yearbook, Personal Collection of Avis and Vermon James.
38. Herlin Riley, interviewed by Kristen Buras, Apr. 12, 2017, New Orleans.
39. 1972 Carver yearbook, Personal Collection of Avis and Vermon James.
40. Trenesse Mosley, interviewed by Kristen Buras, June 10, 2017, New Orleans.
41. "Certified Nursing Assistant–CNA Members," photo, 2001 Carver yearbook, Personal Collection of Avis and Vermon James; "Practical Nursing and the Sciences," photo, 1972 Carver yearbook.
42. Mosley interview.
43. Mosley interview.
44. Mosley interview.

45. Faculty photos, "Mr. B. Pullum–Math," 1978 Carver yearbook, Personal Collection of Avis and Vermon James.
46. Mosley interview.
47. Mosley interview.
48. Kelly O'Guinn, interviewed by Kristen Buras, Apr. 3, 2018, by phone.
49. K. O'Guinn interview.
50. K. O'Guinn interview.
51. Denise O'Guinn, interviewed by Kristen Buras, Feb. 4, 2018, New Orleans.
52. D. O'Guinn interview.
53. D. O'Guinn interview.
54. Dwan Julien, interviewed by Kristen Buras, June 4, 2018, by phone.
55. Hasan Sparks, interviewed by Kristen Buras, June 3, 2018, by phone.
56. Sparks interview.
57. Sparks interview.
58. Adrienne Gladney, Martaz Lynch, and Catherine White, interviewed by Kristen Buras, Apr. 12, 2107, New Orleans.
59. Gladney, Lynch, and White interview.
60. Gladney, Lynch, and White interview.
61. "Building Curriculum Council," 1962 Carver yearbook, UNO, OPSB–147, Carver, Box 5.
62. Avis James, Vermon James, and Marilyn Pierre Degrasse, interviewed by Kristen Buras, Feb. 5, 2018, New Orleans.
63. Lenora Condoll Gray, Carol Righteous, and Clarence Righteous, interviewed by Kristen Buras, June 11, 2017, New Orleans.
64. Condoll Gray, Righteous, and Righteous interview.
65. "Agriscience Program," photos, 2001 Carver yearbook, Personal Collection of James; "Horticulture," photo, 1992 Carver yearbook, with caption, "Under the Supervision of Mr. Cl. Righteous, These Young Ladies Gain Valuable Gardening Experience," Personal Collection of James.
66. Condoll Gray, Righteous, and Righteous interview.
67. For more on Lenora Condoll Gray, see chapter 3.
68. James, James, and Pierre Degrasse interview.
69. James, James, and Pierre Degrasse interview.
70. James, James, and Pierre Degrasse interview; 2001 Carver yearbook, Personal Collection of Avis and Vermon James.
71. "Dillard University Talent Search," 2001 Carver yearbook, Personal Collection of Avis and Vermon James.
72. James, James, and Pierre Degrasse interview.
73. James, James, and Pierre Degrasse interview.
74. James, James, and Pierre Degrasse interview.
75. James, James, and Pierre Degrasse interview.
76. James, James, and Pierre Degrasse interview.

77. "Future Business Leaders of America," photo, 1972 Carver yearbook, Personal Collection of Avis and Vermon James.
78. Danielle Foley, interviewed by Kristen Buras, May 21, 2017, by phone.
79. Foley interview.
80. Foley interview.
81. Foley interview.
82. "Female in a Male Dominated Department," 1982 Carver yearbook, Personal Collection of James.
83. Danille Foley photo, "Female in a Male Dominated Department," 1982 Carver yearbook.
84. Foley interview.
85. Foley interview.
86. Lindsey Moore, interviewed by Kristen Buras, Feb. 6, 2018, New Orleans.
87. Moore interview.
88. Moore interview.
89. For a history of all-white Francis T. Nicholls High School before desegregation, its transformation into the all-black Frederick Douglass High School after mass white resistance, and the school's ultimate closure due to post-Katrina charter school expansion in New Orleans, see chapter 4 in Kristen Buras, *Charter Schools, Race, and Urban Space: Where the Market Meets Grassroots Resistance* (New York: Routledge, 2015). Sadly, the closure of Douglass foreshadowed the dynamics surrounding the closure of the historic G. W. Carver Senior High School.
90. Moore interview.
91. Moore interview.
92. Lindsey Moore commencement photo and biographic sketch, 1992 Carver yearbook, Personal Collection of Avis and Vermon James.
93. Lindsey Moore commencement photo and biographic sketch, 1992 Carver yearbook.
94. Moore interview.
95. Moore interview.
96. Moore interview.
97. Condoll Gray, Righteous, and Righteous interview.
98. "Department of Guidance," 1972 Carver yearbook, Personal Collection of Avis and Vermon James.
99. "Faculty," Carver 1972 yearbook.
100. "Class Night—A Most Unique Affair, May 21, 1992," 1992 Carver yearbook, Personal Collection of Avis and Vermon James.
101. "Annual Awards Breakfast," 1992 Carver yearbook.
102. "Working Together to Build Learning: G. W. Carver Jr./Sr. High School, Student Profile, Top 20% of Senior Class," 1993–1994, UNO, OPSB–147, Carver, 1955–1994, Box 5.

CHAPTER 6: "KNOWING HOW TO MANEUVER THROUGH THE SYSTEM"
1. Ernest Charles, interviewed by Kristen Buras, Apr. 11, 2017, New Orleans.
2. Rhea Joseph, interviewed by Kristen Buras, Apr. 10, 2017, New Orleans.
3. Joseph interview.
4. Trenesse Mosley, interviewed by Kristen Buras, June 10, 2017, New Orleans.
5. Charles interview.
6. Charles interview.
7. Theron Lewis, interviewed by Kristen Buras, Apr. 10, 2017, New Orleans.
8. Mary Polk, interviewed by Kristen Buras, Apr. 10, 2017, New Orleans.
9. Joseph interview.
10. Joseph interview.
11. Joseph interview.
12. Irvin Blackburn, interviewed by Kristen Buras, June 2, 2018, by phone.
13. Blackburn interview.
14. Blackburn interview.
15. Blackburn interview.
16. Leonard Smith, interviewed by Kristen Buras, Apr. 12, 2017, New Orleans.
17. Smith interview.
18. Herlin Riley, interviewed by Kristen Buras, Apr. 12, 2017, New Orleans.
19. Riley interview.
20. Charles interview.
21. Charles interview.
22. Mosley interview.
23. Mosley interview.
24. Mosley interview.
25. Mosley interview.
26. "The Report of the Reviewing Committee for G. W. Carver High School" (Southern Association of Colleges and Schools–Commission on Secondary Education, Mar. 25–27, 1987), 16, UNO, OPSB–147, Carver, 1955–1994, Box 5.
27. "Heroes for 1982," 1982 Carver yearbook, Personal Collection of Avis and Vermon James, New Orleans.
28. Dwan Julien, interviewed by Kristen Buras, June 4, 2018, by phone.
29. Julien interview.
30. Photo, "Students Tour Nation's Capital and New York City," 1973 Carver yearbook; photos, "Close Up at Lincoln Monument," US Supreme Court and Williamsburg, VA, 1992 Carver yearbook, Personal Collection of Avis and Vermon James.
31. Kenneth Royal, interviewed by Kristen Buras, Apr. 13, 2017, New Orleans.
32. "Work Health, Student Life: Support Services for Tots and Students," Mrs. Thomas, director of school-based health clinic, photo with quote, 1996 Carver yearbook, Personal Collection of Avis and Vermon James.

33. Mr. Clinton Ball, photo with quote, 1996 Carver yearbook.

34. Hasan Sparks, interviewed by Kristen Buras, June 3, 2018, by phone.

35. Sparks interview.

36. "Job Training Workshop: Preparing Well for the World of Work," 1986 Carver yearbook, Personal Collection of Avis and Vermon James.

37. "What's Your Claim to Fame?" Carver 1986 yearbook.

38. "Working Together to Build Learning: G. W. Carver Jr./Sr. High School, Student Profile, Top 20% of Senior Class," 1993–1994, UNO, OPSB–147, Carver, 1955–1994, Box 5.

39. Principal Herbert J. McCullum's Farewell, 1978 Carver yearbook, Personal Collection of Avis and Vermon James; emphasis added.

40. "AFNA," 1978 Carver yearbook, Personal Collection of Avis and Vermon James; "Junior Achievement"; McCullum's Farewell.

41. See American Foundation for Negro Affairs, May 19, 1969–Dec. 31, 1969, Horace Mann Bond Papers (MS 411), Special Collections and University Archives, University of Massachusetts Amherst Libraries, http://credo.library.umass.edu/view/full/mums411-b029-f004.

42. "George Washington Carver Senior High School History and Philosophy," Carver yearbook, Personal Collection of Avis and Vermon James.

43. "Preparing to Render Service to Mankind: The Health Professions," 1986 Carver yearbook.

44. "Spotlight on Academics: In the Pursuit of Excellence, We Never Defer," 1986 Carver yearbook.

45. "Tanya Perrier Goes to Washington," 1986 Carver yearbook.

46. Lenora Condoll Gray, Carol Righteous, and Clarence Righteous, interviewed by Kristen Buras, June 11, 2017, New Orleans.

47. Condoll Gray, Righteous, and Righteous interview.

48. Condoll Gray, Righteous, and Righteous interview.

49. Condoll Gray, Righteous, and Righteous interview.

50. Lindsey Moore, interviewed by Kristen Buras, Feb. 6, 2018, New Orleans.

51. Moore interview.

52. Condoll Gray, Righteous, and Righteous interview.

53. Willie Calhoun, interviewed by Kristen Buras, Apr. 12, 2017, New Orleans.

54. "Assistant Principals and Administrative Assistants," 1973 Carver yearbook, Personal Collection of Avis and Vermon James; "Dedication" to Ms. Andrews and Mr. Hoover, 1986 Carver yearbook, Personal Collection of Avis and Vermon James.

55. James Anderson, *The Education of Blacks in the South, 1860–1935* (Chapel Hill: University of North Carolina Press, 1988); William Watkins, *The White Architects of Black Education: Ideology and Power in America, 1865–1954* (New York: Teachers College Press, 2001).

56. Louis Harlan, *Booker T. Washington: The Making of a Black Leader, 1856–1901* (New York: Oxford University Press, 1972).

57. David Levering Lewis, *W. E. B. Du Bois: Biography of a Race, 1968–1919* (New York: Henry Holt and Co., 1993); W. E. B. Du Bois, *The Souls of Black Folk* (New York: Penguin Books, 1969).

58. Donald DeVore, *Defying Jim Crow: African American Community Development and the Struggle for Racial Equality in New Orleans, 1900–1960* (Baton Rouge: Louisiana State University Press, 2015), 146.

59. DeVore, *Defying Jim Crow*, 147.

60. DeVore, *Defying Jim Crow*, 142.

61. DeVore, *Defying Jim Crow*, 145.

62. DeVore, *Defying Jim Crow*, 144.

63. DeVore, *Defying Jim Crow*, 149.

64. DeVore, *Defying Jim Crow*, 147.

65. DeVore, *Defying Jim Crow*, 148.

66. DeVore, *Defying Jim Crow*, 147.

67. DeVore, *Defying Jim Crow*, 148.

68. DeVore, *Defying Jim Crow*, 149.

69. DeVore, *Defying Jim Crow*, 150.

70. Christina Vella, *George Washington Carver: A Life* (Baton Rouge: Louisiana State University Press, 2015).

71. Condoll Gray, Righteous, and Righteous interview.

72. Carver/Lawless Career Development Program, "A Proposal Submitted for ESEA Title III (Mar. 1973)," UNO, OPSB–147, Grants–Preliminary Inventory, Box 5.

73. Carver/Lawless Career Development Program, "A Proposal: Statement of Needs and Objectives," 21.

74. Carver/Lawless Career Development Program, "A Proposal: Statement of Needs and Objectives."

75. Carver/Lawless Career Development Program, "A Proposal: Statement of Needs and Objectives," 22.

76. Carver/Lawless Career Development Program, "A Proposal: Letter by Richard A. Theodore to Members of the Advisory Committee of the Exemplary Program for Occupational Preparation," Mar. 20, 1973.

77. Carver/Lawless Career Development Program, "A Proposal: Financial Requirements," 34–35.

78. Letter by Richard Theodore to Members.

79. See Carver/Lawless Career Development Program, "A Proposal."

80. Carver/Lawless Career Development Program, "Continuation Proposal Submitted for Funding Under Title III," ESEA (May 1, 1975), 51, UNO, OPBS–147, Grants–Preliminary Inventory, Box 5.

81. Carver/Lawless Career Development Program, "Continuation Proposal: Community Agencies That Cooperated in the Project—Fieldtrips," 53.

82. Carver/Lawless Career Development Program, "Continuation Proposal: Community Agencies That Cooperated in the Project—Resource Speakers," 53–54.

83. Danielle Foley, interviewed by Kristen Buras, May 21, 2017, by phone.

84. Foley interview.

85. Lindsey Moore, interviewed by Kristen Buras, Feb. 6, 2018.

86. Moore interview.

87. Avis James, Vernon James, and Marilyn Pierre Degrasse, interviewed by Kristen Buras, Feb. 5, 2018, New Orleans.

88. James, James, and Pierre Degrasse interview.

89. James, James, and Pierre Degrasse interview.

90. James, James, and Pierre Degrasse interview.

91. Moore interview.

92. Moore interview.

93. James, James, and Pierre Degrasse interview.

94. James, James, and Pierre Degrasse interview.

95. James, James, and Pierre Degrasse interview.

96. "It's a Long Day When You're Principal," 1972 Carver yearbook, Personal Collection of Avis and Vernon James.

97. Foley interview.

98. Foley interview.

99. G. W. Carver Junior-Senior High School, School Improvement and Accountability Plan (Dec. 5, 1991), "Parents as Partners in Education" seminar, UNO, OPSB–147, Carver, 1955–1994, Box 5.

100. School Improvement and Accountability Plan, "Improvement Objective: To Develop an Orderly Environment Which Is Free from the Threat of Physical Harm and Is Conducive to Teaching and Learning."

101. Moore interview; "Work Health, Student Life: Support Services for Tots and Students," 1996 Carver yearbook.

102. Moore interview.

103. Moore interview.

104. Moore interview.

105. Moore interview.

106. Moore interview.

107. James, James, and Pierre Degrasse interview.

108. James, James, and Pierre Degrasse interview.

109. Moore interview.

110. "Work Health, Student Life: Support Services for Tots and Students," 1996 Carver yearbook.

111. "Thomas Priestley, Sr.," 1992 Carver yearbook, Personal Collection of Avis and Vernon James.

112. "George Washington Carver Senior High School: Philosophy and Objectives," undated, UNO, OPSB–147, Carver, 1955–1994, Box 1, Folder 1.

113. "C orge Washington Carver Senior High School: Philosophy and Objectives."

114. Photo of Becnel at his desk with a "THINK" sign, "The Principal at Work," 1962 Carver yearbook, UNO, OPSB–147, Carver, 1955–1994, Box 5.
115. 1996 Carver yearbook, Personal Collection of Avis and Vermon James.

CHAPTER 7: "ALL OF ONE ACCORD"

1. Danielle Foley, interviewed by Kristen Buras, May 21, 2017, by phone.
2. Althea Merricks interviewed by Kristen Buras, Apr. 11, 2017, New Orleans; Alma Mater, Carver Senior High School, 1958–1959, Personal Papers of Althea Merricks, New Orleans.
3. Rhea Joseph, interviewed by Kristen Buras, Apr. 10, 2017, New Orleans.
4. Mary Polk, interviewed by Kristen Buras, Apr. 10, 2017, New Orleans.
5. Polk interview.
6. Leonard Smith, interviewed by Kristen Buras, Apr. 12, 2017, New Orleans.
7. Alice Wilkerson, "Carverites Are on the March," *Carver Times* 1, no. 2 (May 1959): 3. University of New Orleans, Earl K. Long Library, Louisiana and Special Collections, OPSB–147, G. W. Carver Junior-Senior High School, 1955–1994, Box 1, Folder 2.
8. Ernest Charles, interviewed by Kristen Buras, Apr. 11, 2017, New Orleans.
9. 1962 Carver yearbook, UNO, OPSB–147, Carver, 1955–1994, Box 5.
10. Charles interview.
11. Willie Calhoun, interviewed by Kristen Buras, Apr. 12, 2017, New Orleans.
12. Trenesse Mosley, interviewed by Kristen Buras, June 10, 2017, New Orleans.
13. "Ms. W. Hogan–Music," faculty photos, 1978 Carver yearbook, Personal Collection of Avis and Vermon James.
14. Dwan Julien, interviewed by Kristen Buras, June 4, 2018, by phone.
15. Julien interview.
16. Kenneth Royal, interviewed by Kristen Buras, Apr. 13, 2017, New Orleans.
17. "Successful Initial Carver Day Classic," *Carver Times* 1, no. 2 (May 1959): 1–2. UNO, OPSB–147, Carver, 1955–1994, Box 1, Folder 2.
18. "Successful Initial Carver Day Classic."
19. 1972 Carver yearbook.
20. "Little Broadway Reports," *Carver Times* 1, no. 2 (May 1959): 5. UNO, OPSB–147, Carver, 1955–1994, Box 1, Folder 2.
21. "Carver Times Staff," 2.
22. Rhea Joseph, interviewed by Kristen Buras, Apr. 10, 2017, New Orleans.
23. Junior Class Officers," 1962 Carver yearbook.
24. Joseph interview; photo by Buras used by courtesy of Joseph.
25. Irvin Blackburn, interviewed by Kristen Buras, June 2, 2018, by phone.
26. Smith interview; "Senior Class Officers," Vice President–Leonard [Smith], photo, 1973 Carver yearbook, Personal Collection of Avis and Vermon James.
27. Trenesse Mosley, interviewed by Kristen Buras, June 10, 2017, New Orleans.

28. 1962 Carver yearbook; Carver Senior High School 1972, 1973, 1978. 1982, 1984, 1985, 1986, 1992, 1996, 1999, 2001 yearbooks, Personal Collection of Avis and Vermon James.
29. Polk interview.
30. Royal interview.
31. Mosley interview.
32. Hasan Sparks, interviewed by Kristen Buras, June 3, 2018, by phone.
33. Polk interview.
34. Smith interview.
35. Alice Wilkerson, "Carnival Comes to Carver," *Carver Times*, 4.
36. "February," 1982 Carver yearbook.
37. Herlin Riley, interviewed by Kristen Buras, Apr. 12, 2017, New Orleans.
38. Riley interview.
39. Denise O'Guinn, interviewed by Kristen Buras, Feb. 4, 2018, New Orleans.
40. Merricks interview.
41. Mosley interview.
42. Mosley interview.
43. Mosley interview.
44. D. O'Guinn interview.
45. Merricks interview.
46. Polk interview.
47. Smith interview.
48. "George Washington Carver Senior High School 50th Year Reunion Keep-sake Booklet, Class of 1963," Personal Papers of Rhea Joseph, New Orleans.
49. "The Class of 1963 20 Years Later," 50th Year Reunion Keepsake Booklet.
50. Joseph interview; "50th Year Reunion, July 12–14 and November 2–7, 2013: The Celebration," 50th Year Reunion Keepsake Booklet.
51. Polk interview; "Dinner Program," Class of 1968, 45th Class Reunion Booklet, Personal Papers of Mary Polk, New Orleans.
52. Irvin Blackburn, "Congratulations to the 1968 Graduates," Forty-fifth Class Reunion Booklet, Personal Papers of Polk.
53. Blackburn, "Congratulations to the 1968 Graduates."
54. "Dinner Program," Forty-fifth Class Reunion Booklet.
55. Riley interview.
56. Riley interview.
57. Riley interview.
58. Sparks interview.
59. Foley interview.
60. Foley interview.
61. Foley interview.
62. Foley interview.
63. Foley interview.

64. Foley interview.
65. Foley interview.
66. Foley interview.
67. Foley interview.
68. Lenora Condoll Gray, Carol Righteous, and Clarence Righteous, interviewed by Kristen Buras, June 11, 2017, New Orleans.
69. Condoll Gray, Righteous, and Righteous interview.
70. Condoll Gray, Righteous, and Righteous interview.
71. Condoll Gray, Righteous, and Righteous interview.
72. Condoll Gray, Righteous, and Righteous interview.
73. Condoll Gray, Righteous, and Righteous interview.
74. Avis James, Vermon James, and Marilyn Pierre Degrasse, interviewed by Kristen Buras, Feb. 5, 2018, New Orleans.
75. James, James, and Pierre Degrasse interview.
76. James, James, and Pierre Degrasse interview.
77. James, James, and Pierre Degrasse interview; "Non-Teaching Personnel—Hall Monitors, Security Guards," photos, 1973 Carver yearbook; "Cafeteria Staff, Maintenance, Security," photos, Carver 1978 yearbook.
78. James, James, and Pierre Degrasse interview.
79. James, James, and Pierre Degrasse interview.
80. James, James, and Pierre Degrasse interview.
81. See chapter 3.
82. Moore interview.
83. James, James, and Pierre Degrasse interview.
84. James, James, and Pierre Degrasse interview.
85. James, James, and Pierre Degrasse interview.
86. James, James, and Pierre Degrasse interview.
87. Condoll Gray, Righteous, and Righteous interview.
88. Condoll Gray, Righteous, and Righteous interview.
89. Collage of Carver faculty signatures, including Willie Mae Andrews, Avis Bierbaum (James), Vermon James, Yvonne Busch, Lenora Condoll Gray, Wilhelmina Hogan, Albert Jordan, Herbert McCullum, Benny Pullum, Carol Righteous, Lucille Simms, and Zenobia Stewart, "Faculty Scribbler's Page," 1978 Carver yearbook, Personal Collection of Avis and Vermon James.

CHAPTER 8: "THEY LOVE THAT GREEN AND ORANGE"
1. Lindsey Moore, interviewed by Kristen Buras, Feb. 6, 2018, New Orleans.
2. Mary Polk, interviewed by Kristen Buras, Apr. 10, 2017, New Orleans.
3. Althea Merricks, interviewed by Kristen Buras, Apr. 11, 2017, New Orleans.
4. Personal Papers of Althea Merricks.
5. Merricks interview.
6. Merricks interview.
7. Polk interview.

8. Herlin Riley, interviewed by Kristen Buras, Apr. 12, 2017, New Orleans.

9. Kelly O'Guinn, interviewed by Kristen Buras, Apr. 3, 2018, by phone.

10. Theron Lewis, interviewed by Kristen Buras, Apr. 10, 2017, New Orleans.

11. Rhea Joseph, interviewed by Kristen Buras, Apr. 10, 2017, New Orleans.

12. Ernest Charles, interviewed by Kristen Buras, Apr. 11, 2017, New Orleans.

13. Charles interview.

14. Irvin Blackburn, interviewed by Kristen Buras, June 2, 2018, by phone.

15. Willie Calhoun, interviewed by Kristen Buras, Apr. 12, 2017, New Orleans.

16. Ella Shaw, interviewed by Kristen Buras, June 11, 2017, New Orleans.

17. Riley interview.

18. Trenesse Mosley, interviewed by Kristen Buras, June 10, 2017, New Orleans.

19. Mosley interview.

20. Mosley interview.

21. See chapter 6 for more on child daycare at Carver.

22. Kelly O'Guinn, interviewed by Kristen Buras, Apr. 3, 2018, by phone.

23. Dwan Julien, interviewed by Kristen Buras, June 4, 2018, by phone.

24. Julien interview; "Faculty," A. Jordan–Biology, photo, 1978 Carver yearbook, Personal Collection of Avis and Vermon James.

25. Hasan Sparks, interviewed by Kristen Buras, June 3, 2018, by phone.

26. Adrienne Gladney, Martaz Lynch, and Catherine White, interviewed by Kristen Buras, Apr. 12, 2017, New Orleans.

27. Gladney, Lynch, and White interview.

28. Gladney, Lynch, and White interview.

29. Gladney, Lynch, and White interview.

30. Personal Collection of Avis and Vermon James.

31. Avis James, Vermon James, and Marilyn Pierre Degrasse, interviewed by Kristen Buras, Feb. 5, 2018, New Orleans.

32. 2001 Carver yearbook, Personal Collection of Avis and Vermon James.

33. 2001 Carver yearbook, Personal Collection of Avis and Vermon James.

34. 2001 Carver yearbook, Personal Collection of Avis and Vermon James.

35. Danielle Foley, interviewed by Kristen Buras, May 21, 2017, by phone.

36. Foley interview.

37. Foley interview.

38. Foley interview.

39. Lenora Condoll Gray, Carol Righteous, and Clarence Righteous, interviewed by Kristen Buras, June 11, 2017, New Orleans.

40. Lindsey Moore, interviewed by Kristen Buras, Feb. 6, 2018, New Orleans.

41. Condoll Gray, Righteous, and Righteous interview.

42. Condoll Gray, Righteous, and Righteous interview.

43. Condoll Gray, Righteous, and Righteous interview.

44. Lenora Condoll Gray, interviewed by Kristen Buras, Apr. 10, 2021, by phone.

45. Condoll Gray, Righteous, and Righteous interview.

46. Condoll Gray, Righteous, and Righteous interview.

47. James, James, and Pierre Degrasse interview.

48. James, James, and Pierre Degrasse interview.

49. Condoll Gray, Righteous, and Righteous interview.

50. Condoll Gray, Righteous, and Righteous interview.

51. Condoll Gray, Righteous, and Righteous interview.

52. Condoll Gray, Righteous, and Righteous interview.

CHAPTER 9: "THE SYSTEM SPREAD FEW RESOURCES VERY BROADLY"

1. Al Kennedy, "The History of Public Education in New Orleans Still Matters," History Faculty Publications, Paper 5 (Feb. 2016): 4, https://scholarworks.uno .edu/hist_facpubs/5/.

2. Presentation by Dr. Mack Spears, President Orleans Parish School Board, to the Business Task Force of the Chamber of Commerce of New Orleans and the River Region, Facts and Finances, "Summary of the 1977–78 Test Scores: New Orleans Public Schools," Gene Geisert, Superintendent, and Ellen Pechman, Department of Research and Evaluation (Oct. 3, 1978), University of New Orleans, Earl K. Long Library, Louisiana and Special Collections, OPSB–147, Samuel Scarnato Papers, Box 14–Carver.

3. Charles Hatfield, interviewed by Al Kennedy, Mar. 12, 1993, Charles Hatfield Papers, Amistad Research Center, Tulane University, New Orleans, Box 4, Item 1; Digital recording of interview obtained from Charles Hatfield Jr., by Kristen Buras.

4. Lenora Condoll in Lenora Condoll Gray, Carol Righteous, and Clarence Righteous, interviewed by Kristen Buras, June 11, 2017, New Orleans.

5. Donald DeVore and Joseph Logsdon, *Crescent City Schools: Public Education in New Orleans, 1841–1991* (Lafayette: Center for Louisiana Studies, University of Southwestern Louisiana, 1991); Donald DeVore, *Defying Jim Crow: African American Community Development and the Struggle for Racial Equality in New Orleans, 1900–1960* (Baton Rouge: Louisiana State University Press, 2015); Liva Baker, *The Second Battle of New Orleans: The Hundred-Year Struggle to Integrate the Schools* (New York: HarperCollins, 1996).

6. James Anderson, *The Education of Blacks in the South, 1860–1935* (Chapel Hill: University of North Carolina Press, 1988); DeVore and Logsdon, *Crescent City Schools*; Keith Medley, *We as Freemen: Plessy v. Ferguson, the Fight Against Legal Segregation* (Gretna, LA: Pelican Publishing, 2003); Kennedy, "History of Public Education in New Orleans Still Matters."

7. James Border, *Marking Time, Making Place: An Essential Chronology of Blacks in New Orleans Since 1718* (Silver Springs, MD: Beckham Publishing Group, 2015); DeVore, *Defying Jim Crow*; Peirce Lewis, *New Orleans: The Making of an Urban Landscape* (Santa Fe, NM: Center for American Places, 2003); Walter Stern, *Race and Education in New Orleans: Creating the Segregated City, 1764–1960* (Baton Rouge: Louisiana State University Press, 2018); Lydia Voigt, Dee Wood Harper, and William Thornton, eds., *Preventing Lethal*

Violence in New Orleans: A Great American City (Lafayette: University of Louisiana at Lafayette Press, 2015).

8. DeVore, *Defying Jim Crow*.

9. Gloria Ladson-Billings, "From the Achievement Gap to the Education Debt: Understanding Achievement in U.S. Schools," *Educational Researcher* 35, no. 7 (2006): 5.

10. Peter Iadicola, "The Chain of Violence and the Lessons for New Orleans," *Preventing Lethal Violence in New Orleans: A Great American City*, ed. Lydia Voigt, Dee Wood Harper, and William Thornton (Lafayette: University of Louisiana at Lafayette Press, 2015), 77–104.

11. Iadicola, "The Chain of Violence and the Lessons for New Orleans," 77.

12. Iadicola, "The Chain of Violence and the Lessons for New Orleans," 77–78.

13. Iadicola, "The Chain of Violence and the Lessons for New Orleans," 78.

14. Iadicola, "The Chain of Violence and the Lessons for New Orleans," 78.

15. Iadicola, "The Chain of Violence and the Lessons for New Orleans," 87; italics added.

16. Iadicola, "The Chain of Violence and the Lessons for New Orleans," 96.

17. Iadicola, "The Chain of Violence and the Lessons for New Orleans," 97.

18. Lovell Beaulieu, "Life Is Crime, Poverty, Fear for Housing Project Dwellers," *Times-Picayune*, Jan. 7, 1980, https://nola.newsbank.com/.

19. Beaulieu, "Life Is Crime, Poverty, Fear for Housing Project Dwellers."

20. *A Place Called Desire*, LS3 Studios, 2021. For more information on this award-winning film, see https://www.aplacecalleddesire.com/.

21. Beaulieu, "Life Is Crime, Poverty, Fear for Housing Project Dwellers."

22. Beaulieu, "Life Is Crime, Poverty, Fear for Housing Project Dwellers."

23. Beaulieu, "Life Is Crime, Poverty, Fear for Housing Project Dwellers."

24. Stern, *Race and Education*.

25. Rhonda McKendall, "Half of Students in N.O. Schools Failing a Class," *Times-Picayune*, Jan. 26, 1986, https://nola.newsbank.com/.

26. DeVore, *Defying Jim Crow*, 127.

27. DeVore, *Defying Jim Crow*, 126–27.

28. DeVore, *Defying Jim Crow*, 128.

29. DeVore, *Defying Jim Crow*, 129; Stern, *Race and Education*.

30. DeVore, *Defying Jim Crow*; chapter 5 of this book; Stern, *Race and Education*.

31. DeVore, *Defying Jim Crow*, 135.

32. DeVore, *Defying Jim Crow*, 135–39.

33. DeVore and Logsdon, *Crescent City Schools*.

34. Alonzo Grace and the Citizens' Planning Committee for Public Education in New Orleans, *Tomorrow's Citizens: A Study and Program for the Improvement of the New Orleans Public Schools* (New Orleans: Orleans Parish School Board, 1940); for more on the Grace Report, see chapter 2.

35. Phillip Johnson, "Toward a Civil Rights Agenda: Charles S. Johnson's Forgotten Study of Black Schools in Louisiana," Louisiana Purchase Bicentennial Series in

Louisiana History, Volume XVIII, Education in Louisiana (Center for Louisiana Studies, University of Southwestern Louisiana, 1999): 406–28; quote on 410.

36. Johnson, "Toward a Civil Rights Agenda," 413.
37. Johnson, "Toward a Civil Rights Agenda," 414.
38. Johnson, "Toward a Civil Rights Agenda," 417.
39. Johnson, "Toward a Civil Rights Agenda," 417.
40. Johnson, "Toward a Civil Rights Agenda," 419.
41. Johnson, "Toward a Civil Rights Agenda," 419.
42. Johnson, "Toward a Civil Rights Agenda," 420.
43. Johnson, "Toward a Civil Rights Agenda," 421.
44. Raphael Cassimere, "Equalizing Teachers' Pay in Louisiana," Louisiana Purchase Bicentennial Series in Louisiana History, Volume XVIII, Education in Louisiana (Center for Louisiana Studies, University of Southwestern Louisiana, 1999): 431–32.
45. Cassimere, "Equalizing Teachers' Pay in Louisiana," 434.
46. Cassimere, "Equalizing Teachers' Pay in Louisiana," 434–35.
47. Cassimere, "Equalizing Teachers' Pay in Louisiana," 435.
48. Cassimere, "Equalizing Teachers' Pay in Louisiana," 437.
49. DeVore and Logsdon, *Crescent City Schools*, 226.
50. DeVore and Logsdon, *Crescent City Schools*, 232.
51. DeVore and Logsdon, *Crescent City Schools*, 232.
52. DeVore and Logsdon, *Crescent City Schools*, 234; Derrick Bell, "Serving Two Masters: Integration Ideals and Client Interests in School Desegregation Litigation," in *Critical Race Theory: Key Writings That Formed the Movement*, ed. Kimberlé Crenshaw, Neil Gotanda, Gary Peller, and Kendall Thomas (New York: New Press, 1995), 5–19.
53. DeVore and Logsdon, *Crescent City Schools*, 235.
54. DeVore and Logsdon, *Crescent City* Schools, 236–37.
55. Louisiana State Advisory Committee to the US Commission on Civil Rights, "The New Orleans School Crisis," 1961, p. 5.
56. Louisiana State Advisory Committee to the US Commission on Civil Rights, "The New Orleans School Crisis," 6, 8.
57. Louisiana State Advisory Committee to the US Commission on Civil Rights, "The New Orleans School Crisis," 7.
58. Louisiana State Advisory Committee to the US Commission on Civil Rights, "The New Orleans School Crisis," 9.
59. DeVore and Logsdon, *Crescent City Schools*, 243.
60. DeVore and Logsdon, *Crescent City Schools*, 244.
61. Louisiana State Advisory Committee to the US Commission on Civil Rights, "The New Orleans School Crisis," 11.
62. Louisiana State Advisory Committee to the US Commission on Civil Rights, "The New Orleans School Crisis," 14.

63. Louisiana State Advisory Committee to the US Commission on Civil Rights, "The New Orleans School Crisis," 15.

64. Louisiana State Advisory Committee to the US Commission on Civil Rights, "The New Orleans School Crisis," 15.

65. DeVore and Logsdon, *Crescent City Schools*, 252.

66. DeVore and Logsdon, *Crescent City Schools*, 266.

67. DeVore and Logsdon, *Crescent City Schools*, 270–71.

68. Gene Geisert, "SCIP: A New Orleans Solution to a National Problem," *Educational Leadership* (1979): 128.

69. Geisert, "SCIP."

70. Geisert, "SCIP."

71. Mark Cortez, "The Faculty Integration of New Orleans Public Schools, 1972," *Louisiana History: The Journal of the Louisiana Historical Association* 37, no. 4 (1996): 405–34.

72. Geisert, "SCIP," 128.

73. DeVore and Logsdon, *Crescent City Schools*.

74. DeVore and Logsdon, *Crescent City Schools*; Peirce Lewis, *New Orleans: The Making of an Urban Landscape* (Santa Fe, New Mexico: Center for American Places, 2003).

75. Presentation by Dr. Mack Spears, "Student Membership Data: Excerpt . . . 'Facts and Finances' 1977–78."

76. Spears, "Student Membership Data."

77. Lewis, *New Orleans*, 125.

78. Presentation by Dr. Mack Spears, "New Orleans Public Schools: Comparative Membership Data by School."

79. Presentation by Dr. Mack Spears, "Summary of the 1977–78 Test Scores: New Orleans Public Schools," Geisert and Pechman (Oct. 3, 1978).

80. Spears, "Summary of the 1977–78 Test Scores."

81. Spears, "Summary of the 1977–78 Test Scores."

82. Spears, "Summary of the 1977–78 Test Scores."

83. Presentation by Dr. Mack Spears, "Demographic Data and Influence on Test Scores: Excerpt . . . 'Student Achievement and Related Data' 1974."

84. Ellen Pechman, "Lessons Learned in the Freedom Movement: A Discussion," transcript, Past and Present: A Gathering with Freedom Movement Veterans at Stanford University, Apr. 11, 2015, p. 9.

85. Presentation by Dr. Mack Spears, "Employee Statistics: Excerpt . . . 'Facts and Finances' 1977–78."

86. Spears, "Employee Statistics."

87. Presentation by Dr. Mack Spears, Memorandum on School Plant Survey from John G. Finney to Gene Geisert (Aug. 4, 1978).

88. Presentation by Dr. Mack Spears, Memorandum on School Plant Survey from John G. Finney.

89. Presentation by Dr. Mack Spears, "New Orleans Public Schools Maintenance Services Proposed Budget 1978–79: 761–Contracted Building Repairs."
90. Presentation by Dr. Mack Spears, Memorandum on School Plant Survey from John G. Finney.
91. Geisert, "SCIP," 128.
92. Geisert, "SCIP," 128–29.
93. Geisert, "SCIP," 128; Mark Cortez, "The Faculty Integration of New Orleans Public Schools, 1972," *Louisiana History: The Journal of the Louisiana Historical Association* 37, no. 4 (1996): 405–34.
94. Geisert, "SCIP," 129.
95. Geisert, "SCIP."
96. Presentation by Dr. Mack Spears, Memorandum on School Plant Survey from John G. Finney.
97. Geisert, "SCIP," 130.
98. Geisert, "SCIP."
99. Geisert, "SCIP."
100. Geisert, "SCIP."
101. Geisert, "SCIP," 133.
102. Geisert, "SCIP."
103. Geisert, "SCIP."
104. Geisert, "SCIP," 134.
105. Geisert, "SCIP."
106. DeVore and Logsdon, *Crescent City Schools*, 278–84.
107. DeVore and Logsdon, *Crescent City Schools*, 271, 278.
108. DeVore and Logsdon, *Crescent City Schools*, 271.
109. DeVore and Logsdon, *Crescent City Schools*, 284.
110. DeVore and Logsdon, *Crescent City Schools*, 279.
111. Michelle Alexander, *The New Jim Crow: Mass Incarceration in the Age of Colorblindness* (New York: New Press, 2012); Michael Omi and Howard Winant, *Racial Formation in the United States*, 3rd ed. (New York: Routledge, 2013).
112. Alexander, *The New Jim Crow*.
113. Alexander, *The New Jim Crow*, 49.
114. Alexander, *The New Jim Crow*, 72–80.
115. Alexander, *The New Jim Crow*, 49–50.
116. Alexander, *The New Jim Crow*, 60.
117. DeVore and Logsdon, *Crescent City Schools*, 286, 290.
118. Alexander, *The New Jim Crow*.
119. "Anti-Drug Retreat Is Planned," *Times-Picayune*, Mar. 11, 1987, https://nola.newsbank.com/.
120. Danielle Foley, interviewed by Kristen Buras, May 21, 2017, by phone.
121. James Borders, *Marking Time, Making Place: An Essential Chronology of Blacks in New Orleans Since 1718* (Silver Springs, MD: Beckham

Publications Group, 2015); Lydia Voigt, Dee Wood Harper, and William Thornton, eds., *Preventing Lethal Violence in New Orleans: A Great American City* (Lafayette: University of Louisiana, Lafayette Press, 2015).

122. Voigt, Harper, and Thornton, *Preventing Lethal Violence in New Orleans.*

123. David Harvey, *A Brief History of Neoliberalism* (New York: Oxford University Press, 2005); John Clark and Janet Newman, *The Managerial State: Power, Politics and Ideology in the Remaking of Social Welfare* (Thousand Oaks, CA: SAGE, 1997); Michael Apple, *Educating the "Right" Way: Markets, Standards, God, and Inequality* (New York: RoutledgeFalmer, 2001); Kristen Buras, *Rightist Multiculturalism: Core Lessons on Neoconservative Reform* (New York: Routledge, 2008).

124. Edward Banfield, *The Unheavenly City: The Nature and Future of Our Urban Crisis* (Boston: Little, Brown, 1968).

125. Harvey, *Brief History of Neoliberalism*; Clark and Newman, *Managerial State*; Apple, *Educating the "Right" Way*; Buras, *Rightist Multiculturalism.*

126. Lindsey Moore, interviewed by Kristen Buras, Feb. 6, 2018, New Orleans; Rhonda McKendall, "Student Health Clinic to Be Opened at Carver," *Times-Picayune*, July 7, 1987, https://nola.newsbank.com/.

127. Division of Planning, Testing, and Evaluation, "School Profiles: 1983–84—G. W. Carver Senior High School," UNO, OPSB–147, Carver, Box 5, Folder 3.

128. Division of Planning, Testing, and Evaluation, "School Profiles."

129. *Report of the Reviewing Committee for G. W. Carver Senior High School*, SACS (1987, Mar. 25–27), UNO, OPSB-147, Carver, Box 1, Folder 1.

130. *Report of the Reviewing Committee for G. W. Carver Senior High School*, 1–2.

131. See *Report of the Reviewing Committee for G. W. Carver Senior High School.*

132. *Report of the Reviewing Committee for G. W. Carver Senior High School*, 18.

133. *Report of the Reviewing Committee for G. W. Carver Senior High School*, 46.

134. *Report of the Reviewing Committee for G. W. Carver Senior High School*, 57.

135. *Report of the Reviewing Committee for G. W. Carver Senior High School*, 3.

136. Trenesse Mosley, interviewed by Kristen Buras, June 6, 2017, New Orleans.

137. Kelly O'Guinn, interviewed by Kristen Buras, Apr. 3, 2018, by phone.

138. Denise O'Guinn, interviewed by Kristen Buras, Feb. 4, 2018, New Orleans.

139. Dwan Julien, interviewed by Kristen Buras, June 4, 2018, by phone.

140. Julien interview.

141. Adrienne Gladney, Martaz Lynch, and Catherine White, interviewed by Kristen Buras, Apr. 12, 2017, New Orleans.

142. Gladney, Lynch, and White interview.

143. G. W. Carver Junior-Senior High School: School Improvement and Accountability Plan (Dec. 5, 1991), "Parents as Partners in Education" seminar, UNO, OPSB-147, Carver, 1955–1994, Box 5.

144. Carver Junior-Senior High School: School Improvement and Accountability Plan.

145. Carver Junior-Senior High School: School Improvement and Accountability Plan.

146. Rhonda McKendall, "Remedial Program Ended at Orleans High Schools," *Times-Picayune*, July 16, 1987, https://nola.newsbank.com/.

147. McKendall, "Remedial Program Ended at Orleans High Schools."

148. Chris Adams, "Students May Find Classrooms Packed This Fall," *Times-Picayune*, May 14, 1992, 43.

149. Aesha Rasheed, "New Superintendent Tours Needy Schools," *Times-Picayune*, Feb. 19, 2003, 15.

150. Rasheed, "New Superintendent Tours Needy Schools," 17.

151. Rasheed, "New Superintendent Tours Needy Schools," 17.

152. Brian Thevenot, "LEAP Scores Get Worse in Orleans," *Times-Picayune*, July 15, 2003.

153. Erika DeCuir, "The Louisiana Educational Assessment Program (LEAP): A Historical Analysis of Louisiana's High Stakes Testing Policy," unpublished PhD diss., Georgia State University, 2012.

154. DeCuir, "The Louisiana Educational Assessment Program."

155. Kenneth Saltman, *Capitalizing on Disaster: Taking and Breaking Public Schools* (Boulder, CO: Paradigm Publishers, 2007), 22.

156. Recovery School District and Orleans Parish School Board, School Facilities Master Plan for Orleans Parish, "Age of School Facilities" (Aug. 2008), 28.

157. Recovery School District and Orleans Parish School Board, School Facilities Master Plan for Orleans Parish, "Building Condition," 31–33.

158. "Building Condition," 33.

159. "Building Condition"; "Master Plan Summary: Recommendations," 43.

160. Everett Williams, "Epilogue: Some Personal Reflections on a Public Institution," in DeVore and Logsdon, *Crescent City Schools*, 298–300.

CHAPTER 10: "THEY DON'T WANT US"

1. Carol Righteous, Clarence Righteous, and Lenora Condoll Gray, interviewed by Kristen Buras, June 11, 2017, New Orleans.

2. Avis James, interviewed by Kristen Buras, Feb. 6, 2018, New Orleans.

3. Kristen Buras, *Charter Schools, Race, and Urban Space: Where the Market Meets Grassroots Resistance* (New York: Routledge, 2015); Raynard Sanders, *The Coup d'État of the New Orleans Public Schools: Money, Power, and the Illegal Takeover of a Public School System* (New York: Peter Lang, 2018); Kristen Buras, Jim Randels, Kalamu Ya Salaam, and Students at the Center, *Pedagogy, Policy, and the Privatized City: Stories of Dispossession and Defiance from New Orleans* (New York: Teachers College Press, 2010); Kenneth Saltman, *Capitalizing on Disaster: Taking and Breaking Public Schools* (Boulder, CO: Paradigm Publishers, 2007); Phoebe Ferguson, *A Perfect Storm: The Takeover of New Orleans Public Schools*, Bayou and Me Media, 2005-), https://www.aperfectstormthemovie.com/.

4. Buras, *Charter Schools, Race, and Urban Space*; Sanders, *The Coup d'État of the New Orleans Public Schools*; Buras et al., *Pedagogy, Policy, and the Privatized City*.

5. See chapter 1; for a comprehensive analysis, see Buras, *Charter Schools, Race, and Urban Space*.

6. James Reiss quoted in Christopher Cooper, "In Katrina's Wake—Old-Line Families Escape Worst of Floods and Plot the Future," *Wall Street Journal*, Sept. 8, 2005.

7. Peirce Lewis, *New Orleans: The Making of an Urban Landscape* (Santa Fe, NM: Center for American Places, 2003).

8. Lewis, *New Orleans*.

9. Representative of Louisiana Federation of Teachers, interviewed confidentially by Kristen Buras, Dec. 9, 2009, Baton Rouge; M. Krupa, "City's Political Landscape Has Shifted," *Times-Picayune*, Apr. 23, 2008, www.nola.com.

10. E. Meese, S. M. Butler, and K. R. Holmes, *From Tragedy to Triumph: Principled Solutions for Rebuilding Lives and Communities* (Washington, DC: Heritage Foundation, 2005).

11. Meese, Butler, and Holmes, *From Tragedy to Triumph*.

12. As part of a study focused on post-Katrina Carver and Collegiate Academies charter school network, I interviewed four Carver-RSD teachers and two Carver-RSD students. In this case, names of interviewees are kept confidential, as stipulated on interview consent forms.

13. George Washington Carver Charter School Association, Non-Profit Incorporation document, State of Louisiana, Commercial Division, July 30, 2012, Personal Collection of Willie Calhoun, New Orleans; The "registered agent" is Alvin Jones, the status of the Carver Charter School Association is "active" and "in good standing," the original file date for incorporation is April 9, 2009, and the most recent report was filed on May 11, 2012; Letter from Internal Revenue Service (IRS) to Carver Charter School Association and Charles Webb, Assignment of Employer Identification Number, 06/02/2009, Personal Collection of Willie Calhoun.

14. Recovery School District, High School Redesign Agreement, Project Roles and Responsibilities Chart, Aug. 21, 2009, Personal Collection of Willie Calhoun.

15. Recovery School District, High School Redesign Agreement.

16. Letter from RSD Superintendent Paul Vallas to George Washington Carver Charter School Association Director Alvin Jones, Aug. 21, 2009, Personal Collection of Willie Calhoun.

17. Visioning Document for a Community-Controlled Carver, circa 2008–2012, Personal Collection of Willie Calhoun.

18. Visioning Document for a Community-Controlled Carver.

19. This was reported by Carver-RSD Teacher 1 interviewed confidentially by Kristen Buras, June 9, 2017, New Orleans; Carver-RSD Teacher 2 interviewed confidentially by Kristen Buras, May 12, 2017, by phone; Carver-RSD

Teacher 3 interviewed confidentially by Kristen Buras, June 11, 2017, New Orleans.

20. Lenora Condoll Gray, Carol Righteous, and Clarence Righteous, interviewed by Kristen Buras, June 11, 2017, New Orleans.

21. Condoll Gray, Righteous, and Righteous interview; New teachers often received a stipend through AmeriCorps, as reported by Carver-RSD Teacher 3 interviewed by Buras.

22. Carver-RSD Teacher 1 interviewed by Buras.

23. Written statement from Carver-RSD Teacher 1 interviewed by Buras.

24. Carver Charter School Association, Meeting Agenda, Jan. 26, 2012, Personal Collection of Willie Calhoun.

25. Carver Charter School Association, Meeting Agenda.

26. Stating the Facts: Getting Rams to Come Out, Feb. 2012, Personal Collection of Willie Calhoun.

27. Carver Charter School Association, *Student Visioning Committee Report*, Mar. 7, 2012, Personal Collection of Willie Calhoun.

28. Carver Charter School Association, *Student Visioning Committee Report*.

29. Visioning Statement: "As a group, we would like to see Carver . . . ," Varnado, Thomas et al., circa 2012, Personal Collection of Willie Calhoun.

30. Vision Committee, "Future/Vision of George Washington Carver Senior High School," S. Stewart, H. Dixon, and E. Charles, circa 2012, Personal Collection of Willie Calhoun.

31. Recovery School District Letter from RSD Executive Director Monica Boudouin and RSD Executive Director of Human Resources Sametta Brown to the Staff of G. W. Carver High School on Phase-Out of Carver-RSD Grades 10–12 and Phase-In of Collegiate Academies' Two New Charter Schools with Grade 9, Mar. 16, 2012, Personal Collection of Willie Calhoun.

32. Save Carver Committee, Meeting Agenda, Mar. 16, 2012, Personal Collection of Willie Calhoun.

33. Visioning Statement, Webb, Lewis, and Frank, circa 2012, Personal Collection of Willie Calhoun.

34. Carver-RSD Teacher 1 meeting transcript from April 18, 2012.

35. Carver-RSD Teachers 1, 2, and 3 interviewed by Buras.

36. Collegiate Academies, "About Us–History," 2017, www.sciacademy.org.

37. Carver-RSD Teachers 1 and 3 interviewed by Buras; Recovery School District Letter from Boudouin and Brown to G. W. Carver High School on Phase-Out and Phase-In, Mar. 16, 2012, Personal Collection of Willie Calhoun.

38. Meeting Transcript, Apr. 18, 2012; italics added.

39. Carver-RSD Teacher 1 interviewed by Buras.

40. Ernest Charles interviewed by Kristen Buras, Apr. 11, 2017, New Orleans; Kristen Buras; photo of "Hands Off Carver" protest sign, Personal Collection of Ernest Charles, New Orleans; Fieldnotes on "Hand Off Carver" protest video, 2012; Andrew Vanacore, "Protesters Gather Outside Carver High

School After New Principal Introduced," *Times-Picayune*, Apr. 19, 2012, www.nola.com

41. Hands Off Carver Petition, circa 2012, Personal Collection of Willie Calhoun.

42. Hands Off Carver Petition.

43. Carver charter school application, 2012, Personal Collection of Willie Calhoun, New Orleans; Gmail Charter Application Submission correspondence from David Shepard, Deputy Director of School Development, Office of Parental Options, Louisiana Department of Education, July 31, 2012, Personal Collection of Willie Calhoun; see also the letter of support for CCSA and its operation of a charter school from Mary Lodge Evans, President of the Carver Alumni Association, to CCSA President Alvin Jones, June 20, 2012, Personal Collection of Willie Calhoun; Letter of support for CCSA charter application from Don Marshall, Executive Director of the New Orleans Jazz and Heritage Foundation, to CCSA, June 20, 2012, Personal Collection of Willie Calhoun.

44. Charter School Board Member Questionnaire Templates, 2012, Personal Collection of Willie Calhoun; CCSA Charter School Application, Appendix M–Resumes of Board Members, 2012, Personal Collection of Willie Calhoun.

45. Kevin Lawrence Henry, "The Price of Disaster: The Charter Authorization Process in Post-Katrina New Orleans," *Educational Policy* 35, no. 2 (2021): 235–58; Kevin Lawrence Henry and Adrienne Dixson, "'Locking the Door Before We Got the Keys': Racial Realities of the Charter School Authorization Process in Post-Katrina New Orleans," *Educational Policy* 30, no. 1 (2016): 218–40; Charter Contract for Carver Collegiate Academy with the Louisiana Board of Elementary and Secondary Education, July 1, 2012, obtained by Kristen Buras from Louisiana Department of Education via public records request; Charter Contract for Carver Prep Academy with the Louisiana Board of Elementary and Secondary Education, July 1, 2012, obtained by Kristen Buras from Louisiana Department of Education via public records request.

46. Carver-RSD Teacher 1 interviewed by Buras.

47. Kristen Buras, "A Legacy That Can't Be Chartered" (forthcoming); Beth Sondel, "'No Excuses' in New Orleans: The Silent Passivity of Neoliberal Schooling," *Educational Forum* 80 (2016): 171–88; Jim Horn, *Word Hard, Be Hard: Journeys Through "No Excuses" Teaching* (New York: Rowman & Littlefield, 2016); Catherine Kim, Daniel Losen, and Damon Hewitt, *The School-to-Prison Pipeline: Structuring Legal Reform* (New York: New York University Press, 2010); Michelle Alexander, *The New Jim Crow: Mass Incarceration in the Age of Colorblindness* (New York: New Press, 2012).

48. George Washington Carver Senior High School ("Carver-RSD") Team Training Binder, Summer 2012, New Orleans.

49. Carver-RSD Teacher 1, interviewed by Buras.

50. Carver-RSD Teacher 1, interviewed by Buras.

51. Carver-RSD Teacher 3, interviewed by Buras.

52. Carver-RSD Teacher 2, interviewed by Buras.

53. Carver-RSD Teachers 1 and 3, interviewed by Buras.

54. Carver-RSD Teacher 1, interviewed by Buras.

55. Danielle Dreilinger, "Shockwaves Continue from Clark, Carver High School Student Protests," *Times-Picayune*, Nov. 26, 2013, www.nola.com.

56. "Dear Collegiate Academies Board and Administration" Demand Letter, Collegiate and Prep Students, Nov. 20, 2013, New Orleans.

57. "Dear Collegiate Academies Board and Administration."

58. Attorneys Eden Heilman and Jennifer Coco, "To the Board and Administration of Collegiate Academies," letter, Southern Poverty Law Center, Dec. 18, 2013, New Orleans.

59. Heilman and Coco, "To the Board and Administration of Collegiate Academies."

60. Karran Harper Royal, Carver Protest, Twitter, Dec. 16, 2013, 7:09 a.m., https://twitter.com/KHRoyal/status/412600391360974848/photo/1.

61. Ben Marcovitz, "Open Letter to the Collegiate Academies Community," Dec. 20, 2013, New Orleans.

62. Heilman and Coco, "To the Board"; Danielle Dreilinger, "New Orleans High School Protests Reopen Suspensions Debate," *Times-Picayune*, Dec. 20, 2013, www.nola.com.

63. Kari Harden, "Civil Rights Complaints Are Filed Against Three N.O. Schools, *Louisiana Weekly*, Apr. 22, 2014, www.louisianaweekly.com.

64. Marcovitz, "Open Letter"; Meredith Simons, "The Student-Led Backlash Against New Orleans's Charter Schools," *The Atlantic*, Feb. 4, 2014. I also interviewed students who attended Collegiate Academies' charter schools during this period of protest, but I do not have the space to include their testimony here. However, it is important to note that student interviews reflected the same concerns written about in this chapter. For more, see Buras, "A Legacy That Can't Be Chartered" (forthcoming).

65. Collegiate Academies, "About Us–History"; Sanders, *The Coup d'État*, "Appendix F: Carver Civil Rights Complaint."

66. Better Education Support Team Rally and Press Conference Flyer, Apr. 15, 2014, New Orleans, Personal Collection of Willie Calhoun.

67. Reverend Willie Calhoun/Better Education Support Team, Attorney Anna Lellelid, and Attorney William Quigley, Civil Rights Complaint submitted to US Department of Education/Office of Civil Rights, US Department of Justice/Civil Rights Division, Louisiana Board of Elementary and Secondary Education, Louisiana Department of Education, and the Recovery School District, Apr. 25, 2014; Danielle Dreilinger, "Civil Rights Complaint Targets New Orleans Charter Group Collegiate Academies," *Times-Picayune*, Apr. 15, 2014; Harden, "Civil rights complaints are filed."

68. Calhoun, Lellelid, and Quigley, "Civil Rights Complaint."

69. Collegiate Academies, "About Us–History."

70. Danielle Dreilinger, "State Investigation of N.O.'s Collegiate Academies Charters on Hold Pending Further Documentation," *Times-Picayune*, May 15, 2014; Anna Lellelid and Bill Quigley, Letter to US Department of Education, Office of Civil Rights, Sept. 4, 2014, Personal Collection of Willie Calhoun.

71. The LDOE superintendent was John White, a graduate of Eli Broad's superintendency program, known for its advocacy of market-based education reform; the RSD superintendent was Patrick Dobard, another charter proponent who later became CEO of New Schools for New Orleans; the BESE president was Chas Roemer, earlier quoted as a school choice advocate; see Calhoun, Lellelid, and Quigley, "Civil Rights Complaint."

72. US DOE, Office of Civil Rights (OCR), Letter to Attorney Anna Lellelid, Aug. 22, 2014, Personal Collection of Willie Calhoun; Lellelid and Quigley, Letter to US DOE/OCR, Sept. 4, 2014.

73. Secretary Arne Duncan headed the US Department of Education (US DOE) at the time and was known for his advocacy of public school privatization in Chicago.

74. Collegiate Academies, CARe Collegiate Academies Restorative Initiative, accessed Jan. 16, 2017, http://collegiateacademies.thecanarycollective.com /page/80/care

75. Former students of Collegiate Academies, interviewed confidentially by Kristen Buras, 2017–2018, New Orleans; photo of Restorative Center, circa 2017, Collection of Ernest Charles; for additional student testimony on Collegiate Academies, see Buras, "A Legacy That Can't Be Chartered."

76. Former student of Carver Collegiate Academy, interviewed by Kristen Buras, June 7, 2017, New Orleans.

77. Carver-RSD Teacher 3 interview.

78. Carver-RSD Teacher 1 interview.

79. Buras, "A Legacy That Can't Be Chartered."

80. Recovery School District and Orleans Parish School Board, School Facilities Master Plan for Orleans Parish, "High School Landbanked: Planning District 8," Aug. 2008: 64.

81. Recovery School District and Orleans Parish School Board, School Facilities Master Plan for Orleans Parish, Superintendents' Amendments and Recommendations to the Louisiana Board of Elementary and Secondary Education, "Phase I High Schools—9th Ward HS (Carver Site), New School," Nov. 6, 2008.

82. Recovery School District and Orleans Parish School Board, School Facilities Master Plan for Orleans Parish; The estimated cost in 2008 was $40 million, but the actual cost was approximately $55 million.

83. In addition to the oral history and archival study completed on the historic Carver for this book, I also completed a study that included confidential

interviews with students, parents, and teachers who had experiences in Collegiate Academies' charter schools, including the ones that replaced historic Carver. This quote is drawn from a former student of Carver Collegiate Academy interviewed confidentially by Kristen Buras, Feb. 6, 2017, New Orleans. For more, see Buras, "A Legacy That Can't Be Chartered."

84. Louisiana Believes, School Performance Scores, 2015 spreadsheet, https://www.louisianabelieves.com/resources/library/performance-scores; in 2016, Sci had a "B" and Carver Collegiate had a "D," 2016 spreadsheet; in 2017, Sci had a "C" and Carver Collegiate had a "D," 2017 spreadsheet.

85. Collegiate Academies was given additional charter school contracts, including Livingston Collegiate Academy in 2016 and Rosenwald Collegiate Academy in 2018 (both in New Orleans), and Collegiate Baton Rouge in 2017.

86. Lenora Condoll Gray, Carol Righteous, and Clarence Righteous, interviewed by Kristen Buras, June 11, 2017, New Orleans.

87. Condoll Gray, Righteous, and Righteous interview.

88. Condoll Gray, Righteous, and Righteous interview.

89. Enos Hick Jr., interviewed by Kristen Buras, June 8, 2017, New Orleans; Lamar Smith Jr. and Douglas Haywood, interviewed by Kristen Buras, June 8, 2017, New Orleans.

90. Condoll Gray, Righteous, and Righteous interview.

91. Avis James, Vermon James, and Marilyn Pierre Degrasse, interviewed by Kristen Buras, Feb. 5, 2018, New Orleans.

92. James, James, and Pierre Degrasse interview.

93. Lindsey Moore, interviewed by Kristen Buras, Feb. 6, 2018, New Orleans.

94. Herlin Riley, interviewed by Kristen Buras, Apr. 12, 2017, New Orleans.

95. Riley interview.

96. Kenneth Royal, interviewed by Kristen Buras, Apr. 13, 2017, New Orleans.

97. Royal interview.

98. Royal interview.

99. Joyce King, Ellen Swartz, et al., *"Re-membering" History in Student and Teacher Learning: An Afrocentric Culturally Informed Praxis* (New York: Routledge, 2014); see also Joyce King, ed., *Black Education: A Transformative Research and Action Agenda for the New Century* (New York: Routledge, 2005).

100. King, Swartz, et al., *"Re-membering" History in Student and Teacher Learning.*

101. Sanders, *The Coup d'État,* "Appendix G: Civil Rights Complaint on School Closings."

102. Sanders, *The Coup d'État,* "Appendix G" (see letter dated May 13, 2014, to Attorney General Eric Holder and Secretary of Education Arne Duncan).

103. Sanders, *The Coup d'État,* "Appendix G."

104. Alliance to Reclaim Our Schools, *Out of Control: The Systematic Disenfranchisement of African American and Latino Communities Through School Takeovers,* Aug. 2015, reclaimourschools.org; Pauline Lipman, *The New Political*

Economy of Urban Education: Neoliberalism, Race, and the Right to the City (New York: Routledge, 2011); Raynard Sanders, David Stovall, and Terrenda White, *Twenty-First-Century Jim Crow Schools: The Impact of Charters on Public Education* (Boston: Beacon Press, 2018).

105. Eve Ewing, *Ghosts in the Schoolyard: Racism and School Closings on Chicago's South Side* (Chicago: University of Chicago Press, 2018), 1.

106. Ewing, *Ghosts in the Schoolyard*, 104.

107. Ewing, *Ghosts in the Schoolyard*, 106.

108. Kennedy, "The History of Public Education Still Matters in New Orleans," History Faculty Publications, Paper 5 (Feb. 2016): 19, https://scholarworks .uno.edu/hist_facpubs/5/.

109. Elizabeth Heavrin, *Recordation of Certain Buildings at the George Washington Carver School Campus, New Orleans, Louisiana* (Washington, DC: FEMA, June 28, 2010), 1, University of New Orleans, Earl K. Long Library, Louisiana and Special Collections, FEMA G. W. Carver School Collection, Box 1, Folder 1.

110. Lenora Condoll Gray, interviewed by Kristen Buras, Apr. 10, 2021, by phone; Dwan Julien, interviewed by Kristen Buras, June 4, 2018, by phone.

111. "Famous Quotes from Carver Teachers," *Carver Times* 1, no. 2 (May 1959): 5, UNO, OPSB–147, Carver, Box 1, Folder 2.

112. Gloria Ladson-Billings, "From the Achievement Gap to the Education Debt: Understanding Achievement in U.S. Schools," *Educational Researcher* 35, no. 7 (Oct. 2006): 3–12.

113. Visioning Document for a Community-Controlled Carver, c. 2008–12, Personal Collection of Willie Calhoun.

EPILOGUE: "A REALITY OF LIFE FOR BLACK PEOPLE IN CITIES ALL OVER"

1. Ebony Duncan-Shippy, ed., *Shuttered Schools: Race, Community, and School Closures in American Cities* (Charlotte, NC: Information Age Publishers, 2019), 1.

2. Duncan-Shippy, *Shuttered Schools.*

3. Terrance Green, "'We Felt They Took the Heart Out of the Community': Examining a Community-Based Response to Urban School Closure," *Education Policy Analysis Archives* 25, no. 21 (Mar. 2017): 1–26.

4. Eve Ewing and Terrance Green, "Beyond the Headlines: Trends and Future Directions in the School Closure Literature," *Educational Researcher* 51, no. 1 (Jan./Feb. 2022): 58–65.

5. Ewing and Green, "Beyond the Headlines."

6. Journey for Justice Alliance, *Death by a Thousand Cuts: Racism, School Closures, and Public School Sabotage*, Voices from America's Affected Communities of Color, May 2014, p. 1, https://dignityinschools.org/resources/death-by-a -thousand-cuts-racism-school-closures-and-public-school-sabotage/.

7. Journey for Justice Alliance, *Death by a Thousand Cuts*, 1–2.

8. Journey for Justice Alliance, *Death by a Thousand Cuts*, 2.

9. Journey for Justice Alliance, *Death by a Thousand Cuts*, 2.

10. Journey for Justice Alliance, *Death by a Thousand Cuts*, 3.

11. Journey for Justice Alliance, *Death by a Thousand Cuts*, 4.

12. Journey for Justice Alliance, *Death by a Thousand Cuts*, 18.

13. Journey for Justice Alliance, *Death by a Thousand Cuts*, 19.

14. Journey for Justice Alliance, *Death by a Thousand Cuts*, 12.

15. Journey for Justice Alliance, *Death by a Thousand Cuts*, 12.

16. Gail Sunderman, Erin Coghlan, and Rick Mintrop, *School Closure as a Strategy to Remedy Low Performance* (Boulder, CO: National Education Policy Center, 2017), 14, http://nepc.colorado.edu/publication/closures; see also Molly Gordon et al., *School Closings in Chicago: Staff and Student Experiences and Academic Outcomes* (Chicago: University of Chicago Consortium on School Research, 2018).

17. Alliance to Reclaim Our Schools, *Out of Control: The Systematic Disenfranchisement of African American and Latino Communities Through School Takeovers*, Aug. 2015, p. 7, http://www.reclaimourschools.org/sites/default/files/out-of-control-takeover-report.pdf.

18. Alliance to Reclaim Our Schools, *Out of Control*, 11–12.

19. Alliance to Reclaim Our Schools, *Out of Control*, 4.

20. Domingo Morel, *Takeover: Race, Education, and American Democracy* (New York: Oxford University Press, 2018).

21. See chapter 3 in Kristen Buras, *Charter Schools, Race, and Urban Space: Where the Market Meets Grassroots Resistance* (New York: Routledge, 2015).

22. Buras, *Charter Schools, Race, and Urban Space*, 78.

23. See chapter 3 in Buras, *Charter Schools, Race, and Urban Space*.

24. Buras, *Charter Schools, Race, and Urban Space*, 67.

25. Green, "'We Felt They Took the Heart Out.'"

26. Green, "'We Felt They Took the Heart Out,'" 10.

27. Green, "'We Felt They Took the Heart Out,'" 11.

28. Green, "'We Felt They Took the Heart Out,'" 16.

29. Green, "'We Felt They Took the Heart Out,'" 18.

30. Felecia Briscoe and Muhammad Khalifa, "'That Racism Thing': A Critical Discourse Analysis of a Conflict over the Proposed Closure of a Black High School," *Race Ethnicity and Education* (2013), http://dx.doi.org/10.1080/13613324.2013.792798.

31. Briscoe and Khalifa, "'That Racism Thing,'" 10.

32. Briscoe and Khalifa, "'That Racism Thing.'"

33. Pauline Lipman, *The New Political Economy of Urban Education: Neoliberalism, Race, and the Right to the City* (New York: Routledge, 2011), 51.

34. Lipman, *The New Political Economy of Urban Education*, 51.

35. Lipman, *The New Political Economy of Urban Education*, 52.

36. Lipman, *The New Political Economy of Urban Education*, 54.

37. Lipman, *The New Political Economy of Urban Education*, 55.
38. Lipman, *The New Political Economy of Urban Education*.
39. Lipman, *The New Political Economy of Urban Education*.
40. Ewing, *Ghosts*, 18.
41. Ewing, *Ghosts*, 20.
42. Ewing, *Ghosts*.
43. Ewing, *Ghosts*, 21.
44. Ewing, *Ghosts*, 22.
45. Ewing, *Ghosts*, 23–24.
46. Ewing, *Ghosts*, 25.
47. Ewing, *Ghosts*.
48. Ewing, *Ghosts*, 25–27.
49. Ewing, *Ghosts*, 28.
50. Ewing, *Ghosts*, 34.
51. Ewing, *Ghosts*.
52. Ewing, *Ghosts*, 43.
53. Ewing, *Ghosts*, 46.
54. Ewing, *Ghosts*, 47.
55. Ewing, *Ghosts*, 51–52.
56. Jitu Brown, "#FIGHTFORDYETT: Fighting Back Against School Closings and the Journey for Justice," in *Lift Us Up, Don't Push Us Out: Voices from the Frontlines of the Educational Justice Movement*, ed. Mark Warren with David Goodman (Boston: Beacon Press, 2018), 48.
57. Brown, "#FIGHTFORDYETT," 49.
58. Brown, "#FIGHTFORDYETT," 50.
59. Brown, "#FIGHTFORDYETT," 53–54. It should also be noted that the City Fund, led in part by the former CEO of New School for New Orleans, is a new initiative funded by the pro-charter school Arnold Foundation and Hastings Fund. With $250 million, City Fund leaders aim to seed grassroots charter support in target cities and transform urban public school districts into heavily privatized charter school markets. In short, they aim to destroy the very institutions at the heart of our communities. For more on the City Fund, see Kristen Buras, "The City Fund Takes It to 'The People': How Top-Down Reforms Imposed on New Orleans Will Be Bankrolled as Bottom-Up Initiatives in Cities," in *Conservative Philanthropies and Organizations Actions Shaping U.S. Educational Policy and Practice*, ed. Kathleen deMarrais, Brigette Herron, and Janie Copple (Gorham, ME: Myers Education Press, 2020), 119–52.
60. Derrick Alridge, Jon Hale, and Tondra Loder-Jackson, eds., *Schooling the Movement: The Activism of Southern Black Educators from Reconstruction Through the Civil Rights Era* (Columbia: University of South Carolina Press, 2023).

INDEX